LONG WEN

MH370
SHOULD BE HERE

Translated by Peng Lingyang and Yang Bo

LONG WEN

MH370
SHOULD BE HERE

Translated by Peng Lingyang and Yang Bo

Mereo Books

1A The Wool Market Dyer Street Cirencester Gloucestershire GL7 2PR
An imprint of Memoirs Publishing www.mereobooks.com

MH370 Should Be Here: 978-1-86151-906-1

First published in Great Britain in 2019
by Mereo Books, an imprint of Memoirs Publishing

Copyright ©2019

Long Wen has asserted his right under the Copyright Designs and Patents
Act 1988 to be identified as the author of this work.

This book is a work of fiction and except in the case of historical fact any
resemblance to actual persons living or dead is purely coincidental.

A CIP catalogue record for this book is available from the British Library.
This book is sold subject to the condition that it shall not by way of trade
or otherwise be lent, resold, hired out or otherwise circulated without the
publisher's prior consent in any form of binding or cover, other than that in
which it is published and without a similar condition, including this condition
being imposed on the subsequent purchaser.

The address for Memoirs Publishing Group Limited can be
found at www.memoirspublishing.com

The Memoirs Publishing Group Ltd Reg. No. 7834348

Typeset in 9/12pt Century Schoolbook
by Wiltshire Associates Publisher Services Ltd.
Printed and bound in Great Britain by Biddles Books

About the Author

Long Wen, whose real name is Gong Xiaoxiao, was born in August 1948 and is from Nandong Town, Gaocheng District, Shijiazhuang City, Hebei Province. After graduating from a military academy, he served in the army for 26 years and in the police for more than 20 years. Now engaged in assets evaluation, he is also qualified as a research assistant, a data analyst and an insurance surveyor.

A member of Shenzhen Writing Association, he has edited and produced several major works, including the Annals of Nandong Town, a great work of over a million Chinese characters published in January 2015; it won first prize in the Excellent Annals of Counties & Towns of Hebei Province. He has also written many short articles and has won several prizes for them.

The Translators

Peng Lingyang has been teaching English in China for fifteen years. He is fond of conducting research on English-Chinese and Chinese-English translation & interpretation. Mr. Peng has successfully chaired a number of Chinese-American inter-school exchange activities and ceremonies.

Yang Bo has been working in Shenzhen as a civil servant since September 2005.

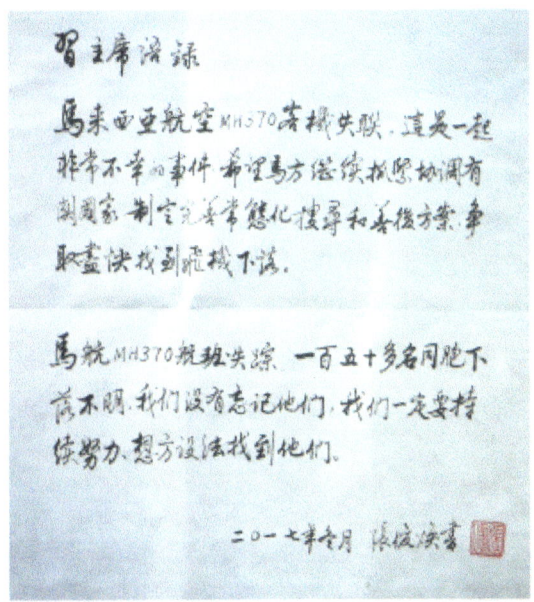

'The disappearance of Flight MH370 was a very unfortunate event. I hope that Malaysia takes the time to coordinate relevant countries, to make plans for regular search and how to deal with problems arising from the event, and to finally find the whereabouts of the aircraft.'

Selected from President Xi Jinping's words when meeting with the Malaysian Speaker of the House of Representatives, Pandikar Amin Mulia, on June 24, 2014.

'After the disappearance of MH370, over 150 of our compatriots were missing. We will never forget them, and we should keep trying hard by all means to find them.'

From President Xi Jinping's New Year 2015 speech delivered via China Radio International, China National Radio and China Central Television.

Calligraphy from Junhuan Zhang
December, 2017

Preface

On March 8 2014, the disappearance of Malaysian Airlines Flight MH370 shocked the world. Despite years of searching at a cost of many millions of dollars, the aircraft has still not been found.

On July 17th 2014 another Malaysian Airlines flight, MH17, was shot down by a missile in eastern Ukraine. MH17's wreckage has been confirmed to be located on Ukraine's border with Russia. Was the culprit the Ukraine government army or local anti-government armed forces? Who was the real culprit? The UN has been involved in the investigation, and it is believed that soon the truth will be found.

On December 28, 2014, another aircraft, Indonesia Air Asia Flight QZ8501, disappeared when flying over Jawa, Indonesia. 15 days later, the debris was found in the 30-metre deep waters under the area of disappearance. According to the investigation, the disaster was caused by the pilots' operating errors.

Within ten months, three aviation disasters had happened to a small country's airline companies. We may not say it will never occur again in the future, but it is definitely unprecedented.

Malaysia, Australia, the United States and the international maritime satellite organisation held that MH370 crashed in the Southern Indian Ocean, west of Perth, Australia, and they adopted a variety of means to search thoroughly for the plane, but so far all their efforts have been in vain. Where and why MH370 disappeared remains a mystery.

The Mystery of Flight MH370, published in May 2014 by an Australian author, argued that the disappearance of MH370 was an accidental shoot-down.

In August 2014, New Zealand author Taylor Swift published *Goodnight Malaysia Airlines Flight MH370*, which suggested that the pilot was mentally ill and that the plane had crashed into the sea, but the book failed to elaborate.

In November, 2017, Chen Tiexia, an American, wrote *Investigation of MH370 (Closure)*. The book claims that MH370 was hijacked to a certain base via electronic remote control and all the people had been imprisoned alive, kept as hostages.

Since the disappearance there have been scattered Chinese accounts on the Internet and on individual media, but no one in China has yet written a book on the matter.

Flight MH370 was carrying 239 people, of whom 154 were Chinese. For such an important event, Chinese people should voice their attitude to the world and let it be heard. That's why I wrote this book.

I don't think a satellite is a star, and an instant 'handshake' is not a complete reflection of the plane's dynamics, let alone the truth. The seven-handshake data of the Indian Ocean satellite lacks logic and uniqueness; there are many alternative explanations for the irregularity and inconsistency of the information available. For this reason I don't agree with the conclusion that the plane disappeared in the Southern Indian Ocean waters west of Perth, Australia, which was based on the satellite 'handshake'.

Based on radio direction-finding and positioning principles, combined with the Pacific radar and satellite data, removing layers of obscurity and excluding many fallacies, I have finally concluded through careful research and analysis that Flight MH370 did not splash down in the Southern Indian Ocean, west of Perth, Australia, but in other waters. It was a 'traffic accident', and there was no intrigue. Its whereabouts will be revealed when you finish reading this book.

I predict that MH370 may be found intentionally or 'unintentionally' at some 'appropriate' time, perhaps by some fishermen, a ship's crew, explorers, shepherds, hunters or animals, and is likely to be made known in some 'smart' way. Time is the touchstone of judging the right or wrong, and so it will tell us who is right.

I especially appreciate the selfless help from the leaders and colleagues of the Shenzhen Zhong Xiang property appraisal Co. Ltd. I want to thank my friends who have worked on my writing, and thank them for their support and their views.

A blessing

On the one hundredth day after the disappearance of MH370
March 8th, for all the women a celebration day,
A Malaysian airliner disappeared half way.
The whole world was mobilised searching for a trace,
Not on the earth, did it fly out into space?
It has been lost for a hundred days
Sorrow crept onto the caring person's face.
No sign of it in the Indian Ocean sea.
Poles apart it certainly couldn't be.
The passengers came widely from fourteen nations,
Everywhere are people who have lost relations.
They await the news of the missing plane,

Broken hearts, tearful eyes, a day feeling like a year.
Wisdom search, like another gate,
Plus our amassed efforts decides on its fate.
Money and efforts should not be wasted in Australia's west
Searching the South China Sea is best.

An Anniversary Memorial
March 2015

There arrived another Women's Day,

The Malaysian airliner is still far, far away.

Land, seabed have been searched for a trace,

Not on the earth, did it fly out into space?

Satellites orbit day and night,

Ships are also busy searching for a sight.

To board humans, Heaven is not among the places,

But we lost the sight of 239 faces.

In the same year on Malaysia many times disasters fall,

Three planes in succession crashed in all.

The shocked world began to guess,

While Malaysia was completely in a mess.

Disappearing and missing three planes

Indonesia and East Europe found some remains.

Only flight MH370 was still unseen,

But it may appear if another search of the South China Sea begins.

Note:

'a family' here only refers to Malaysia.

'Three flights' refers to the three Malaysian flights 2014, MH370, MH17 and QZ8501 which crashed in succession. MH370 disappeared in the South China Sea on March 8th; flight MH17 was shot down by a missile on July 17th, 2014 in Ukraine, Eastern Europe; flight QZ8501 crashed in Indonesia on December 28, 2014 due to the pilot's operating errors.

Eastern Europe here only refers to Ukraine.
Nanyang here only refers to Indonesia.
'Three seven' here only refers to the missing flight MH370.

Contents

Chapter One — P.1
Various opinions about the disappearance of MH370

Chapter Two — P.25
What really went wrong on MH370?

Chapter Three — P.35
MH370, where are you?

Chapter Four — P.47
The clues that MH370 crashed at Scene 1

Chapter Five — P.63
Evidence that MH370 never left Scene 1

Chapter Six — P.69
MH370 may lie somewhere in Scene 1

Chapter Seven — P.72
Why was no debris found at Scene 1?

Chapter Eight — P.79
It was a big mistake to give up the search at Scene 1

Chapter Nine — P.97
Why were there no clues to MH370 at Scene 2, the Indian Ocean west of Perth?

Chapter Ten P.128
Was it wrong at the very beginning to move
to the Indian Ocean?

Chapter Eleven P.136
Guesses about the debris of BB670

Chapter Twelve P.158
Why the search policy for MH370
should be changed

Chapter Thirteen P.166
What will happen next?

Chapter Fourteen P.181
The cheats and crooks exploiting MH370

APPENDICES:

Appendix 1 - Introduction to Flight MH370, P.185
passengers and crew members

Appendix 2 - The communication and P.199
tracking systems of MH370

Appendix 3 - Major relevant events after P.207
MH370's disappearance

Appendix 4 - A common-sense approach P.271
to radio communication

Appendix 5 - A selection of readers' comments P.275

Acknowledgements P.284
Postscript P.285

CHAPTER ONE

Various opinions about the disappearance of MH370

March 8, 2014 is a day we can never forget. Early in the morning, a Malaysia Airlines flight numbered MH370 took off to fly from Kuala Lumpur, Malaysia to Beijing, China. There were 239 people on board, 154 of whom were Chinese, taking up 64% of all on board.

The flight punctually departed Kuala Lumpur, capital of Malaysia. 42 minutes later, it lost contact with ground. It remains lost.

The disappearance of Flight MH370 shocked the world. The plane had been shot down by Vietnam and broken up in the sky, some forecasters of The Book of Changes said; some suggested it had been attacked or hijacked by terrorists; some claimed it had been captured by an alien UFO. Some argued that the plane had not splashed down but was being controlled by an unknown organisation, falling into the hands of others. Some officials indicated that the plane was carrying the fruit mangosteen, and there were bombs in the mangosteen, the explosion of which caused the plane to crash. Some believed the pilot had killed himself or hijacked the plane and all the passengers for political reasons. Some still held it had all been caused by the flight crew. In short, opinions varied, and they still vary. There is continuing speculation, analysis and reasoning, with various new hypotheses. 'Experts' from all fields actively express conflicting opinions.

In summary, their theories fall into 15 kinds, as follows:

SUGGESTION 1 – AN INTELLIGENCE CAMPAIGN

Someone who declared he had long served as an official of the US State Department and was one of the world's most experienced international crisis handlers and hostage negotiators pointed out that when Flight MH370 went missing, the United States was withdrawing troops from Afghanistan. He suggested that the Taliban had hijacked and ambushed their guards and seized the commander and a control system which weighed about 20 tons and was packed in six boxes. The Taliban planned to sell the control system to Russia and China. But Russia was busy with its own crisis, and China seized the opportunity to talk about the control system.

The system could make all US unmanned aircraft fail! China sent eight scientists to check the system before making payments. The eight scientists and six boxes came to Malaysia and the goods were placed in the embassy. In order to safely transport the goods, they used the civilian aircraft which flew as MH370, thinking the

United States would not do anything to a civilian aircraft.

The United States asked the Israeli intelligence service to reclaim the goods, and then sent five Americans and two Israelis to board the plane at the same time. Officials had also announced that there were two Iranians on board MH370, using stolen passports; they were actually Israeli spies.

When MH370 was about to leave Malaysia's airspace, the US AWAC intercepted the signal to the air controller in Vietnam, disabling the pilot's control system and switching it to remote control mode, causing it to fall immediately. US and Israeli agents then turned off the transponder and other communication systems, changed the plane's course and flew it west. The plane flew south of Sumatra, Annanbas and southern India, and landed in the Maldives. Some local residents saw the plane landing. They also saw the cargo on the plane and the black box being removed, and the plane being filled with fuel. It then continued its course to Diego Garcia, where the US Air Force Base in the middle of the Indian Ocean is located.

When MH370 set off again it crashed in the Southern Indian Ocean. The United States made everyone think that the plane had run out of fuel and put the blame on the pilot.

This man – we will call him X – said that the United States had staged a good show, and Australia had joined the show too.

SUGGESTION 2 – AN INTERNATIONAL CONSPIRACY

Somebody has read a lot of books. He opened the wings of imagination, and the version he created for the disappearance of Flight MH370 was as boundless as the sea and sky.

1. The international background behind the disappearance of MH370. It started from the financial crisis in 2008. The dramatic change in the international situation occurred when the United States declined from its flourishing past. To transfer its crisis, the US made Greece bankrupt, brought disasters to the European Union and exceeded its credit by quantitative easing. The world felt bitter. When it intended to strike Syria with the hope of reversing the situation, Russia ruthlessly suppressed its desire, thus exposing the weakness of the United States' disguise.

   When Chinese leaders did not hide their intention of reviving China's dream, the United States feared the challenge. In 2014, the United States provoked Ukrainian civil war in a bid for success, and Russia struggled to counter the US and occupied the Crimea - a heavy, direct blow to the international system, including the US dollar. This was system the United States had spent more than 20 painstaking years to establish since the disintegration of the Soviet Union. Now the US is facing a grim domestic economic situation: the gigantic amount of debt and the high unemployment rate as a result of industrial decline. Where should the United States go? A life and death decision. It had to do something.

2. The motives of the MAS flight event—to restrain Russia and China. When the former US Republican presidential candidate appeared in the Kiev streets for anti-government demonstrations, he was in a position to blatantly interfere in the internal affairs of other countries, provoking disputes and creating Russian-European contradictions, as well as an excuse for the United States to rally. Russia strongly

counterattacked by seizing the Crimea, directly giving the US a slap in the face and challenging its authority.

Under the watchful eyes of the world, the United States must give its response. Its choices regarding Russia may include public condemnation; military strike; or economic sanctions.

Option 1 is superficial, so Russia is not afraid. For Option 2 facing Russia, the United States lacks courage. Option 3 the most ideal but is impractical. If the US wants to implement it, it needs China's support.

China's ability is enough to make the United States' sanctions on Russia. In this context, the sudden disappearance of MSA aircraft shocked the world.

3. The clever timing of the MSA event. March 8 2014 was just before the United Nations vote on the Crimea issue and China's attitude was the most critical. If China stands on the US side and implements joint economic sanctions on Russia, Russia may find it too hard to bear and will eventually yield. The United States can grab the chance to rally and to restore glory. As for China, Sino-Russian relations will be severely damaged, and if Russia is over, China will certainly be the next to suffer US sanctions, just as the old Chinese saying goes: if the cunning rabbit is killed, the chasing dog will soon be cooked.

If China is on the side of Russia, contrary to China's consistent policy of 'respect for the territorial integrity of other countries,' China will suffer the public humiliation of slapping its own face, arousing the world's outrage, seriously damaging China's international image and giving the United States a good excuse to discredit China.

If China abstains and stays neutral, the best choice, it will not participate in the US-led sanctions against Russia, nor damage Sino-Russian relations, nor be accused of self-destroying its image. However, China's abstention is also unacceptable to the United States, which means that China will not participate in sanctions against Russia, which means the US sanction against Russia will not really work and the US will have to swallow the bitter pill of being blocked and slapped down by Russia. For a leader, credit and authority are of vital importance. If the US loses face and trust before the world, the only result will be its decline.

So we understand the significance of the United Nations vote on the Crimea issue — about the fate of the US, extremely important to the US. What will the United States do? It must resort to unconventional means to force China to submit – hence the disappearance of MH370.

4. The MSA flight event had been planned for a long time. The man X continued that the plane was from Malaysia and the event occurred between Malaysian and Vietnamese airspace. The plane was produced in the United States and most of the passengers were Chinese.

The event was first called a 'disappearance', not a hijacking, nor a crash; 'disappearance' can be converted into hijacking, crash, 'contact restored', but it can also remain forever 'disappeared'. The whole event must remain in the hands of experts, after repeated consideration, deduction and with a number of alternative hypotheses. The implementation was so waterproof that the whole world could not find out who did it.

The event, on the one hand, seemed to attract the attention of China, but on the other hand, it did not seem to be directly against China. After all, it is a conspiracy which once brought to light will outrage the world, and may even cause a war, a great risk. It is necessary to play along with China, but not to play across the line.

5. The MSA flight event was of ingenious design. X pointed out that China was not notified until five hours after the event, in order to leave the United States enough time to deal with the aircraft and passengers. India's military radar did not work; Malaysia muttered and mumbled; Singapore and Thailand remained silent; US intelligence agencies warned unrelated people not to utter a single word. They released a variety of false information to confuse the public.

China, very clear-sighted, rapidly responded to the event, sending ships and aircraft straight to the South China Sea – Scene 1, as I shall call it - and mobilizing 10 satellites for surveillance. Vietnam was keen to help open its air space to China.

The expansion of the situation: after the battlefield was transferred to the Indian Ocean, China increased the number of satellites, additional ships, aircraft and personnel to expand the search.

The United States threw out another route, the North Pakistan, Kazakhstan and South Australian route, to test China's strategic direction. China did not hesitate to reject the north route, expressing confidence about its influence on Central Asia; instead, China chose the southern line and sent its teams directly to areas supportive to America, including Australia, adopting an offensive posture: Tell the US that if you dare to challenge, China will not defend, but will launch counter-attacks. If you want to play, play big.

With no progress in events, Malaysia Airlines rushed to unload its burden under the guidance of satellite data provided by the relevant countries. But what is the truth? Malaysian Airlines cannot say, at least not now, but soon it has to say! The conspiracy makers played a big game, but they still could not stop Russia from successfully solving the problem of the Crimean.

History is a mirror, a precipitation. History is history. Things seem better at home. It can be said that there is a big push behind the MSA flight event, playing with the feelings of people involved. At a time of life or death, they are still playing with so-called military secrets, clearly showing that they are working for one force. The future of Malaysia has been ruined by these events and the country is in deep sorrow.

6. The MSA flight arrangements were very complicated.

In the information announced about these related events, Malaysia was used as a pawn. In fact, everything considered, Malaysia, on its own, cannot come up with or infer what is the right thing to do, so it was just speaking for others.

Malaysia Airlines' announcements are basically playing tricks and showing no respect for the Chinese people. However, a case involving human life must be treated with the utmost care. In an event concerning so many Chinese passengers' lives, Chinese people's feelings must be taken into account.

In accordance with current technology, IT was also an important technical factor that caused the aircraft's disappearance, in addition to man-made factors. 'Back doors' in the software programmes of relevant aircraft offer security and military departments a way of controlling the programmes, especially when the plane is on autopilot. Once the airliner is controlled by a hacker, the plane becomes a tool, for even the pilot cannot really control his or her own aircraft then.

It should be said that the debris now found by the satellites of various countries may be from the missing aircraft, but at this stage the deaths of all on board cannot be confirmed. If anyone insists otherwise, it is extremely irresponsible. That is to say, it is hard to ascertain whether the aircraft debris and the people on the plane were together. The aircraft may have landed and taken off again and then crashed into the sea on automatic pilot, to give a false impression to people so as to end the search and rescue work. Within a certain period of time after landing, the passengers may have been replaced, for the real purpose behind it was not the lives of these people, but the effect behind them.

In some respects, the West excludes China again and again, and China adheres to the principle that 'the right to survive' is the most important thing. Now some people have deprived so many people of the right to live, China should take action, and it is clear that this time China will really deal a heavy blow.

In the maintenance of national interests, Russia set a good example for China. Encountering strong offensives, the previous promises suddenly came to nothing, just like a crashing plane.

So, what should be protected should be protected; one should return to history and respect it. It is no longer possible to muddle along on sheer luck. Some people will be very anxious, especially those behind the disappearance. They will be anxious to find a scapegoat to take responsibility for the event. In other words, the first one to come out is not the criminal, it is the next.

SUGGESTION 3 - HIJACKING

After the MH370 event happened, some thought it had been hijacked. There are many versions, of which these are the six main ones, which all belong to Theory 3:

VERSION 1 – SIX SIGNS THAT THE PLANE WAS HIJACKED

1. The communications systems were deliberately shut off: two sets of airliner communications systems were switched off 14 minutes apart. Apparently, there were obvious signs of human involvement.

2. The airliner disappeared from civil aviation radar first. If an airliner fails or disintegrates, it will disappear from military radar first and then from civil radar. MH370's abnormality meant people on board had artificially shut off the communication systems.

3. MH370 still sent messages to a satellite after its disappearance: after the airliner went missing, its SatCom transmitter continued to signal to the satellite, which could only be achieved if the aircraft was intact and under power.

4. The altitude of the aircraft also indicated that only professionals could be responsible: the final flight height was 29,500 feet, not the standard height of 10,000 feet,

indicating that the aircraft did not want to collide with other aircraft, and may even have turned off the collision system.

5. The aircraft changed its route many times: Malaysia military radar signal showed that the aircraft first turned to the west and then north west, an indication of deliberate manipulation.

6. After losing contact for seven hours, the Malaysian government admitted that the final contact with satellites was at 8:11 am, seven hours after the aircraft took off.

VERSION 2: MH370 WAS SECRETLY HIJACKED BY THE USA

This theory states that MH370 did not crash, nor was shot down by Malaysian army or Vietnam forces (they did not have the courage) but was secretly hijacked by the USA. Before we discuss this theory, we might note the following news: Associated Press reported on March 12 that the US civilian defence contractor Benjamin Bishop, at the headquarters of US Pacific Command, admitted to having disclosed military secrets to his Chinese girlfriend. According to an Associated Press report on March 12, Bishop's lawyer said he would admit to having given the military information to his girlfriend. It is expected that Bishop will admit two crimes: passing defence information to those who are not entitled to it, and illegally preserving defence documents and plans.

According to an article in the US *Time* magazine, Bishop was arrested in March 2013 at the headquarters of the US Pacific Command. The US Federal Bureau of Investigation (FBI) last year accused Bishop, then 59 years old, of leaking the operational plan and other confidential information such as nuclear weapons, missile defence and the like to his 27-year-old Chinese girlfriend. The FBI said that Bishop met the woman in Hawaii at an international defence meeting and they started a 'close romantic relationship' in June 2011. Bishop was originally a Lieutenant Colonel in the US Army Reserve. Pacific Command Chief of Staff Anthony Kraedfield said that Bishop was familiar with gaps in Pacific Command's highest priority capability and was proficient in the use of Pacific Command's cyber security. According to Kraedfield, from 2010 to 2012, Bishop had access to 'top secret' information about United States defences against ballistic missile attack by North Korea.

This news came on March 12, four days after the disappearance of MH370. What does that mean? It has been so long since Flight MH370 went missing, but we still do not know where it is. It sounds incredible to many people that a plane could have disappeared without trace, given today's technology. So what is the truth? We may as well make a bold assumption.

There was a huge secret on board Malaysia Airlines MH370. Intelligence officers of some country or other obtained top military information, made the handover in Malaysia, and then tried to mingle with the ordinary passengers (note that this flight had more than 100 passengers from that country) in order to return home secretly. Unfortunately, shortly after the plane took off, the United States obtained certain information and immediately put pressure on the Malaysian government or the Malaysian military. Malaysia Airlines, knowing that its objections would be overruled, secretly instructed the pilot to shut off all the signals over the South China Sea. Of course, there is another possibility: that the United States dispatched a stealth fighter, which is why the Malaysian Air Force radar detected a UFO after the disappearance of MH370's signal and reported that it was friendly, so they did not shoot it down. In fact, the Malaysian Air Force knew the UFO was the US aircraft. It quickly approached flight MH370 and set up electromagnetic interference. That is why the Vietnamese ATC heard 'a lot of static interference' from another flight in the vicinity when the flight tried to contact MH370 under the request of Vietnam ATC. If the electromagnetic interference was due to the weather, why did the plane nearby which attempted to contact MH370 not encounter any? The purpose of the interference was to establish separate communication with the pilot, and to avoid being detected by a certain country's spies who would inform their country through technical means. There was also the intention of making the other side, Vietnam, also believe that the plane was lost.

Under the hijacking of the US military fighter, aircraft MH370 flew to the Diego Garcia American military base in the Indian Ocean. All the people on the aircraft had their phones confiscated and sent back to the United States for detection; that is why some people who tried to call their relatives on the flight said their calls could actually be connected, but were immediately cut off. That is why experts picked up the signal in the United States.

Malaysia Airlines, under the pressure of the military, pretended to have no knowledge of the aircraft, and then released to the outside world the news of its disappearance. For one thing, probably Malaysian Airlines was not really clear what had happened; for another, in order to play for time, it deliberately released the wrong location to the outside world.

When a certain country learned that its spies had been arrested, it was so angry at Malaysia that, although it was not appropriate to attack it publicly, it sent a large number of warships and planes to put pressure on Malaysia in the name of search and rescue. According to the United States, Malaysia also issued a search request to its neighbouring countries, not only to make the situation complicated, but also to avoid being humiliated by a certain country.

To show its innocence and also to improve its international image, Vietnam was very active in this issue, opening its territorial waters and airspace to more than 10 countries. Malaysia initially said that the airliner had lost contact in the South China Sea, and when more than 10 countries crowded in to search there, the US Army went to the Malacca Strait. There was only one reason: to block the channel into the Indian Ocean to prevent a country's warships moving forward. So that country could only sent its merchant ships to search around the Malacca Strait, but at the same time, it also resorted to a trick: demanding an International Charter for space and major disasters, and calling the 15 space agencies to use their satellites to search for MH370.

The Guardian in the UK reported that a group of Earth surveillance satellites had already joined the search for the missing flight. China has called for the launching of the so-called International Charter on Space and Major Disasters. Under this agreement, 15 space bureaux or national space agencies will assist in emergency or rescue efforts by transmitting images taken by satellites flying over that location. This is to make the issue bigger, big enough for the whole world to know.

With the passage of time, the US military's trial on the Diego Garcia military base in the Indian Ocean has made progress. It is estimated that a certain country's spy confessed, so there was some Associated Press news on March 12; US military officials admitted to a leak. The US military got what they wanted.

What about the people on the plane? There was the following news: the White House confirmed that the United States would search for the lost aircraft in the Indian Ocean. Why did the

Americans go there? Did the news from Malaysia carry the slightest suggestion that the plane had flown there? The reason is very simple. The Americans acted badly, but still wanted praise. Actually they knew that the plane had landed on a small island in the Indian Ocean, and they pretended to search there and find it accidentally. Something that attracted the world's attention; something the families would be grateful for; something some country had only to express thanks for, at least on the face of it. So, it is expected that the plane will soon come back, and that will be the end of the matter!

VERSION 3: HIJACKED BY SOMEONE ON BOARD

One Malaysian official said that MH370 had been hijacked and confirmed that the communication system of the disappearing airliner had been deliberately shut down, the route had been deliberately changed and the last communication between the satellite and the plane was at 08:11, March 8. For the final position of the airliner, he gave two possibilities: the corridors of Kazakhstan and the Turkmenistan border to Thailand, or the corridor from Indonesia to the Indian Ocean.

They said that the satellite and military radar data-based survey report released by Malaysia on March 15 showed that the lost plane had first been flying according to the scheduled route but did a U-turn over the South China Sea, across, turned west across the Malay Peninsula, and then turned north-west towards the Andaman Sea, following a strange Z-shaped route. Reuters quoted the source, saying that MH370 was last seen by civilian radar on March 8, near a location code-named Igor, at 01:21. Through the analysis on the Malaysian military radar data, the aircraft suddenly made a sharp turn to the west toward a navigation point named Wampi, the only way for an airliner to fly to the Middle East. Then, the plane flew towards Keval, south of Phuket, Thailand. When the plane was last detected by the military radar, it was flying towards the Iglesias navigation point, on a route across the Andaman Islands to Europe.

At one point the plane moved up and down frequently as if there were signs of fighting. The radar data showed MH370 changing its flight height abruptly and changing its flight route twice. When the airliner rose to more than 13,700 metres (overrun), it suddenly turned westward, flew unevenly down to about 7,000 metres, turned again to the Indian ocean and rose to a higher altitude. This means that the pilot – or hijacker – changed course, or the plane flew without a pilot. Based on satellite data, the location of the last communication between the aircraft and the satellite could be in one of two 'corridors': one from Kazakhstan and Turkmenistan to the northern part of Thailand, the other from Indonesia to the Southern Indian Ocean.

VERSION 4: HIJACKED BY THE PILOTS

An expert said that there are few things that can go wrong when flying smoothly 11 kilometres above the ground. As a result, the sudden disappearance of MH370 has made people puzzled.

The first question is, at 1:07 am on the 8th, the cockpit said the plane was cruising at 35,000 feet, and the same information had just been released six minutes before. This did not need to be mentioned, so the communication about the flight altitude was a purposeful communication, before the ACARS (Aircraft Communications Addressing and Reporting System) was cut off.

The second suspicious thing is that the flight lost contact at the junction between the Malaysian flight control area and the Vietnamese air traffic control area. The air traffic control boundary between the two countries might have a dead spot, which might mean the ground could not see the plane. The plane's communication response system was artificially closed, and it was after that that the plane was stolen.

VERSION 5: HIJACKED BY TERRORISTS

A group of people have claimed that various signs show that the disappearance may be related to terrorism. This event happened during the time ISIS was rampant. It was making trouble in any way it could to show its existence, so it hijacked MH370.

They said that Thailand had recently been in a state of chaos; its military's control was concentrated in the vicinity of the capital. If the terrorists swooped in the southern jungle, it was likely that their forced landing might succeed. After all, the Islamic forces in southern Thailand had been hoping for independence, and they were highly active.

Others say that Cambodia is the closest country to the flight channel, but the country's military power is the weakest, being one of the least developed countries. It has almost no air defence identification ability except through the military facilities of China. So the hijacked aircraft was forced to land at a secret airport in Cambodia's jungles, or in Laos, which has a population of less than one million and a large jungle. And as for Burma, the Coral State in southern Burma is not more than 20 kilometres from the Gulf of Thailand, and the plane could have flown at low altitude through Thailand's air defence system and landed in newly-united southern Burma without being known to the government of Burma.

VERSION 6: HIJACKING BY ELECTRONIC REMOTE CONTROL

A person in authority who wrote about the 9/11 investigation claimed, after investigation, that the lost MH370 had been hijacked by electronic remote control, and taken to the American Diego Garcia military base in the Indian Ocean. He said there was a passenger on MH370 named Philip Wood. He quoted Mr Wood's words: 'I became a hostage when the plane was hijacked. I worked at IBM, and I put my cellphone in my ass at that moment. Now I am in a jail, and separated from other passengers.' He said he had succeeded in taking a picture and sending it out from his iPhone. Although the photo image is dark, nothing can be seen, but the technical staff found, through the photo parameters, that it had been taken on a US military base. The principle of tracking the address through the photo is that the basic part of the image format contains exif metadata, recording the geographical information, including latitude and longitude, height, direction and so on. The latitude and longitude data of the photo can be figured out with specialized software and then the shooting location can be ascertained in Google Maps. The location was the US Diego Garcia military base. The passengers on MH370 were kept there.

A map showing the location of the Diego Garcia American military base

The airport at the Diego Garcia American military base

SUGGESTION 4 - TERRORIST ATTACK

An India Airlines flight in 1985 and Pan Am flight No. 103 in 1988 had been destroyed by bombs. Some people used that as a reference and guessed that those who had used other people's passports rushed into the cockpit and forced the pilots to turn off the communication system or set off bombs, to finally cause the disappearance of MH370.

SUGGESTION 5 - THE AIRCRAFT WAS SHOT DOWN

A book about the missing aircraft, *The Mystery of Flight MH370,* appeared on July 19, 2014 in the New South Bookstore shelves in Sydney. The book gives a reason for the loss of the aircraft, that is, the United States and Thailand were implementing a joint military exercise in the South China Sea and the plane was accidentally shot down.

SUGGESTION 6 - THUNDERSTORM AND TURBULENCE

Some say MH370 might have encountered bad weather, resulting in a failure in the aircraft's equipment and the pilot's error in regarding the sea as the sky, leading to the tragedy. This situation is more likely to occur over the sea at night. One reasons is pilot fatigue; the second is that the sky and the sea often look the same colour, making them difficult to distinguish.

After flying up to more than 10,000 metres, an aircraft enters the cruise phase, immediately out of the troposphere, above the level of lightning, thunderstorms and the like, so it is basically flying in clear sky, on the edge of the troposphere. Only 9% of disasters occur during the plane's smooth flight phase. There might also be turbulence.

SUGGESTION 7 - MECHANICAL FAILURE

Scott Hamilton, managing director of Leeham Co., an American aerospace consultancy, said that for an 11-year-old Boeing 777, there is no aging problem, but if the aircraft lacks good and timely maintenance and repair, there might still be fatigue problems. Judging from the available information, if the aircraft disintegrated in the air, it was very likely that the aircraft might not have had time to report to the ground. If the plane crashed into water, the wreckage would be very concentrated.

SUGGESTION 8 - THE PILOT'S SUICIDE

The US media said the plane had been lost because the pilot had committed suicide. They said that in the 1990s an Egyptian pilot deliberately flew his plane into the sea to commit suicide. They thought that because he had inadvertently lifted the aircraft's autopilot function and caused a crash, the aircraft may have hit the sea outside the distance of 5 to 6 hours from its last contact point.

SUGGESTION 9 - STATIC INTERFERENCE

According to foreign media reports, before MH370 lost contact, another Boeing 777 airliner pilot, at the request of the Vietnam Air Traffic Control Centre, had made contact with the aircraft. This pilot, requesting anonymity, pointed out that the answer at that time might be from MH370's pilot or co-pilot. 'There's a lot of interference... electrostatic interference, but I heard mumbling from the other end. This was the last time we got in touch with them and then we couldn't get in touch with them any more.'

SUGGESTION 10 – LOSS OF CONSCIOUSNESS DUE TO LACK OF OXYGEN

Someone who participated in the search thought that Captain Zahari had mental problems. Forty minutes after the plane took off, he told the co-pilot to rest and closed the air-to-ground contact system. After breaking the contact, he pulled the plane up to 39,000 feet, and decompressed the cabin, so that the lack of oxygen made everyone in the cabin lose consciousness within 60 seconds and could not resist. All the people on board, including himself, died of hypoxia. Then the plane ran out of fuel and crashed into the sea.

SUGGESTION 11 – CAPTURED BY ALIENS

A less intelligent person has provided some interesting explanations. He said that since no clues had been found on the ground for such a long time, the plane might have been hijacked by aliens. Probably, FAST (the Five-Hundred-Metre Aperture Spherical radio Telescope) in Guizhou, China, could be used to help look for MH370, and the plane might have landed on Mars or Jupiter.

SUGGESTION 12 - AN EXPLOSION IN THE BAGGAGE

Some people who analysed events said that on board were four tons of the fruit mangosteen, the wrapping carton of which might contain a bomb. Under this theory, the plane had exploded shortly after take-off. No visible debris was found in the search because the plane disintegrated in the air.

SUGGESTION 13 - A HIDDEN AIRCRAFT

One pilot thought that 40 minutes after MH370's take off, the pilot had turned off the answering machine and positioned his aircraft under another plane, so that two planes displayed only one spot on the radar. The plane might then have flown to North Korea, Pakistan, or a country in Africa, and landed at an airport in a self-governed country. They had used the latest stealth technology, so the aircraft could not be detected.

One aircraft hides another (drawn by Liu Panpan)

SUGGESTION 14 - A COLLISION

A capable pilot called Chris Goodfellow pointed out on Wired that the plane might have experienced an electrical fire in the air. There was also the possibility that the aircraft had suddenly encountered outside objects such as space garbage, a meteorite or other object, resulting in the crash of both. This led to the plane not sending out a signal any more and losing contact with the ground.

SUGGESTION 15 - CRIMINAL ACTION

Malaysian police have defined the investigation about the disappearance of MSA passenger MH370 as a criminal investigation. More than 170 surveys have so far been conducted on MH370. As for the investigation into the pilot's flight simulator, there is still no final conclusion. Police are waiting for experts to give a report. If the investigation results were released now, they might have an influence on later indictment. The investigation into the reasons for the loss of MH370 is still ongoing.

CHAPTER TWO

What really went wrong on MH370?

The whole world was shaken by the disappearance of MH370. Many concerned countries and well-meaning people were quickly engaged in an unprecedented international search for the aircraft, while trying to figure out the cause of its disappearance. So far, 26 countries are reported to have sent planes, warships and merchant ships to the suspected sites. Hundreds of millions of people in our country are concerned about the search results and are ready to serve in the search and rescue. But up till now, the search has yielded no results. Is the missing Malaysia airlines flight one of the biggest mysteries of all time? What happened to you, MH370?

According to reports, Flight MH370 took off from Kuala Lumpur airport on March 8, 2014. Originally it was scheduled to arrive in Beijing at 6:30 am, but the plane lost contact with the air traffic control centre over the Malaysian state of Subang shortly after take-off. The Civil Aviation Administration of China learned that it had lost contact with the control department in Ho Chi Minh City, Vietnam and lost radar signals. The passenger plane had not been in contact with China's regulatory authorities or the Chinese intelligence community.

Time has shown that these reports were objective, authentic and credible. The plane took off at 00:42 March, 2014 and disappeared at 1:25, just 43 minutes later. What happened to flight MH370 in those 43 minutes?

The aircraft was in a normal cruise state after 0:50; at 01:19:29, the co-pilot spoke to the tower and said 'All right, good night.' 104 seconds later, at 01:21:13, MH370 disappeared from the Kuala Lumpur airport radar. It disappeared from the Suratthani military radar at 01:22, and from the Ho Chi Minh City air control radar at 01:25. Then the aircraft's altitude went down from FL350 (35,000ft) to 0. Within three minutes the flight had disappeared. The actual valid time was between 62 and 180 seconds, but for ease of expression, we will call it three minutes.

At 1:37, when the ground should have been receiving messages from the ACARS system at 30-second intervals but didn't, the flight 'disappeared'. What might have happened during those three minutes, and what might the disappearance of the radar signal at the same time and the flight altitude returning to zero indicate? From 01:19 to 01:37 is just 18 minutes. What did it suggest? If you hold these details in mind, it is not hard to discover the mystery.

MH370 took off from Kuala Lumpur airport at 0442 local time on March 8, 2014, and all was normal half an hour after take-off. This indicates that all preparations were normal before departure, and all the personnel and equipment on board were normal.

What might have happened during those three minutes is the point we should look into.

FOCUS 1: EXPLOSION IN THE AIR OR ATTACKED BY WEAPONS.

Whether a fatal crash was caused by an explosion because someone took the mangosteen fruit on board combined with a bomb, or a bomb was set off by fake passport holders who mingled with the passengers and crew members, or an attack was made with various weapons such as missiles, in terms of time, it could have happened within the three minutes. However, with an explosion in the air there are two considerations: first, there will be a lot of drift; the second is the 'air fireball.' Whether the drift falls on the sea or land, when an aircraft falls from an altitude of 11,000 metres, the debris will be scattered over an area of more than 150 square kilometres. For nearly four years, the sea has been searched for floating objects, and there have been no reports of fallen objects on land.

MH370 was a 63-metre-long jumbo jet, and there should have been a 'fireball' if it exploded in the air. With so many spy satellites in the air and other monitoring satellites, it is completely unreasonable that such an explosion would have been undetected.

US intelligence agency senior officials said on March 12, 2014, that the US spy satellite did not monitor any signs of an air explosion. The US 'Global Search Flash System' also did not show any evidence of an explosion. Nor did any other satellites around the world. Therefore, the 'air explosion' possibility can be ruled out.

FOCUS 2: THE PLANE WAS ABDUCTED BY ALIENS FROM ANOTHER PLANET.

MH370 weighed 250 tons and was 63 metres in length, a huge plane, and even at 1000 kilometres altitude it would still be subject to the same force of gravity. I am afraid that this could happen only in a fairytale.

FOCUS 3: HIJACKING, SUICIDE OR TERRORISTS ON THE PLANE.

If MH370 was hijacked, one possibility is that the plane was not able to land or make an emergency landing because the potential hijack was detected by passengers or because the plane was out of control when the passengers were fighting against the terrorists. In that case, the plane could possibly have crashed into the sea or a high mountain. In recent years there have been precedents to this. Some planes landed successfully, some crashed; in other cases the acts of terrorism were foiled.

This aircraft plane suddenly went missing in normal operation. This could be caused by hijacking, pilot suicide or a fight between the passengers and the terrorists. Whichever it was, it is against common sense that not one of the 239 people sent any message out. Moreover, hijacking an aircraft requires a number of people to make preparations over a long period. After a hijacking, relevant organisations or people would soon claim responsibility via the media, Internet or other means, or they would ask for a ransom, for someone to be release, or similar. Yet years have passed, and no response or evidence has been found.

Some say the pilot killed himself. There were two people in the cockpit, and they could not both have committed suicide within a few minutes. There is no chance that one pilot was armed with a gun to shoot the other and then kill himself. The possibility of a hijacker, a terrorist attack or pilot suicide was largely ruled out after investigations.

FOCUS 4: BIRD STRIKE

The plane could also have crashed because the pilots reacted wrongly after the plane had hit birds, but no birds fly at 10,000 metres, so this possibility too can be ruled out.

FOCUS 5: THE PILOT'S SUDDEN DEATH OR LOSS OF CONSCIOUSNESS

Did this happen to Captain Zahari, who was 53 years old? Between co-pilot Hamid's last call at 01:19:29 on March 8th and 01:22, aircraft information disappeared from the radar of Thailand, Vietnam and Kuala Lumpur. If one pilot suddenly died and the other reacted incorrectly, it might lead to the aircraft losing control. This is a possibility, but the team should have been familiar with this kind of emergency situation through intensive training, and it is very unlikely that the plane would fall within three minutes. If the crew of MH370 were surprised by a sudden death or loss of consciousness, the aircraft could have flown by itself until the fuel ran out. If so, the plane would strike the surface of the sea or the ground, forming a large area of debris. The 'eyes' of the many satellites in the sky have not seen such debris, making it unlikely. There were also medical staff among the passengers.

FOCUS 6: ENCOUNTERING ABNORMAL WEATHER

While the weather was well suited for flying, a storm may arise from a clear sky, and unexpected thunderbolts and storms are both unpredictable and difficult to avoid. In this situation, the plane could lose control and suffer rapid mechanical failure.

If an aircraft runs into the eye of a storm, it will rise and fall almost instantaneously. There have been cases of this happening. On July 24 2014, Algerian Airlines flight AH5017, a McDonnell-Douglas MD-83, flew into a storm 50 minutes after take-off. The engines are thought to have iced up because the pilots did not active the anti-icing system, and they did not take appropriate action when the aircraft began to drop. Within three minutes it fell from 10,000 metres into the jungles of Mali, killing all 116 people on board. When the plane hit the ground, it broke up into small pieces.

If MH370 happened to encounter this kind of abnormal weather, a crash within three minutes because of a thunderbolt or entering the eye of a storm is entirely possible. In terms of time, it is reasonable and logical for the plane to crash within three minutes.

FOCUS 7: A HACKER GOT INTO THE COMPUTER AND SENT THE AIRCRAFT OUT OF CONTROL

Hackers or crackers may have cracked the computer control systems of the aircraft, gaining access to electronic equipment or the remote control system. They could have reprogrammed the plane, reversing the polarity of the cockpit display system or lift system, changing course, shutting down communication or the engines, cabin oxygen supply, power outage and so on. In the face of such a situation, the pilot's own abilities are not sufficient to identify, correct or alter the situation. They would only be able to play with it, and the result was a shocking human tragedy.

Hacker harassment may also be related to politics. The disappearance of Flight MH370 occurred on International

Women's Day on March 8, and it was suggested that hackers had acted in opposition to feminism.

The Boeing 777-200 first flew in 2002 and had been in use for nearly 12 years, with some equipment ageing, especially the black box, which was supposed to be changed but was not. In any case it is not possible to find the black box if a plane disappears.

Forty minutes after take-off the aircraft flew up to 10,668 metres, where the plane was in auto-cruise and mostly computer-controlled, and the pilot would be at his most relaxed and most prone to carelessness. At this point, if the computer system on the plane was affected by hacking, or passengers on the plane used mobile phones, computers or other electronic communication equipment, it could cause a malfunction in the computer system, leading to power blackouts, a communication system malfunction or mechanical failure, making the pilots' manual operation useless. It takes a 250-ton object only 49 seconds to fall from a 12,000-metre altitude to the ground in free fall, and this makes the plane disappear without trace.

There were related reports in 2005: a Boeing 777 aircraft, flying over the Indian Ocean, was cruising at a height of 10,000 metres when its computer software failed to calculate speed and acceleration, causing the plane to suddenly rise 915 metres. Malaysia's military radar showed that Flight MH370 had been 'sharply rising and suddenly falling'. Did the same thing happen to MH370 this time?

At the same cruising altitude, if the plane suddenly rises from 10668 metres to 11583 metres, all the people on board will lose consciousness in a moment as they would on a roller coaster. From 11583 metres back to 10668 metres, the pilot probably lost consciousness. Combined with improper operation and computer failure, the aircraft will be destroyed in minutes.

FOCUS 8: EQUIPMENT FAILURE

In addition to being harassed by hackers or computer malfunction, the plane may also have had problems of mechanical failure, failed wires or lines, or parts falling from the plane itself. When these problems arise and the pilots don't take the correct action, the plane may lose speed and fly out of control until it crashes.

According to air crash statistics for the 40 years from 1974 to 2014, after problems caused by mechanical failure, electrical failure, undercarriage failure, detector failure, fuselage skin peeling, the hatch door opening, wings falling off, cabin on fire, the rudder getting stuck, wings getting iced and so on, crashes and casualties caused by improper handling and operation by pilots take up over 55%.

The same kind of situation occurred to MH370 over 40 minutes after take-off: a pilot's mistake, even pressing one button wrong, could cause critical loss of speed and crash in an instant.

FOCUS 9: A MISHANDLED 'ROADBLOCK' ENCOUNTER

Flight MH370 took off from Kuala Lumpur airport at 0:42 and reached cruising altitude at 050:50. Before 1:19:29, for all 227 passengers and 12 crew members, everything was normal. But after 1:20, there was no more communication. Surveillance radar signals disappeared; the communication addressing signals were gone; the logging data could no longer be found from the auxiliary Pacific satellite; and the aircraft's altitude dropped from 35,000 feet to zero. Within that short time, all communications of Flight MH370 were aborted and radar signals disappeared. The internal and external monitoring system of MH370 reported data consistent with the disappearance of the plane.

I think this is very possibly what happened: the pilot was caught off-guard when the plane suddenly encountered an unexpected event in the normal cruising flight of MH370. The pilot did not have the skills to handle this, or he dealt with it inappropriately, causing the plane to stall quickly, sending it out of control and making it dive into the sea.

This event would be what is called a 'roadblock'. During normal cruising, the pilots or aircraft radar suddenly detected some obstruction in the way, something which could hinder normal flight or endanger aircraft safety. The roadblock could be space debris, a meteor shower, a mirage, a tornado, another flying object. In this case, the pilot will instinctively take evasive action to avoid the problem and continue flying. Of course, if this is done properly, the plane will avoid the obstacle. But if he encounters something unexpected during the operation, the pilot's instinct is to immediately brake, pull up and turn right or left. The wrong action could cause a crash in an instant.

It's like the way we ordinary people drive on a highway. When the driver suddenly sees an obstacle ahead while he is cruising at a speed of 150 kilometres per hour, his first reaction is to brake to slow down, and then turn the wheel right or left. Properly handled, he may avoid a terrible traffic accident; improperly handled, the car could hit the obstacle or roll over, potentially causing a terrible accident. Such tragedies abound in the history of road transportation. This, not an exceptional case – it happens hundreds of times every day in China alone.

According to the saved data from MH370 showing that the temperature went from 24° to 333°, there must have been evasive action. And it was this deadly evasive action that caused MH370 to disappear.

From what has been discussed above, I think:

1. MH370's disappearance was not because of the pilots' suicide; it was not because of hijacking or sabotage; it was

not because of being shot down, or exploding in the air; it was not because of being carried away by aliens; it was not because of being hit by birds.

2. The pilot's sudden death or loss of consciousness could not be completely excluded, but it is very unlikely.

3. Internet hacking cannot be ruled out.

4. The most likely explanation is that the aircraft encountered a 'roadblock' or entered the eye of a storm, or there was a computer malfunction or abnormal speed, together with faulty operation, leading to a major accident. The accident caused the disappearance of the aircraft.

CHAPTER THREE

MH370, where are you?

The disappearance of Malaysia Airlines Flight MH370 on March 8, 2014 has become a mystery. On March 9, some said it had crashed in the Gulf of Thailand in the South China Sea. After the 12th, it was said that because of the length of runway a Boeing 777 needs, the plane may have made a forced landing on Christmas Island or Cocos Island in the Southern Indian Ocean. On the 17th, another guess was that the plane might have landed in central Asia's Kizrekum desert or the Muyunkum desert.

On March 19, China's Ministry of Defence said that in China's Nansha Waters and the million square kilometres of land covered by China, 'No signs have been found in the territory of the missing Malaysian airliner'. Countries such as Afghanistan and Laos also said they did not have any traces of MH370.

On March 24th, Malaysia issued a statement saying the final

location of the flight was 'within a kilometre' of the Indian Ocean, about 1,800 kilometres west of Perth.

On March 8, 2014:

At 00:42, MH370 took off from Kuala Lumpur International Airport

At 00:50, MH370 entered cruise mode.

At 01:07, the ACARS system communicated normally.

At 01:19:29, the pilot left his last message to the control centre via the air communication system: 'Good night'.

At 01:21:13, Kuala Lumpur airport radar reported: 'MH370's signal has disappeared.'

At 01:22, the Suratthani Air Force radar also reported: 'MH370's signal disappeared.'

At 01:25, the Ho Chi Minh city radar reported: 'MH370's signal disappeared.' Meanwhile, the flight altitude dropped from FL350 (35,000 feet) to 0.

At 01:37, the ACARS system and the ground control centre reported: 'MH370's signal disappeared.'

At 02:03:41, the Pacific satellite logging data disappeared. Now all signals from MH370 had ceased. Something abnormal had happened in the 18 minutes between 1:19:30 and 1:38. At least the wireless transmission equipment on the plane failed, and there was no call made; the addressing signals were not sent. If the problem didn't lie in the ground receiving equipment, it must have lain in the communication transmitting system on the aircraft.

The communication signals told us that we should not consider 01:20 (when the last conversation took place) to be the time when the plane began to disappear. Instead, 01:37 would be more reasonable.

The authorities said that the communication on the plane had been artificially turned off, while the 'handshake' signals still existed; according to the last handshake signal at 08:19 on March 8, the time of disappearance should be 09:19. The disappearance of MH370 should be characterized as a 'missing plane' event.

Radar signals told us the plane was not detected after 1:25.

Communication signals reflect the local operation of the aircraft in the air or the ground. Radar signals reflect the presence of aircraft in the air or on the ground. They are two different systems. One is a radio response system and the other is a radio reflection system. When the two different systems went wrong at the same time, an accident must have happened. If only the communication signal was not available, it could be explained by the aircraft flying into a 'blind zone' or the pilot switching off or deactivating the transmission system. And it would explain this well.

If only the radar signal disappeared, it could be said that the pilot had changed the flight position of the aircraft, beyond the radar signal control range. Other possibilities could be super low/high altitude flight or radar failure. So when the two different kinds of tools had the same reaction while the plane was cruising, there is only one explanation: the plane had crashed. But nobody heard or saw it. When the plane disappeared in the air at that time, it must have crashed either into the sea or into the ground. There has never been any exception to this in aviation history.

As the saying goes, seeing is believing, but hearing is not. Within three minutes, both 'hearing' and 'seeing' disappeared, based on which, it must be concluded that MH370 disappeared at the junction beneath Route 24° north-east to Kuala Lumpur, where the radar beams sent by Thailand, Vietnam and Malaysia disappeared. This passes the test.

If we are sure we know what happened on board and when the aircraft disappeared, we know where it has gone: under the aircraft's route, the joint location where the radar beams transmitted by Thailand, Vietnam and Malaysia disappeared. Then it is not hard to find out where it is.

The plane took off at 00:42 March 8, 2014 and disappeared at 01:25, just 43 minutes later. Assuming the speed was 900 km/h, we can calculate the flight distance as 900/60×43=645km. So the area 645 kilometres away from the take-off should be the key area. In general the key search area should be determined as follows: draw an arc, Kuala Lumpur being the centre of the circle, Kuala Lumpur-Hòn Khoa as one right-angle side, Kuala Lumpur-Serasan as the other, the radius being 600 km. The waters, deep mountains, or some inaccessible areas 100 km left and 100 km right to the arch should be the resting place of MH370 (as illustrated on the graphics below).

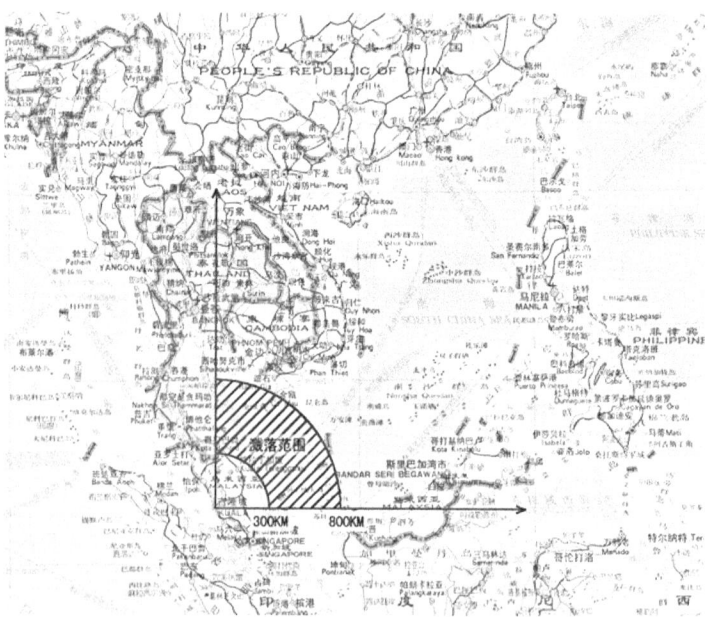

Diagram of MH17's splashdown and floating range
(drawn by Liu Panpan)

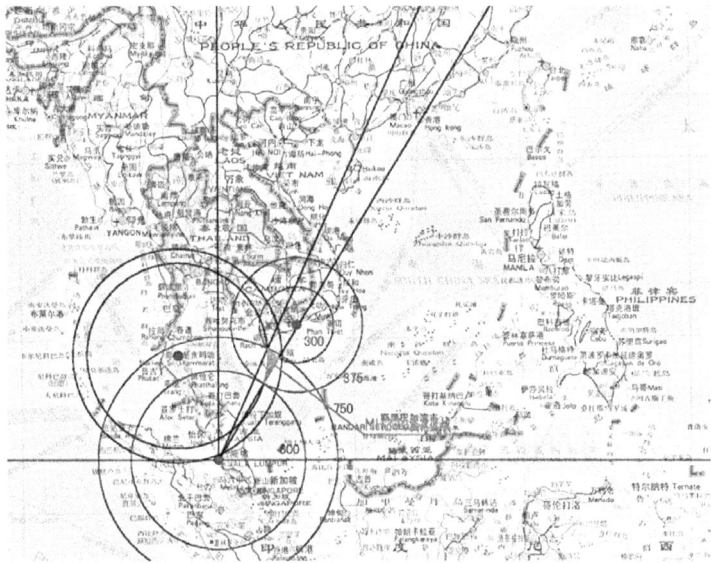

Diagram of MH370's estimated splashdown area, a triangular area of approximately 13,000 square kilometres (drawn by Yu Haibo)

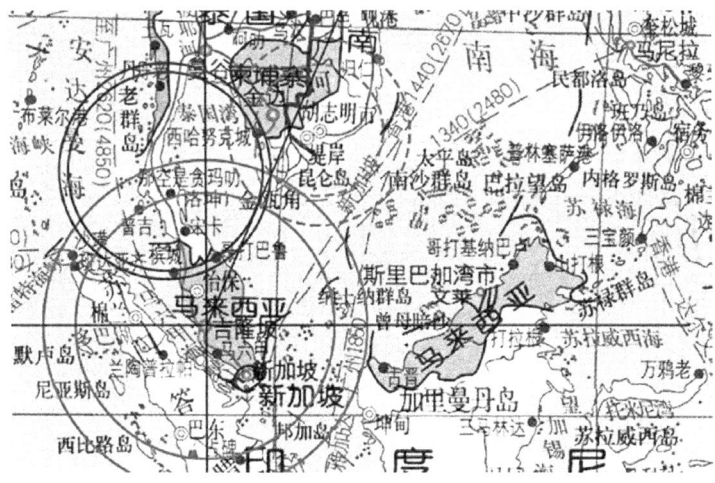

Diagram of MH370's location suggested by the radars of Malaysia, Thailand and Vietnam (about 1800 square kilometres) (drawn by Yu Haibo)

Diagram of the joint point of the three azimuth angles from the direction-finding stations of the radars of Malaysia, Thailand and Vietnam (drawn by Yu Haibo)

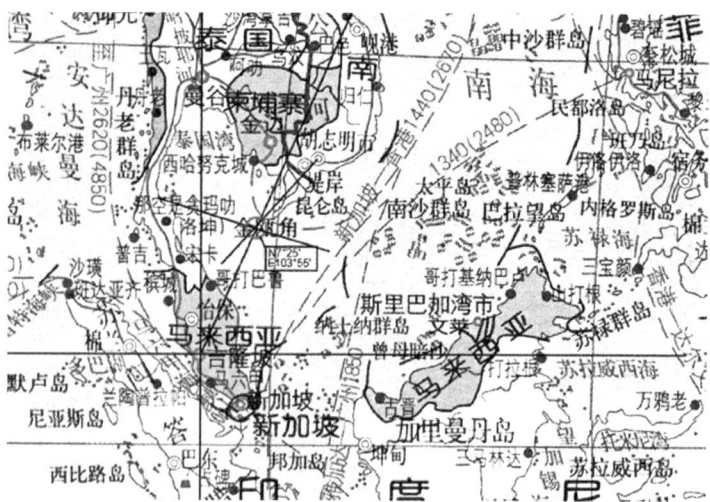

Diagram of the area where MH370 crashed (about 200 square kilometres) determined according to the direction-finding theory (waters around N07° 25' E103° 55' with a radius of 50 km (drawn by Yu Haibo)

The author proposes that the current whereabouts of MH370 should be determined according to the principle of radio direction finding, which is both scientific and accurate.

The scientific principle of radio direction finding is based on the propagation characteristics of electromagnetic waves and the process of determining the direction of radio waves by means of instruments and equipment. The wave direction is the direction of the radio wave in the electromagnetic environment of the direction-finding machine. Determination often requires several different direction-finding stations at different places working jointly to determine the direction. They make all three azimuth angles join, and the ultimate goal is to determine the direction and location of the radiation source.

MH370 is like a radio transmitter (a source of radiation); Kuala Lumpur, Ho Chi Minh City, and Surat Thani are three direction-finding stations. The intersection of the three azimuth angles at the same time, 01:25, was at N7° 25', E103° 55'. This is where MH370, the source of radiation, must be.

The more direction-finding stations there are from different distances and directions, the more azimuth angles there will be, the more concentrated the intersections will be, the more precise the location will be and the more precise the source of the radiation's location will be. On the contrary, the fewer direction-finding station there are, the fewer azimuth angles there will be, and the less accurate the intersections and location of the source of radiation will be. If only one or two stations display the three azimuth angles, only an approximate direction could be offered instead of a location. With just one azimuth angle at one time from a station, the reference value is very limited, even misleading. If a station provides one azimuth angle multiple times, this is worth referring to. Sometimes, two stations form a 180° angle, so it is hard to choose between them. There being a number of skills in the choice of azimuth angles, experienced people will select out a few angles with high credibility, discard the false azimuth angles and draw conclusions about the exact location.

Inexperienced people sometimes get confused by the false azimuth angles, so their conclusions may be far from the truth. The author has many years of successful experience in the selection of azimuth angles. The three-point location method can be used to determine the whereabouts of MH370. Azimuth angles from Kuala Lumpur, Suratthan and Ho Chi Minh City are adopted. Among the three, the one from Thailand is critical as a 'tangent', in addition to the angle formed by Ho Chi Minh City and Kuala Lumpur. Therefore, where MH370 has gone is solved by looking at the junction of these three lines.

Where are you, MH370? The answer is: the waters around N7° 25', E103° 55'. Taking into account ocean currents and many other elements, the actual position of the wreck could not be exactly there, but certainly within 100 kilometres.

Let me turn to radar, which determines positions based on radio direction-finding theory. When the radar signals show normally on the monitor, it suggests that the object being tracked still exists; if the signals on the monitor are gone when all the equipment functions well, the tracked object must have escaped from sight or disappeared. MH370 belongs to this type of case: it disappeared suddenly from the radars of three different regions within three minutes at the same time, definitely no coincidence. Therefore, MH370 must have been away from the designated route. It is certain that the aircraft has crashed under the route.

So according to the three-point location method, we have decided that the aircraft fell somewhere near N7° 25', E103° 55'. The location, as shown on the map, is the waters south of Nam Can, Vietnam or deep mountains (see previous page).

Reasoning conversely to the reset flight direction and time of disappearance, we find that they approximately match the time of the signals' disappearance from air traffic control in Ho Chi Minh City and Thailand radar. What's more, the distance is reasonable (200-300 km away from Ho Chi Minh City, 500-750 km away from Kuala Lumpur, 600-800 km from Thailand radar). It is not going to be hard to spot the wreck of the aircraft in this key area with a wide and thorough search.

Considering that there was a discrepancy in the reported time of the radar signals' disappearance from Vietnam, Thailand and Malaysia, when searching for their whereabouts, appropriate corrections should be made according to the actual verified data. Considering the drift factor, to be on the safe side, the searched area can be slightly expanded. During the search, the influence of waves, currents, topography and landforms should be fully considered, such as the possibility of it having fallen into a trench or basin at the bottom of the sea, or a silt bed or cliff crack. Perhaps too little of the aircraft is exposed to be detected; the plane is buried by thick silt or magma, or the splashdown area is within a small range. Those factors may all range beyond our expectations. There is hope only if a thorough search is conducted. The search in Nam Can-related areas like the Cambodia-Vietnam and Vietnam-China border should not be given up easily either.

If nothing is found in this area, to eliminate doubts, there are two other possibilities, although these are unlikely. One is the coordinate the Malaysian military last detected, the area between N6° 58'60', E117° 1' 59' and N5° 30', E107° 37'. This area includes waters around Laut Island, the Great Natuna Besar, James Shoal, the Nansha Islands and Mount Kinabalu in Malaysia.

Although it was reported on March 8 that the Malaysian army had found an unidentified civilian airliner heading west towards the Indian Andaman Sea, the area between 2,300 km south-west of Perth, Australia and 2,600 km north-west of Perth, which is well away from the preset route, is not very likely. As it turned out, nothing has been found after four years of searching.

Another key point is that from April 5 to 10, more than once in the area of 2,300-2,700 km north-west of Perth, Australia's ADV Ocean Shield and China's Coast Guard Vessel both detected signals suspected to be from the black box. According to factors such as the transmission features of pulse signals and their frequency, I confirmed as early as April 10, 2014, that these were addressing signals, balloon signals, beacon signals or signals of some equipment set at the bottom of the sea rather than signals from MH370's black box.

So-called satellite-aircraft handshake signals might also be a kind of illusion caused by features of satellite systems. It would be a mistake to take satellite-aircraft handshake signals as evidence.

If one to three planes are in the same area covered by the maritime satellites at the same time, then which is the one shaking hands with the satellites? Data show, at 00:00 - 02:00, March 8, Flight 3K514 from Bangkok to Singapore and Flight CX137 from Hong Kong to Perth, another flight from Kota Kinabalu to Penang, all in the same flight area as MH370. During that period, did the Indian Ocean Satellite handshake MH370, CK137 or 3K514? (See illustration p. xx) Moreover, fixed-point synchronous satellites are neither the sun nor the fixed stars. Their positions are influenced by various elements, like floating and swinging, resulting in shifts in frequency, angles of depression and angles of elevation. It is quite unreliable to prove the positions with instantaneous, irregular changes – you need a period of continuous, regular frequency shift and changing data of angles of depression and elevation. Some data are not usable at all.

In an area covered by two satellites, it not rare for a station to communicate with Satellite A and Satellite B alternately. In the professional field, this is called 'Frequency Shift' or 'Satellite Shift.'

The last satellite signal from MH370 was at 8:19, March 8. Is this questionable? I don't think this was the time MH370 dived into the sea after running out of fuel after seven hours of flight. It might be the time flight crew members switched off the power after arriving in Perth. In other words, the plane crashed before 1:37, and its signals transmitter died six hours later, which matched the designed service of a transmitter, in terms of time. It has nothing to do with whether it is flying.

It was also possible that the handshake signals terminated after the addressing system was powered off when the plane crashed, while the location of the plane did not change. So the handshake signals went on working for a few more hours until the power ran out. The existence of handshake signals from only one synchronous satellite is not reliable. If there are two or three satellites sending the same signals, it will be another story.

Now the search focus is on the Southern Indian Ocean. The focus is on unidentified, out-sync PING data 'heard' by an Indian satellite rather than on the three countries' radar signals (equal to three satellites), which is dwelling on the abstract and avoiding real issues. What's coming out of it could not be more obvious. It is seeking what is far away and neglecting what lies close at hand to determine that the aircraft crashed into the waters west of Perth in the Southern Indian Ocean just because of the seven 'handshake' signals from the Indian Ocean satellites (one satellite cannot help locate; at least two are needed, because one may cause error).

Ever since the search focus was moved to a vast area west of Perth, Australia on March 14, 2014, 26 countries were engaged, using all kinds of methods. The floating pieces and suspected black box signals found in the area were finally excluded. Many days of omnidirectional three-dimensional search should be able to prove that MH370 did not fall into the Indian Ocean.

A search was done in the Gulf of Thailand, and nothing was found. A search was done in islands like Kalimantan Island, and nothing was found. In the Straits of Malacca, nothing was found. In the western waters of Indonesia and Australia, nothing was found. So where is Flight MH370? Now it's suggested the search should be drawn back to the South China Sea. A thorough search is needed, especially the waters and land south to Nam Can, which was on the way to the flight's destination. That area should be the top priority, worth searching repeatedly. I think MH370 will be found, as has been expected by all.

CHAPTER FOUR

The clues that MH370 crashed at Scene 1

After the disappearance of Flight MH370, both Malaysia and Australia organised experts and relevant personnel to conduct a long and serious investigation into the event. On October 8, 2014, the Australian Traffic Safety Administration issued a safety report numbered AE-2014-054; on March 8, 2015, the Malaysian 13th Security Investigation Team published a Safety Survey of Factual Information MH370; on October 3 2015, the MH370 Search & Rescue Committee issued a search & rescue final summary report. These reports, as well as relevant information, provide us with a lot of valid data.

1   Radar data prove that MH370 crashed vertically at Scene 1 (South China Sea)

After Flight MH370 went missing, Malaysia released a 584-page survey report. The report shows that its flight altitude was more than 200 metres lower and its flying direction changed from 24° to 333°, according to the last data transmitted from the plane to the ground. Some experts believe that the aircraft heading changed from north-east to north-west flight; some think it did a U-turn southward, during which it gracefully performed a few left turns and right turns. So naturally the plane was guided to the Indian Ocean. Search and rescue commanders are also very inclined to shift the search effort to the Indian Ocean.

The author holds no doubts about these data. Meanwhile, he argues that these data validly proved the fact that the plane crashed at Scene 1.

How do we interpret the data? Flight MH370 changed its heading from 24° to 333°, a sharp turn from the north-east to the north-west. The aircraft could be interpreted as flying north-west, flying to the south in a U-turn or, flying to the Indian Ocean. All are possible. You could see it as evasive action. However, the data are interesting. Now let us look at the changes in the heading degree from an different angle.

Note that 333° is the heading in a clockwise direction; if anti-clockwise, shouldn't it be -27°? Flight MH370 suddenly changed its normal heading of +24° to -27°; can it be seen as the flight changing its state? That is to say, the state was changed from a horizontal one into a vertical one.

And then the flight altitude was reduced by 200 metres. What if it was further reduced by 500 metres or more? Does that mean its angle changed from 333° to 360°, also called 0°, and its flight altitude was 0?

At that time, Flight MH370 was cruising over the South China Sea. If it changed its posture from horizontal one to vertical, the results can be imagined. In the horizontal state, the flight is heading into unlimited blue sky. In the vertical state, it is heading straight for the deep blue ocean!

If so, when the aircraft changed the horizontal state into a vertical dive, the angle with the sea is changed from +24 to -27, the intersection angle 93, ie Flight MH370 dived into the sea at an angle of 93°!

The radar signals of the three countries, a direct reflection of Flight MH370's state, lost their contact with the flight in blink of an eye – a plane in the air was like a stone falling into the sea, untraceable.

Moreover, Flightradar 24, assisted by Google Maps and aviation information, can directly see the position of the flight. While travelling by air, many people are worried about flights being delayed. An innovative APP named Flightradar 24 can solve users' problems. The APP can provide users from all over the world with real-time flight information data. There are three versions, webpage, IOS (payment needed) and Android. With the assistance of Google Maps (microblog) and aviation information, one can not only see the position of the flight and click on or search for a particular flight, but get access to the airline company, flight altitude, whether it is on time and so on. The database above even includes the flight's historical log and data. Switch to the Cockpit View mode, and one can obtain simulated flying experience as if you were on the scene.

At 10:43 on March 8, 2014, an iPad user of Flightradar 24 passed on some information worthy of attention. He said 'The last datum our radar received was the flight altitude returning from FL350 to 0.' The last altitude of MH370 before its disappearance was 0, while the second to last was FL350 (35,000 feet, normal cruising altitude), so the interruption of the flight's signals was sudden.

Wasn't the fact that the flying direction and altitude changed so consistently proof of what had happened? At this point, the flight crashed into the sea!

It is really like what a classic Chinese poem depicts: from the side, it looks like a whole range; from the end, a single peak: far, near, high, low, no two views are alike. Why can't I tell the true shape of the mountain Lu-shan? Because I am on Lu-shan.

Some experts, according to the radar data, believe Flight MH370 went down in the Southern Indian Ocean, but the author, based on the same data, believes it went down in the South China Sea. If a plane dives at a steep angle into the water, it will not be crushed by the resulting impact but will sink into the sea in one piece. So there will be few floating objects and little oil on the surface, making it traceless. The mystery of MH370 was most probably caused by big waves. In diving, an angle of 90° generates the smallest splash.

2 The satellite data show Flight MH370 went missing before 41 seconds of 2:03 at the first site.

According to the published Malaysian Interim Report and the Australian Report, Flight MH370 used the Pacific satellite for communication (POR) from 20:50, March 7, 2014 - 1:20 pm. From the last call at 01:19:29 on March 8 to 02:31:41, when all communication was terminated, there were no Pacific satellite data. The above data show that at this point, Flight MH370's link to the outside world ended. Communication is as vital to a plane as breath is to a human being.

The three outside radars, Kuala Lumpur, Ho Chi Minh, and Suratthani, which had been observing Flight MH370, reported almost simultaneously after the last call that the flight was gone from their sight. These 'eyes of a thousand miles' witnessed the end of Flight MH370 on the air. At that point it made a spin in the air (from 24 degrees to 333 degrees) and then disappeared. Even if the plane was still flying for those minutes or even for an hour, it could not have flown out of the South China Sea into the Indian Ocean. Unless its speed changed from Mach 0.84 to a cosmic velocity – after a lapse of 65 minutes.

At 2:25:27 on March 8, 2014, satellite communications logged in again, but during the login process this time:

1. The logging satellite was changed from the Pacific satellite to the Indian Ocean satellite.
2. The ground station did not receive the flight number.
3. The registration request of a satellite communication system and the state of the signal's synchronous pulse frequency were abnormal.

No reception of the flight number can be regarded as no official ID; the abnormal synchronous pulse frequency is the same as an unmatched footprint. These two pieces of evidence are enough to confirm that this flight was not Flight MH370. The registered login, often referred to as the 'first handshake', was no longer the Pacific satellite, but the Indian Ocean satellite. Since the login satellite was not the original one and the flight number was not identified, neither the aircraft nor the satellite could get synchronized. On what basis was this aircraft claimed to be flight MH370?

In satellite communication activities, the author understands that no subject would ever transfer from the Pacific satellites to the Indian Ocean satellites in the absence of synchronization and a registered login to recognize a flight number identification. This would be contrary to communication principles. In a uniform coverage area, even though the communication jump is normal, neither the identifier nor the sync pulse will change – unless the subject has been changed.

After that, the seven handshakes, sometimes from the aircraft to the satellite and sometimes from the ground stations to the satellite, were seemingly tailored. Trying to make them fit together could not be sustained, since they did not belong together. Although the two sets of data are in the shared coverage of the Pacific and the Indian Ocean communication satellites, it is artificial and unconvincing to treat the latter and the former as an integrated whole. 'Self-willed' is how the leader of the maritime satellite organisation defined the investigation authorities' behaviour in insisting that Flight MH370 splashed down in the Southern Indian Ocean based on mathematical models.

After carefully studying the data from the seven handshakes, I think reference to such data requires not only going through the processed and sorted data for the 24-hour period from March 7, 2014 to March 8 but also checking, over 72 hours, the original data from the shared channel of the two satellites in the Pacific and the Indian Ocean. If more of the original data reflect communications with the paired ground station and these data are released to the public, it will be more convincing.

Based on the seven handshake signals within no more than six hours from 02:25 to 08:19, we can draw at least four different explanations:

Explanation 1: the seven handshakes had nothing to do with Flight MH370. As mentioned above, the Pacific satellite stopped all connection to MH370 at 02:03:41 local time. The Indian Ocean handshake signals didn't match it, nor did logging registration; there was no exclusive connection. They should be regarded like two cars in two different lanes. They were totally unrelated.

Explanation 2: the seven handshake signals were not transmitted by one device. They might be transmitted by several devices, including various types of aircraft, other vehicles, boats or warships. Some might be vessels or aircraft heading for Perth.

There might be direct satellite communications; some might communicate by cable to wireless, or wireless to wireless.

The four communications from 03:41 to 06:41 were possibly signals from a transmitting station which was sending standby signals to the ground station of the Perth satellite, which in turn forwarded the signals to the Indian Ocean satellite. So there were communications via cable to wireless and wireless to wireless. The other three times had different time intervals, supposed not to be transmitted by same devices.

Explanation 3: a hacker group was playing tricks such as 'car deck'(involving fake licence plates) or a disguised telephone number. This trick of hacker groups is sinister and ruthless. In order to mislead subsequent searches, they counterfeited Flight MH370 and transmitted some 'fake data' via a maritime satellite public channel to the Indian Ocean maritime satellite and the Perth satellite ground station. They aimed to make the mystery of MH370 more confusing. If that was the case, it could be technically superior to the Alpha dog that beat the Go champion. If they used their intelligence for military purposes or terrorist activities, they could change, in the sky, the tracks of satellites, flying missiles, planes and ships. If they were engaged in terrorist activities, they would not launch such simple actions as the 'lonely wolf' type suicide attack, but horrible, unimaginable attacks like crashing the Pentagon's command system, the Japanese economy or the world's stock market. When the false becomes true, the true becomes false. This incessant evolution of true and false promotes social progress and technological development.

Explanation 4: on October 8, 2014, the Australian Transport Safety Bureau issued a Security Report, external aviation survey (file no. AE-2014-054) — Analysis Progress of MH370's Flight Path, which stated: 'According to A radar data analysis and a signal received by the satellite communications (SATCOM) system, the plane is located in Australia in the Southern Indian Ocean search area arc. The arc is also the position closest to where the aircraft ran out of fuel.

The definition and analysis of the satellite and flight data continued as MH370 lost contact. The analysis was carried out independently and jointly by Britain, the United States, Australia and Malaysia. According to data built on the mathematical models of probability and hypothesis, MH370 would have exhausted its fuel in its 'zombie flight' and come down at the previously indicated 60,000 square kilometre area, later changed to the 'Seventh Arc', 120,000 square kilometres away in the Southern Indian Ocean. There are more explanations, but I won't go into unnecessary further detail.

From the above text, it is not difficult to see that I can draw a totally different conclusion according to an analysis of the same radar data and signals received by the satellite communications system (SATCOM), contrary to the Australian authorities. They concluded that Flight MH370 crashed in the Southern Indian Ocean, while my conclusion is that it is in the South China Sea just past where the aircraft lost contact.

One says this, another says that. Who is right? The answer will be self-evident when the main body of the aircraft is finally found and salvaged. For the official conclusion that MH370 collapsed in the Southern Indian Ocean, of the four institutions and experts involved in the investigation and study for the survey report, Britain, the United States and Australia basically share the same view and voted for this conclusion. The fourth, Malaysia, may vote to abstain rather than against this conclusion. They hold different views but do not dare to argue.

I read the report 'Safety Survey of Factual Information MH370' by the International Civil Aviation Organisation affiliated to Malaysia, directed at the interim investigation report issued by the 13th Security Investigation Group on March 8, 2015, and the Australian Department of Transportation's report on October 8, 2014, feeling that Malaysia's report was more objective, while the latter was more opinionated and chilling. The reader may obtain the relevant reports and the original data to consider them at leisure.

The radar data and satellite data tell us that it is right to look for the whereabouts of Flight MH370 according to their data. It is the correct decision not to take seriously the handshakes with the Indian Ocean satellite. Some only referred to the change of radar data of the Malaysian military, disregarding the common reflection from the radars of the three countries. They didn't judge, distinguish and analyse together the data from the Malaysian military, 'leading' MH370 to diverge from the route to Beijing. The plane 'turned around', 'reversed' and crashed into the Indian Ocean after 'making circles'. This is because someone deliberately involved the Indian Ocean satellite and the Perth ground station in the event and they 'shook hands', but they shook the wrong hands! The result is that over four years on, hundreds of millions of dollars have been spent and not a single piece of debris from MH370 has been found in the search area. They then spread the news that if it was not found by the end of June 2016, they would put the plane's disappearance down to the pilot's abnormal behaviour, and his intention to make the plane crash. What happened to justice?

If Flight MH370 was loaded with enough fuel, I fear that the handshake data from the 'unidentified flights' and 'non-synchronized sync pulse' would extend past 08:19, probably to 10:19 or 11:19 or even later. There would be more than seven handshakes – maybe eight, maybe even more, and the search would follow from the Indian Ocean to the Atlantic. They might as well search Holland!

What is the difference between this and the idea that Iraq had weapons of mass destruction? In addition to satellite data, the satellites' advocates should find more data evidence, even circumstantial evidence, to prove the relevance and exclusivity of the communication data between Flight MH370 and the Indian Ocean satellite and the Perth ground station. That would be the best way to convince people!

THE CIRCUMSTANTIAL EVIDENCE OF THREE WITNESSES

Now let's talk about the clues. One witness is a New Zealand oil worker who witnessed MH370 'on fire'. According to a newspaper report on June 9, 2014, a 55-year-old New Zealand oil worker named Mike McKay was working for a Japanese corporate. On the morning of March 8, 2014, he was working on 'Songa Mercur', a drilling platform near the port of Vung Tau, Vietnam. At the time when MH370 disappeared from the radar screen, he saw an 'orange light' in the night sky above the water border between Malaysia and Vietnam, and it continued for 10-15 seconds. McKay asserted that it was the lost Flight MH370. He sent emails about what he had seen to his employers and the Vietnamese authorities. However, his statement was treated as false and mischievous. Later, some Australian media found McKay, and established that two police insiders were treating him as 'a reliable witness to the disappearance event of Flight MH370'.

The second is a British woman who believes she saw MH370 on fire. In June 2014 a 41-year-old British sailor, Catherine Tee, reported that in March that year when she was sailing with her husband across the Indian Ocean from Cochin, India to Phuket Island, Thailand, she saw a plane flying by emitting black smoke from its tail. She suspected the plane was on fire. Mrs Tee reported that she also saw, higher in the sky, two other aircraft flying in the opposite direction. Later, after she had figured out, through GPS, the sailing position of her yacht at the time, she found the time and place were consistent with the time and place of the disappearance of MH370, so she reported the matter to the local authorities. This woman's GPS data could help locate the crash site of MH370 more accurately.

The author investigated and found that in addition to Flight MH370, there were indeed three aircraft passing the same area at the time the woman mentioned: one was Flight 3K514 from Bangkok (21:20) to Singapore (0:50), one was Flight CX137 from Hong Kong (22:45) to Perth (06:30), and the other was a flight from Kota Belud (22:35) to Penang (01:15). This witness's intersection is consistent with the radar.

Mike McKay was standing on a drilling platform offshore of Vung Tau Port, Vietnam, so he must have seen the suspected on-fire Flight MH370 aircraft from east to west. Mrs Tee was sailing towards Thailand, when she spotted the smoking aircraft, so she must have observed it from west to east.

One of the meeting points on the graph from the mutual intersection results is in the waters 100 kilometres south of Nam Can, Vietnam, coinciding with the previously described meeting point of the three countries' (Malaysia, Vietnam, Thailand) radar signals at N7° 25', E103° 55'. They were basically at the same position.

A reverse computation of the oil worker's standing height according to the visual observation formula for the human eye on the sea, $S^2 = 16.88h$, derives that the drilling platform is 15 metres above the sea. The distance observed by the woman sailor was relatively great, so her visibility range was farther than that of the oil worker. The time she spotted the aircraft was also earlier, and the aircraft then was flying at a relatively high altitude. Both calculations are logical. With the same approach, we cannot find, in the Southern Indian Ocean, the shared visual point of the two observers or their mutual intersection point. Even if there is an artificial intersection, the conclusion based on it will be completely illogical.

Also, the query confirmed that, within 24 hours from 0:00 March 8, 2014 to 0:00 March 9, no other civil plane or military aircraft disappeared, crashed or caught fire anywhere in the world except Malaysia Airlines Flight MH370. Therefore these exclusive clues show that the evidence provided by the two witnesses have a certain value.

The coincidence of the two witnesses' mutual visual intersection with the meeting point where Malaysia, Thailand and Vietnam's radar signals disappeared once again supported the inference that the radar intersection was the location of MH370's crash site. The disappearance of satellite data and radar signals, the change of radar plane data from 24 to 333 degrees, and the two eyewitness' sightings, a chain of closely linked and logically reasonable evidence, should be reliable.

Diagram of MH370's crash into the sea at 93° (drawn by Liang Guanglin)

MH370 swallowed by huge waves (drawn by Yu Haibo)

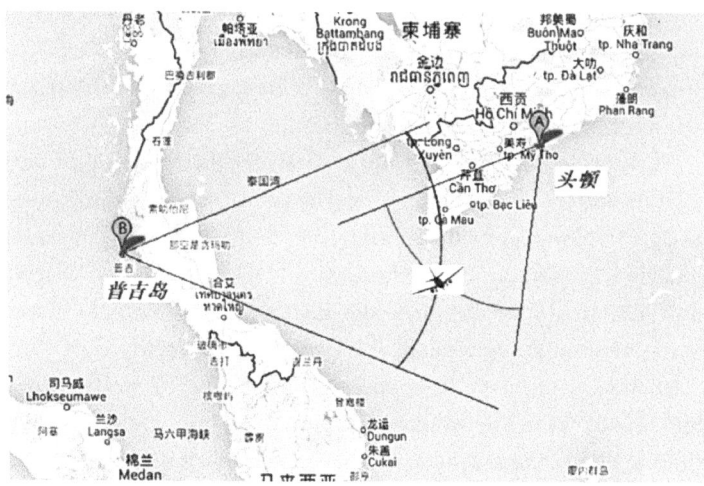
Diagram of the intersection of the two witnesses' view of what appeared to be MH370 (Drawn by Liu Panpan)

WHERE IS MH370?

In conclusion, the author believes MH370 should be at this location. First, the assumption that Flight MH370 fell into the Indian Ocean is untenable. After Flight MH370 lost contact with the Pacific satellite, the Indian Ocean satellite's 'handshakes' were not a restoration of communications and there is no relationship between the two; the inference based on the Indian Ocean satellite's communication data that Flight MH370 splashed down in the Indian Ocean is incomplete and only guesswork and lacks hard evidence, so it is not credible.

The resting place of Flight MH370 is not in the Indian Ocean, but in the South China Sea, Scene 1, perhaps in a seabed cave or trench within about 50 km radius of N7° 25', E103° 55' as the core, 80-120 metres from the sea surface (The height of the aircraft itself is 40 metres, so it was calculated to be 40-80 metres away from the sea surface), not on a flat area of ocean floor. This location is based on scientific and technological positioning, not out of guesswork, inference, deduction or assumption.

It is calculated that the air capacity in the cabin could only sustain 239 people for 15 minutes. The aircraft crashed into the sea at 01:25, so by around 01:40, all in the cabin would die. The water shielded, eroded, absorbed, and prevented radio communication and air circulation between the inside and the outside of the plane; the communication devices were not artificially shut off.

On that same day, the pilot of a Boeing 777 aircraft, which had taken off for Narita International Airport 30 minutes earlier than MH370, had a conversation during flight with Vietnam Air Control. He said when he contacted MH370 at 01:30 on March 8, 'there were noises, sounds of static electricity and some undistinguished words'; after 01:30, 'it was out of touch'. This is the solid evidence.

(Author's note - those phenomena are exactly the features when one side of a radio conversation, either on the land or in the air, is abruptly lost. If it goes into tunnels or buildings, the signals received would be different. If MH370 crashed into the sea at about 01:25, it would be gradually submerged by water. At 01:30, five minutes later, there were "some undistinguished words", "sounds of static electricity", "noises" and it was "out of touch"; at 01:37, the addressing signals stopped connection. All the things above were closely linked to each other, and support each other as evidence. If there were no such things as "noises, sounds of static electricity and some undistinguished words", "the crash into the sea at 01:25" and "the stopping of connection" didn't match, so we couldn't draw the conclusion in that situation. If MH370 was still flying at 01:25, and two planes were both in the air, the air communication was normal and there couldn't be the features mentioned above although the two planes were several hundred kilometres away from each other because of the 30 minutes take-off time difference.

THE DISAPPEARANCE OF FLIGHT MH370

1. Definition: the aircraft is 'missing', (in other words contact was lost), it did not 'disappear', or it went missing first, then disappeared. 'Missing' led to 'disappearing'.

2. Positioning: South China Sea (referring to the pictures on pp 38-40)

1 This range covers about 13,000 square km splash range:
N06° 50'—07° 30'
E103° 30'—104° 35'。'

2 This range covers about 1,800 square km Key areas:
N07° 10'—07° 25'
E103° 50'—104° 25'。

3   Core areas: This range covers about 200 square km N07° 25'、E103° 55' as the centre with a radius of 50 km.

3. Timing

   Missing time: 01:25

   Disappearance time: 01:37

   Time Chain: 00:42 take-off - 00:50 cruise - 01:25 missing - 01:37 disappearance.

4. Flight altitude when missing: FL350—0

5. Posture when missing: 24° —333° (-27°)

6. Causes and effects of the disappearance: encountering 'accidents' during normal 'cruise'. An inappropriate 'right escape turn' led to the plane's sudden disappearance.

The word 'accidents' used by the author the analyses are extremely serious 'broken-down' problems, so the crew have no time or ability to handle or report. They could be suddenly encountering acceleration and speed errors, meteorites, space junk, mirages, storm centres, sudden diving and so on. To discover the real causes, we might have to wait till all the data in the black box of MH370 are found and analysed, if that is possible.

However, the author is a little pessimistic because an interim report by Australia says the black box of MH370 had already run out of power by December 2013. If the black box was powered off, how could it record data? If that was the case, even if the flight is found, the cause of the disappearance is likely to be an eternal mystery.

CHAPTER FIVE

Evidence that MH370 never left Scene 1

On December 28, 2014, the first edition of this book was printed and released. By coincidence, on the same day, another Malaysian airliner disappeared. That made three within a single year.

At 05:32 on December 28, 2014, local time, a flight of Indonesia AirAsia numbered QZ8501, an Airbus A320-216, set off from Surabaya airport and was bound for Changi International Airport, Singapore. Just like MH370, it lost contact with the ground 42 minutes after take-off. It had been six years since the aircraft was put into service. The flight contained 162 people including the two pilots, five crew members and 155 passengers, including 16 children and one baby. In terms of nationality, there were 155 Indonesians, 3 Koreans, 1 British, 1 French, 1 Malaysian and 1 Singaporean. Its pilot had 6100 hours' flight experience and the co-pilot had 2275 hours.

The last time the pilot contacted the air traffic control tower was at 6:12 am, local time, when he asked to turn left and raise the flight height to 34,000 feet to avoid the clouds. Later he did not send signals asking for help. At 05:32, the flight departed. At 06:12 came the last verbal communication. At 06:16, it was still visible on radar. At 06:18, only two minutes later, it disappeared from radar.

The year 2014, the 'year of the Ma' (horse) was catastrophic for Malaysia. From March 8 to December 28 is just 9 months and 10 days. Within 280 days, there were three air disasters. One aircraft disappeared; one suffered an accident; one was shot down. Natural and man-made disasters took away 699 innocent lives (MH370: 239 people; MH17: 298 people; QZ8501:162 people). Malaysia Airlines encountered the severest disaster. Chinese superstition says that Malaysia will incur bad luck in the year of horse.

Throughout history, the various types of air crashes can be attributed to just three basic causes: natural disasters, man-made and a combination of the two. Which case was Flight QZ8501? American aviation expert Keith McKee said bad weather was likely to be the culprit, but in his view it was unusual for the pilot to try to increase height in that situation. A colleague of McKee also believes that the QZ8501 is likely to have encountered bad weather, but in general, the pilot will choose to bypass it rather than climb to the top of a thunderstorm cloud to avoid the risk. He also pointed out that flying through a thunderstorm at an altitude between 31480 feet or 9450 metres and 38,000 feet or 11,500 metres, the aircraft will usually encounter a strong air jolt and that once the control surface ices up, the pilot will not be able to take timely remedial measures, causing the aircraft to fall, within a minute, more than 5000 feet or 1500 metres. In this case, the pilot will usually take the first emergency measures to regain control of the aircraft, and then send the tower a distress signal.

On December 1, 2015, the Indonesian Traffic Safety Committee released the investigation report into Air Asia flight QZ8501s crash. The report concluded that the pilots' handling of the technical failures was the main cause. The survey found that the year before the crash, the FAC (flight stabilization computer system) had 23 faults involving cracked solder joints, commonly known as 'poor contact'. The records of the last three months showed that the interval between faults was getting shorter and shorter.

Perhaps in the past when encountering a fault, the pilot would leave his position to shut down the FAC switch and resolve the fault. This time the aircraft's FAC was in such a critical state that turning off the switch instantly changed the aircraft's attitude to a degree far beyond the pilot's handling capacity, which led to the crash (Note: Flight MH370's instant change of its flying posture from 24° to 333°, and the change of flight altitude from 35000 to zero, also seemed to be beyond the pilot's handling capacity and led to its crash).

The disappearance of QZ8501, just like that of MH370, aroused all kinds of suspicions in the world within a short period of time. Fortunately, due to the Indonesian officials' accurate judgement, proper command, quick actions and effective measures, their search and rescue of QZ8501 won fruitful results in a short period of time. On December 30, 2014, 48 hours after the disappearance of QZ8501, the rescue work had already made significant progress. The Indonesian military aircraft found the wreckage and more than 40 bodies and luggage, emergency rafts and other items 10 km away from where QZ8501 disappeared from the radar screen.

On December 31, 2014, the Indonesian National Search and Rescue Centre, through sonar equipment, identified the wreckage of the plane's main body. Sonar images showed that the plane lay upside down on the sea bed 24 to 30 metres down. 'The aircraft's wreckage looks quite complete and the bodies of the victims are still neatly dressed,' said the aeronautics experts. 'These facts indicate that the airliner did not disintegrate in the process of falling before it hit the water.'

On January 9, 2015, 14 days after the disappearance, the searchers detected the black box signal. Aviation experts explained that when an aircraft touches the water, the black box will automatically activate its underwater positioning beacon. The aircraft is usually equipped with two such beacons, which are respectively the flight data logger of the black box (including records of flight altitude, speed, heading and so on) and its cockpit voice recorder. The underwater positioning beacon will send a pulse signal of 37.5 kHz, which can only be received within one mile of the surface of the water, and therefore cannot be received by satellites but only by aircraft or ships.

Power in the black box can enable the beacon to work for about 30 days. In order to find the black box as soon as possible, Indonesia sent three ships and detected its signal 1km east of the tail wreckage. They launched a search of the four square kilometres around the location of the signal. On January 12, 16 days after the disappearance, a black box and later 12 pieces of aircraft wreckage were found 1 km around the tail. On the 13th, another black box was also discovered under 32 metres of water. On the 14th, the main body of the plane was found 3 km from the tail.

On December 1, 2015, the Indonesian investigators announced that the crash of passenger QZ8501 was mainly due to flight control system failure and the incorrect handling of the pilots. The electrical wiring had been damaged, due to a temperature difference between the ground and the sky, but ground maintenance personnel did not take that into account. Such a failure is not dangerous; the main cause of the crash was the pilots' improper tackling of the problem. After the line fault occurred, the pilot cut off the autopilot power and changed to manual operation. During the subsequent voyage, the co-pilot misunderstood the pilot's questioning and pulled the plane up, causing it to stall and eventually to crash.

Only two weeks passed before the wreckage of flight QZ8501 and the first black box were found. Allowing for the first two days during which the high waves and the strong wind made it impossible to search and rescue, it only took 15 days to find the disappeared plane.

From the Indonesian commander's judgement of the crash site, the positioning of the black box and the measures they took, it is not hard to see that the Indonesian search and rescue commander thinks in the same way as the author of this book.

According to the *Shenzhen Special Zone Daily News* on September 27, 2015, an AT-3 two-seater trainer 0851 from Taiwan Air Force Academy disappeared in the course of conducting the 'instrument flight' courses 27 minutes after it took off at 11:57 on September 22. Four days after its disappearance, the search and rescue personnel found its wreckage 2-3 km from where it had disappeared from the radar screen.

From the two examples above, it is correct to determine the plane's whereabouts with radar signals (which can also be seen as azimuth angles) plus the data of the flight course, flight speed and flight time. According to this idea, MH370 didn't leave Scene 1 or fly far. I believe that the whereabouts of MH370 can be found within 30 days if the search is carried out, with appropriate equipment and methods, in the given areas with coordinates like N7° 25 ', E103° 55' in the South China Sea as described in the previous chapters. Then it is not too late to study the causes of the crash. The successful search and rescue of the QZ8501 flight should be considered an example of determining the whereabouts of MH370.

It is worth mentioning that the current search for MH370 in the Southern Indian Ocean, whether with submarines or a Bluefin search vessel, or the submarine mapping approach, are quite right in either the choice of search equipment or the employment of search methods. However, the correct method does not necessarily produce good results. Politically and philosophically, when the effect is not consistent with the method, the reasons lie in the ways of thinking and the corresponding guiding principles. If these two issues are not solved, it is impossible to yield ideal results.

For instance, if you are looking for wild pandas, go to such places as Sichuan or Shaanxi. Even if you use a stupid search method, will surely find them as long as you don't give up. But if you are going to look for wild pandas in California, no matter what advanced equipment and scientific method you use, no matter how many people you mobilize, no matter how much money you are willing to spend, you will not find them (except in zoos). Wrong directions and guidelines will certainly yield unsatisfactory results!

CHAPTER SIX

MH370 may lie somewhere in Scene 1

According to a report on March 9, 2016, a Boeing B-17, an F6F, an Inferno fighter and Mitsubishi fighters shot down in World War II were found in the Solomon Islands. Immersed in the seabed for years, these fighters have rusted and are covered with seaweed. The fighters now lie peacefully on the shallow seabed, about 56 metres (185 feet) down. Some of the fighters were almost intact as shown in the following picture.

Sunken WW2 fighter aircraft in the South Pacific Ocean

It has been nearly four years since MH370 disappeared. No floating objects from the flight have been found either in the South China Sea or in the tens of thousands of square kilometres in the Seventh Arc of the Southern Indian Ocean which has been searched many times. This shows that MH370 did not break up when crashing into the sea, no matter what5 the cause, whether it was 'zombie flight' or any other, and that none of the cabin doors was open when the plane went into the sea, otherwise various objects would have been found floating on the surface. For instance, one of the things it carried was nearly five tons of mangosteen fruit. The buoyancy of the fruit would leave it on the surface and its floating range would be 300-500 square metres. When several square metres of old and useless decks could be found by scoutplanes, satellites and warships, how could a large quantity of floating mangosteen not be found? Moreover, since the volume of mangosteen was small, it would float free as long as there were cracks of 10-20 centimetres in the plane; the stalks were smaller, so they only needed cracks of 5 centimetres to float with great buoyancy. Nothing was found. This suggests that the whole plane, after crashing into the sea, was completely covered with sediment or similar. So we can imagine the difficulty in using unmanned underwater vehicles' airborne sensors detection equipment like sonar and electronic infrared to look for it.

In consideration of the view that the aircraft crashed into the waters around N7° 25', E103° 55' at an angle of 93°, its condition on the 80-120 metres deep seabed may be complete like those World War II warplanes found at the bottom of the Southern Pacific Ocean. It may also be in the sediment, oceanic trenches, seabed caves or some corner where it will not be easy to find. In short, it can be forecast that no matter how difficult it is, no matter in what form the wreck is, no matter how long it takes, the whereabouts of Flight MH370 will be found, beyond all doubt.

When it is found (my belief is that it will be some time in 2020), it will be known to all who is right and who is wrong. We are waiting to see whether it crashed in the Southern Indian Ocean or the South China Sea. We are looking forward to finding the whereabouts of MH370 and the people on board as soon as possible. We are looking forward to laying the myth of MH370 to rest as soon as possible. And we are praying!

CHAPTER SEVEN

Why was no debris found at Scene 1?

After MH370 disappeared on March 8, 2014, Vietnam started the search that day, while China and some other countries arrived in the area where contact had been lost on the 9th. From March 10th to 12th, there assembled many warships and aircraft; on the 12th, Vietnam began to scale down its search; on the 14th, US warships and other countries withdrew from the area where contact had been lost. From March 8 to 14th, ten countries – China, Vietnam, Malaysia, Singapore, Thailand, the Philippines, the US, Indonesia, Australia and New Zealand – sent 65 warships and 46 types of aircraft to conduct a wide search in an area of 70,000 square kilometres around the point where MH370 disappeared near Gulf of Thailand.

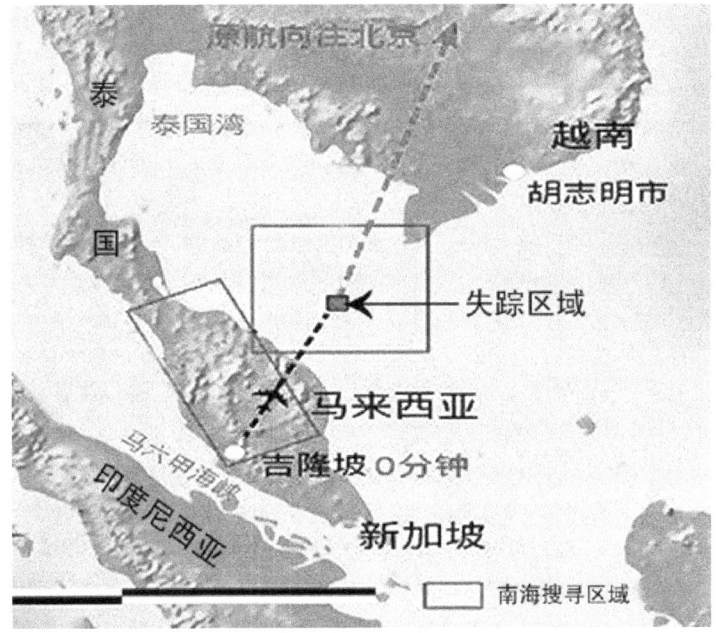

Diagram of the search area in the South China Sea (drawn by Yang Jun)

The search at Scene 1 lasted for no more than seven days and ended up with nothing found. The reasons are as follows:

REASON ONE: WRONG DEFINING, TIMING AND POSITIONING.

First, was the MH370 event a case of a 'missing aircraft' or a 'disappearance'? Before March 15, 2014, everyone judged it as a disappearance, meaning it might reappear. Therefore, the prior concern was about whether it had changed its contact means, whether the communication devices were artificially turned off, whether it had been hijacked, or whether it had flown to somewhere else. From March 8 to 15, there was no mention of the word 'missing'.

This wrong definition certainly influenced the search. Although ten countries sent many warships and aircraft, searching the sea surface and watching for floating objects, most of the search was superficial. Some areas of the seabed were glanced over hurriedly. There was no surveying, and mapping and detection before the search was ended hurriedly.

Second, the accurate time of the 'missing' or 'disappearance' event was not precisely determined. What was the exact time of MH370's 'disappearance'? What was the exact time when MH370 went 'missing'? There has been no clear official definition so far. The Malaysian authorities announced to the world the disappearance time as 01:20, which was confirmed after the multi-verification not to be so. The disappearance time should be 01:37. The aircraft has since been declared 'missing'. It is more important to determine the time when it went missing than to determine its disappearance time.

The Australian survey concluded that the disappearance time was at 8:20 pm on March 8, 2014 (they determined the last handshake was 08:19), but the time it went missing has not yet been clearly identified. I assume that the missing time of Flight MH370 (when contact was lost) was before 01:25, March 8, 2014.

Because time and distance are closely linked, different times will generate different distances, and different distances will result in different directions.

Third, inaccurate positioning. The orientation point issued by the authorities was where IGARI had the conversation, N6° 55□15',E103° 34□43'. After the verbal communication at 01:19:29 local time, the flight was still cruising on its scheduled route. It didn't disappear from the radar until it passed BITOD, also called (BITODS) navigation point. The BITOD point is N07154, E104071. IGARI and BITOD are two navigation points,

60-80 kilometres away from each other. It's not hard to imagine the result if the positioning is inaccurate and consequently the searched area is inaccurate.

Only when the nature, the time, and the position of this event are definitely determined and are highly consistent can people derive the correct fall point of Flight MH370 and thereby can decision-makers formulate a scientific and reasonable programme.

Flight MH370 went missing earlier than it lost contact, not the other way around. It is very important to understand this. According to the time of 01:20, the determined position for MH370 was N06°55'15 ', E103° 34 '43'. In fact, 01:20 was the end of the pilot's voice call, neither the contact-losing time of the aircraft's communication nor the missing time of the aircraft. This position was the last-call position, not the missing position.

There was a five-minute interval between the call at 01:19:29 and the missing time at 01:25, during which the plane was still in its normal cruise, that is to say, it was five minutes later that the aircraft disappeared from the radar and the flight altitude returned from 'FL350' to '0'; the flight had gone missing.

Flight MH370 cruised from the so-called 'lost' point (N06° 55'15', E103°34'43') for another five minutes or so, resulting in a natural extension of the range of 60 to 80 km or so and a change of the splash-down position of its main body to near N7° 25 ', E103° 55' or farther. Therefore, it would be impossible to find the missing plane at the place it disappeared without inappropriate equipment and the wrong search method, with a search range not wide enough and insufficient depth. This is especially true when searching under the sea. Only when the scanning equipment is aimed right at it can we hope to find it. Side detection may not be detected. Thus, we might turn a blind eye and a deaf ear to it even if it is within our range.

So it is not difficult to judge that the key reason for failing to find Flight MH370 in the South China Sea lies in inaccurate defining, timing and positioning.

REASON TWO: A SERIOUSLY INADEQUATE SEARCH PERIOD

After Flight MH370 disappeared, 60-70 ships and dozens of reconnaissance aircraft from 10 countries searched the South China Sea for less than 7 days, and the active time was only three days. You would spend 10-15 days looking for a missing hen before you gave up, let alone a missing aircraft carrying more than two hundred people!

Searching the South China Sea waters this time lasted for no more than a week and the search teams hastily moved to the Southern Indian Ocean. How can Flight MH370 be found in such a way? There is a serious shortage of search time, so some people have asserted that they cannot find MH370 even if it lies there.

REASON THREE: SIMPLE SEARCH EQUIPMENT, INAPPROPRIATE SEARCH APPROACHES AND METHODS

The average depth of the Gulf of Thailand is 50 metres. American oceanographer David Gallo has said that although this area is shallower than the mid-ocean ridges, probably no more than 100 metres, the seabed is very likely to be covered with sediment. An aircraft is relatively small, and even a small bump may make the search complicated. There are difficulties in searching shallow water. Acoustic navigation and measuring devices cannot see far, and the equipment faces strong tides and poor visibility.

So the search in the South China Sea was very superficial. After the scanning of the sea surface and examination with telescopes, the conclusion was drawn that this was not the whereabouts of

Flight MH370, and the search teams left. Have they interviewed the people near the waters where MH370 disappeared? No! Have they repeatedly probed the sea bed with the most modern sophisticated submarine detection equipment? No! Have they searched using the surveying and mapping methods employed in the Southern Indian Ocean? No! Have they deeply and repeatedly explored the remote areas of the seabed? No! Without even taking a look, they slipped away. Apparently, their searches were a mere formality just to appease the public.

In addition to the above three points, the search commanders were clearly distracted, using the wrong search method. In other words, they took the attitude that even if they knew where MH370 splashed down, and could easily find it in the South China Sea, they did not want to find it, or they did not want to find it as soon as possible. So it is quite understandable that Flight MH370 was not found in the area.

REASON FOUR: POOR SEARCH ORGANISATION AND CARELESSNESS IN INVESTIGATION AND RESEARCH

After the disaster, appeals for help with the search were responded to everywhere; Malaysia and Vietnam both opened their doors. Many rescue teams were sent. Everybody, well-intentioned, was searching, and ships, warships and aircraft were all used. Everyone did what they thought was right. What a mess! Back then, there was no unified organiser; there was no interviewing the local people, no investigation and no screening. Needless to say there was poor research and judgement on every aspect of the event and they did not work out a scientific search plan. They just went there, took a look, searched, and left. They found no valuable clues on the surface. Were there any clues on the seabed within the range of search? We have no idea!

REASON FIVE: THE LOCATIONS DETERMINED BY DIFFERENT SEISMOMETERS WERE DIFFERENT

After the disappearance, two seismometers from the University of Science and Technology of China were put around the area, 116 kilometres north-east of where it disappeared. During the search from March 8 to 14, 2014, the search team focused its search in this key area, but nothing was found. How do we explain this? The author believes that the direction was right, but the precision was not great enough.

Let's analyse this by using the radio direction finding principle. The two seismometers had only two measuring lines, or in other words, two azimuth angles. The included angle of the two lines was an acute angle. According to past experience, this provided a rough direction, with a rather big difference from the actual location, but it was within a reasonable range if the difference was 50-60 kilometres. It was right only when the actual distance of the 'vibrator point' was no more than 116 kilometres. If we search according to the points, it may not work. There is hope only if we extend the search range.

As for the time difference, it should be the difference between Beijing Time and Malaysia Time as well as the difference between the ups and downs of the flight and the timekeeping of measuring lines.

Conclusion: The reason why no debris or clues were found at Scene 1 lay in the search time, approaches, methods, techniques and so on, not the search direction.

CHAPTER EIGHT

It was a big mistake to give up at Scene 1

Today, the fact that Flight MH370 crashed has been largely accepted by the public and their governments. However, people's opinions vary as to where MH370 crashed. Most people hold it fell into the ocean; some argue it crashed on land; still others think it could be either. As to whether the place where MH370 crashed (hereinafter referred to as the crash spot) is the same as the location where it went missing, most agree they are roughly the same, though some disagree. There are seven major suspected locations, which we refer to as seven scenes:

Scene 1: the South China Sea south of Nam Can, Vietnam (referring to the picture in Chapter 1).

Scene 2: the waters in the Southern Indian Ocean west of Perth (referring to the picture on page 164).

Scene 3: Diego Garcia (referring to the picture on 159).

Scene 4: East Malaysia and the coast.

Scene 5: the Andaman Islands in the Indian Ocean.

Scene 6: the North Corridor of Kazakhstan.

Scene 7: 600 km south of Albany, Australia (the opposite direction from Beijing).

Given these seven possibilities, what should we do? Malaysia organised experts from various countries to conduct research into the possible crash spot. Their current conclusions and adopted measures locked onto Scene 2, ignoring Scene 1. As for the other scenes, they fail to arouse much interest and are basically excluded, though considered possible by some official or non-official organisations. In contrast to the above, I think all seven scenes are possible, until we find useful clues.

If the search was relaunched, it should be more scientific and reasonable to consider Scene 1 as the first choice and make every effort to search for Flight MH370. If we still cannot find it and all the possibilities are excluded, then we may consider moving to the other scenes. The current situation is that hasty searches of Scene 1 only lasted three to five days. Before the searchers' resources were exhausted, they decided to dwell on the 'abstract' to avoid the 'real' (the definitions of 'abstract' and 'real' were explained before) and relaunch searches at Scene 2 based on speculation or guesses, which is questionable.

A comparison of the similarities and differences between the traces found at Scene 1 may reveal something.

Scene 1 and Scene 2 comparison

Order	Content	the first scene	the second scene
1	Missing time	01:25, March 8, 2014	not determined yet
2	Disappearance spot	N06°55´15″、 E103°34´43″	the Seventh Arc of the Southern Indian Ocean
3	Missing spot	area near N7°25´, E103°55´	within 120 thousand square km west of Perth, the South Indian Sea
4	Evidence	communication and radar live record and data	speculation from radar and satellite data
5	Search time	less than 7 days	1,040 days
6	Search range	70,000 square kilometers	millions of square kilometers
7	Search equipment	warships, aircraft, merchant ships	warships, aircraft, merchant ships, submarines, submersible robots, mapping devices, etc.
8	Follow-up plan	no	till the end of January, 2017
9	Search leader	Malaysia	Australia
10	Search directors	Malaysia and USA	USA and Australia
11	Search teams	10 countries including Malaysia	26 countries including Australia
12	Cost	tens of millions of US dollars	hundreds of millions of US dollars
13	Search results	No findings	No findings

It's everyone's agreement that we should take further measures and continue the search. The question is whether the priority should go to those programmes that can meet the requirements of the missing passengers' family members and the companies. However, the measures we now see run against that.

To start the second round of searching, we should draw up programmes observing the basic principles of looking in the right place, deploying enough resources, and we must keep devoting energy and financial resources to the search until we find the whereabouts of MH370. In the second round of searching, Scene 1 should be preferred since it enjoys great reliability for its both 'visual' and 'audio' conclusions, a great variety of data and consistent chains of evidences evidence.

The fruitless results of the first searches are mainly due to improper control, bad coordination, too short a search time, not fully using the available search methods, insufficient search range and depth, biased data, inappropriate search equipment and inaccurate timing and positioning. In contrast, in the first round of searching Scene 2, forces all over the world were mobilized and all equipment was used, all search methods were applied and the search range was broad enough, but still there was no result. The main reason is that the search work got politicized, many things were deliberately ignored, formality was preferred and pragmatism was cast aside. There was not enough evidence for the crash site, the evidence chain was not consistent and the data were ambiguous.

What would be gained and lost by re-employing professional companies to search Scene 2? What will the programme yield this time? One predictable result is that Australia will get the long-desired seabed map for her own territorial waters, at others' cost. Perhaps the search results may prove again that the sea west of Perth is not the final resting place of Flight MH370. Without any hard evidence, they have decided that the Southern Indian Ocean west of Perth is the crash location of MH370. According to the so-called seven 'handshakes' with the satellite, the seventh and last is recalculated at about 1800 kilometres away from the west coast of Australia. If so, where are the positions of the first six handshakes? Can we push back to Kuala Lumpur airport? Even a position nearby?

With only a part of the synchronous satellite data and no circumstantial or other evidence, it is not enough in law to accept the evidence, because no one can be sure whether the handshake contact made by the satellite was from Flight MH370 or from some other flight. The inference of the position at each handshake is derived by a trace of incoherent, frequently shifting data, which lack the GPS data as circumstantial evidence. Can this inference stand the test of the factors such as time, distance, height, environment and so on?

Can we simply suppose that Flight MH370, filled with fuel, followed its scheduled route to the South China Sea, suddenly turned around for the Southern Indian Ocean, exhausted its fuel seven hours later, and finding nowhere to land, crashed into the Southern Indian Ocean? Although the seven signals may basically match the aircraft's cruising time and so does the fuel use, this seemingly perfect inference is full of loopholes.

If when the radar signals of Flight MH370 disappeared, the plane had crashed in South Vietnam, and the several 'handshake' sounds were pulse signals, only reflections of the dynamics of the system battery rather than a report of Flight MH370's state, then the claim that MH370 splashed into the Southern Indian Ocean will become a standing joke.

Some officials speculated that the plane was on automatic pilot - also known as 'zombie flight' – when crossing the Indian Ocean. Some experts claimed that if the aircraft maintained 'zombie flight' till the fuel ran out and its engines shut down, then the aircraft would be tilted and would break into pieces with its fragments widely distributed. Forty years of data tell us that in such air crashes, the fragmented wreckage of such planes is, without exception, widely distributed, and floating objects could easily be found by searchers.

Assuming Flight MH370 maintained 'zombie flight' till it ran out of fuel and crashed into the Southern Indian Ocean, how come the aircraft, warships, and satellites from 26 countries could not find a fragment of the crashed plane? It is inexplicable. If the plane was on automatic pilot for a long time till it ran out of fuel, what were the 239 people on board doing until then? They didn't eat? They didn't go to the bathroom? They didn't walk? Was that possible?

As we all know, during the search for MH370, the aircraft involved in the search would suspend their flight in bad weather, fearing the stormy Indian Ocean. Was Flight MH370 lucky enough to fly through a cloudy and stormy Indian Ocean and withstand the strong winds unscathed till its fuel ran out? If it cruised for seven or eight hours and shifted to automatic pilot (without any data support) after turning back, the crew on board must all have been dead or unconscious. The time when they became dead or unconscious should have been between 01:20 and 01:50. The satellite data since the seventh handshake can only be explained by a state of 'zombie flight'. Otherwise, they were contradictory.

There are too many arguments against and too little evidence for the conclusion (based on satellite data and some assumptions) that Flight MH370 ended up in the Southern Indian Ocean, west of Australia (the author's note: with the exception of the area 600 km south of Albany, Australia).

Even Chris McClarklin, vice president of the International

Maritime Satellite Organisation, said that the clues should be carefully and scientifically analysed. The 'handshake' signals do not contain information such as positioning data, time, location, and so on. The automatic cruising speed is assumed. 'We also screened a large amount of electronic signal information based on the fuel and voyage data of the flight,' he stated. 'Flight MH370 was not forced to send its position signal, so its positions were all speculated, something that had never been done before.' In short, the decision to search the waters west of Australia bears hidden motives!

In addition to the above 'handshake' signals, there is possible evidence supporting the decision to search Scene 2: the suspected black box signal, the suspected floating objects and the 'special signal', probably of an earthquake, from Lu Yan Kok monitoring station, West Bank of Australia, at 9:30 on March 8.

Coincidentally, at 02:55:06 March 8, the Wen Lianxing research group from the Earthquake Laboratory, University of Science and Technology of China also detected an undersea event at N7° 25 ', E104° 30', 116 km north-east of the missing aircraft. The location of this event can be used as supporting evidence or indirect evidence for Scene 1. They did not define this submarine event as an earthquake signal. As far as I understand, only a considerable amount of shock is reflected, so its time accuracy and position accuracy may not be as precise as seismic data. The gap in time may be for other reasons, but it can still serve as a reference for the circumstantial evidence; its orientation data can be used as an amendment basis for the crash location of MH370, a reference far more credible than the 'special signal' of Lu Yan Kok.

Let's talk about the six pieces of direct evidence for Scene 1. The first is that the 10 sets of communication equipment on the aircraft, direct reflections of the plane's running state, were discontinued at 01:37 pm on March 8. Since take-off, The flight had been using the Pacific Communications satellite to communicate, but after the last call at 01:19:29, there were no satellite data.

The second is that after Flight MH370 took off, the three radar signals respectively from three different direction, Kuala Lumpur in Malaysia, Ho Chi Minh in Vietnam and Suratthani military radar of Thailand, which directly reflected MH370's state in the air, disappeared before 01:25 on March 8 and were not recovered. The flying angle changed from 24° to 333° and the flight altitude from FL350 to 0.

After 1:25, Ho Chi Minh City, Sanya and Hong Kong, ahead of MH370, Singapore city, Indonesia, behind MH370, Phnom Penh, Bangkok, left of MH370, the Philippines, right of MH370; Pacific Ocean satellites, above MH370, all declared that MH370 was not visible and did not enter their respective territory. Only the South China Sea had not given clear information.

Thirdly, the ATC call reflects both the time and position of the missing aircraft.

The ATC of Ho Chi Minh City called his counterpart in Malaysia to report that Flight MH370 had just passed BITODS air point (N07154, E104071) and disappeared from their radar with a 'flash' phenomenon. The plane was then at 35,000 feet and the time was 01:25. Flight MH370 was seen no more after 01:25. The Civil Aviation Control Centre of Ho Chi Minh City, Vietnam did not receive Flight MH370 at the junction of its air control area. After the flight took off, there were many lengthy wireless calls between the Malaysian Air Transport Command Centre (MAS OPERATIONS, hence M), Kuala Lumpur (KLATCL, hence K) and the Vietnamese Ho Chi Minh District (HCMATCC, hence H). Excerpts are as follows:

At 1:39:08, K: Malaysia 370 has been handed over to you.

At 1:39:12, H: Yes, it was transferred at 20 (this referred to 01:20), but we have lost contact after the BITOD navigation point. Our radar lost the trail Flight MH370; another aircraft was identified on our radar.

At 1: 46:57, H: We can receive the radar signal though without voice communication when it passed the IGARI (navigation point). But after the BITOD navigation point, its radar signal and ADS-B (broadcast automatic correlation monitoring) signal were both gone.

At 1:58:31, H: We didn't enquire from you until seven minutes after it passed BITOD.

At 3:50, K: Actually, after the IGARI point, no flight intelligence area tracked it or knew which intelligence area it flew to.

H: Up till now, we have checked with many airlines as well as the flights at our frequency, and there was no reply. No one has known about MH370.

K also reported that almost at 01:25, H said he 'saw a flash'. M immediately responded: 'that's bad!'

Fourth, when Flight MH370 disappeared at 01:37, Vietnam gave an immediate response at 01:38, the very first. The ATC at Ho Chi Minh District actively communicated with the surrounding cities, including Kuala Lumpur, Phnom Penh, Medan, Singapore and Hong Kong, and reminded Kuala Lumpur that MH370 had disappeared on their radar and did not arrive in the sky area of Ho Chi Minh City.

After the disappearance, the Vietnamese government responded promptly and accurately and took effective measures to open their territorial airspace and territorial waters on the day so that other countries could search. Its military, air force, navy, border-guard forces and fishery administration all headed off to the disappearance area to search. Their positive attitude and generous behaviour were admirable. However, three days later, on March 11, 2014, they wasted this good start, not only by reducing their search level but also declaring that they would not allow other countries' warships or aircraft to search their waters any more. Their open door was closed again.

Fifth, at the disappearance of Flight MH370, six of the seven countries (Malaysia, Thailand, Cambodia, Laos, China, the Philippines and Vietnam) around its scheduled routes all issued a statement that Flight MH370 had not fallen in their territory. Only Vietnam failed to issue a clear statement.

Sixth, since the disappearance of Flight MH370, no country or organisation (such as Malaysia Airlines or Boeing) or any of the 239 families have received a ransom demand or a threat to kill hostages. Nor have any terrorist organisations or anti-government forces claimed responsibility.

The above is direct evidence, forming a close, logic, interlocking and seamless chain; reversing the data, their convergence is also appropriate, which is enough to prove that the general direction of the missing MH370 should be in the northern hemisphere and in the South China Sea.

According to the difference between the missing time and the disappearing time, it is entirely possible to determine accurately the final position of MH370, which should be in the waters south of Nam Can, Vietnam , N7° 25 ', E103° 55', or the nearby high mountains and forests. In view of the factors affecting the drift, the search range should be moderately expanded.

In my opinion, MH370 made a turning movement, but not towards the Indian Ocean. Instead, it turned to the lower right and dived vertically into the sea. The Malaysian Air Force reviewed the radar video, and the conclusion drawn was contradictory between the radar data collected by the civil radars respectively from Vietnam, Thailand, Indonesia and Kuala Lumpur. The plane which Malaysia said had made a turning movement and flown to the Indian Ocean was not MH370, but another flight or aircraft. It is very likely that some people concerned confused MH370 with the route of another flight, mistakenly judging that MH370 had flown across the Indian Ocean until it ran out of fuel.

Aside from the direct evidence, there were six other pieces of indirect evidence:

First, when we compare the 81 cases of civil air crashes (including private planes and transport aircraft), with 84 planes crashed, 10,765 people dead and 1,034 people injured in the 40 years from January 1, 1974 to December 31, 2014, though their causes were quite varied, they bore two major similarities. One, the communication signals and radar signals of the same plane disappeared simultaneously and were not recovered. The plane ended up crashing. Two, after the crash, the main body of the aircraft fell within 50 km of where the radar signal disappeared with no exceptions (not including floating debris. Please refer to the following table for details.

Number	Time	Flight number	Type	Departure—destination	Crash site	Causes	Communication and radar	Casualties
1	1974.03.03	981	DC-10	Paris—London	Ermenonville, France	Explosion of the plane	Communication suspended, radar disappearing	346 people killed
2	1975.04.04	airfreighter	C-5A	Saigon—Manila	Near Saigon, Vietnam	Cabin doors falling off	Null	153 people killed, 175 people injured
3	1977.03.27	PA1736	747	LA, US—Las Palmas, Spain	Los Rodeos Airport, Spain	Two planes colliding with each other due to thick fog	Communication suspended/Null	583 people killed
4	1977.04.04	242	DC-9-31	Alabama—Atlanta, US	State of Georgia	Windstorm	0	72 people killed
5	1978.09.25	PSA182	727	Sacramento—San Diego	San Diego International Airport	Collision due to vision deviation	Null	146 people killed
6	1978.12.28	173	DC-8	Kennedy International Aiport—Oregon	Near Portland Airport	Out of fuel	0	10 people killed, 24 people injured
7	1979.05.25	191	DC-10-10	Chicage—LA	Chicago Airport	Engine falling off	Null	273 people killed
8	1980.06.27	870	DC-9	Bologna—Palermo, Italy	Sea near Ustica	Suspected attack by a bomb or a missile	Communication suspended, radar disappearing	81 people killed
9	1982.01.13	90	737	Washington—Miami	Potomac River	Ice and snow buildup on the plane	0	74 people killed, 5 people injured
10	1983.06.02	797	DC-9-32	Dallas/Fort Worth International Airport, US—Montréal-Dorval International Airport, Canada	Cincinnati International Airport	An in-flight fire behind the washroom	Null	23 people killed

MH370 SHOULD BE HERE

Number	Time	Flight number	Type	Departure—destination	Crash site	Causes	Communication and radar	Casualties
11	1983.09.01	KAL007	747	Kennedy International Aiport—Seoul, Korea	Sea near Sakhalin, Soviet Union	Attacked by Soviet Union	Communication suspended, radar disappearing	269 people killed
12	1984.10.11	3352	图-154	Krasnodar—Novosibirsk Tolmachevo Airport	Crashing into maintenance vehicles on the runway	an air traffic controller falling asleep on duty	0	178 people killed
13	1985.06.23	182	747	Montreal, Canada—Mumbai, India	Atlantic Ocean	Explosion in cargo bay	Communication suspended, radar disappearing	329 people killed
14	1985.08.02	191	L-1011L-1011	Fort Lauderdale, Florida—LA	Dallas/Fort Worth International Airport	Thunderstorm attacks	00	136 people killed, 27 people injured
15	1985.08.12	JAL123	747	Tokyo—Osaka	Crashing into Mount Takamagahara	tail fall-off	Communication out of touch, radar disappearing	520 people killed
16	1985.08.22	28M	737	Manchester, England—Island of Corfu, Greece	Runway of take-off	Engine on fire	Null	55 people killed, 15 people injured
17	1985.12.12	1285	DC-8	Cairo, Egypt—Kentuky, US	Newfoundland Island, Canada	plane iced up and overweight	0	256 people killed
18	1986.08.31	498	DC-9-32	Mexico City, Mexico— LA, US	Los Angeles International Airport	A piper archer entering "Terminal Control Area"	Communication suspended, radar disappearing	82 people killed
19	1987.08.16	255	MD-82	Michigan—Orange County, California	Airport of take-off	Lack of power in the early-warning system	0	156 people killed
20	1987.11.28	295	747	Chinese Taipei—Johannesburg, South Africa	Indian Ocean	Cargo bay on fire	Communication out of touch/Null	159 people killed
21	1987.12.07	1771	BAe146-200	LA—San Francisco, US	California	Former employee of PSA shooting the pilots	Communication suspended, radar disappearing	43 people killed
22	1988.06.26	296	A320-111	Basel— Basel, France	Airport of take-off	Human errors of the pilots	0	3 people killed, 133 people injured
23	1988.07.03	655	A300	Bandar Abbas, Iran—Dubai, The United Arab Emirates	Persian Gulf	Shot down by US army	Communication suspended, radar disappearing	290 people killed
24	1988.12.21	103	747	Heathrow Airport, England—Kennedy Airport, US	Scotland	Explosion in the cabin	Null	270 people killed
25	1989.03.10	1363	F28-1000	Ontario—Winnipeg	Near theAntario Airport	Ice accumulated on the wings	0	24 people killed
26	1989.07.19	232	DC-10	Stapleton International Airport—Philadelphia	Sioux City, Iowa	Explosion of the engine	Null	111 people killed, 185 people injured
27	1989.09.08	394	CV580	Oslo, Norway—Hamburg, Germany	Open seas near Denmark	Screw bolts broken	Communication out of touch/Null	55 people killed
28	1990.01.25	052	707	Colombia—Kennedy International Airport	Near Long Island Airport	Out of fuel	0	73 people killed, 85 people injured
29	1991.02.01	1493	737	New York—LA, US	LA Airport	Local controller distracted	0	34 people killed, 77 people injured
30	1991.03.03	585	737	Denver—Colorado Springs, US	Runway	Rudder power control loss	0	25 people killed
31	1991.07.11	2120	DC-9	King Abdulaziz International Airport, Saudi Arabia—Sadiq Abubakar III International Airport, Nigeria	Airport of take-off	Low tyre pressure, fire caught when one tyre stopped rotating	0	261 people killed

Number	Time	Flight number	Type	Departure—destination	Crash site	Causes	Communication and radar	Casualties
31	1991.07.11	2120	DC-9	King Abdulaziz International Airport, Saudi Arabia—Sadiq Abubakar III International Airport, Nigeria	Airport of take-off	Low tyre pressure, fire caught when one tyre stopped rotating	0	261 people killed
32	1991.09.11	2574	EmB-120	Laredo—Houston, Texas	Colorado County	Screws forgotten to be replaced	0	14 people killed
33	1992.01.20	148	A-320	Lyon—Strasbourg	Vosges Mountains, France	Wrong setup of descent data	Communication out of touch, radar disappearing	87 people killed, 9 people injured
34	1994.03.23	593	A-310	Moscow—Hong Kong	Siberia	misoperation	Null	75 people killed
35	1994.09.08	427	737-200	O'Hare International Airport—Pennsylvania	Near the airport	Rudder fault	0	132 people killed
36	1994.10.31	4184	ATR-72	Indiana—Chicago	Near Indianapolis International Airport	Ice accumulated on the wings	0	68 people killed
37	1995.08.21	529	EmB-120	Atlanta—Mississippi	Near Carroll County	Propeller fault	0	9 people killed, 20 people injured
38	1995.12.20	965	757	Miami, US—Aragón, Colombia	Valle del Cauca, Colombia	Crew members forgetting to put away spoilers	Communication out of touch/Null	159 people killed, 4 people injured
39	1996.02.06	301	757	The Dominican Republic—Frankfurt	Near Dominican Airport	Pitot tube clogged	Null	189 people killed
40	1996.04.03	IF021	737	Zagreb—Dubrovnik, Croatia	Near Dubrovnik Airport	Errors in Navigation altitude diagram	0	35 people killed
41	1996.05.11	592	DC-9	Miami—Atlanta, US	Florida	Cabin on fire	0	110 people killed
42	1996.07.17	800	747	Kennedy Airport, US—Rome, Italy	The Atlantic Ocean near Long Island, New York	Tank on fire, and the explosion afterwards	Communication out of touch, radar disappearing	230 people killed
43	1996.10.02	603	757	Lima, Peru—Arturo, Chile	The Pacific Ocean near Lima	Static vent fault in the pitot tube	Null	70 people killed
44	1996.11.12	763	747	Indira Gandhi International Airport, India—Az Zahran Saudi Arabia	Charkhi Dadri, India	Colliding with Flight 1907	Communication suspended, radar disappearing	349 people killed
45	1997.08.06	801	747	Gimpo Airport, Korea—Guam	Near Guam Airport	fatigue driving, communication interference	0	228 people killed
46	1997.12.19	185	737	Soekarno–Hatta Airport, Indonesia—Changi Airport, Singapore	Musi River, Indonesia	Suspected captain's action or hydraulic unit fault	Null	104 people killed
47	1998.09.02	111	MD-11	Kennedy Airport—Geneva, Switzerland	Crashing into the Atlantic Ocean	Cabin on fire caused by electrical short-circuit	Communication out of touch/Null	229 people killed
48	1999.06.01	1420	MD-82	Dallas—Little Rock City, US	Near the Little Rock City Airport	Thunderstorm and the spoilers unable to be opened in time	0	11 people killed
49	1999.10.31	990	767	LA, US—Cairo, Egypt	The Atlantic Ocean	Suspected co-pilot's action or elevator defection	Communication out of touch, radar disappearing	217 people killed
50	1999.12.22	8509	747	Tashkent, Uzbekistan—London Stansted Airport	Essex	Attitude director indicator malfunction	Null	4 people killed
51	2000.01.10	CRX498	340B	Zurich, Switzerland—Dresden, Germany	Niederhasli	Pilots' fault & passengers making phone calls	Communication out of touch, radar disappearing	10 people killed

MH370 SHOULD BE HERE

Number	Time	Flight number	Type	Departure—destination	Crash site	Causes	Communication and radar	Casualties
52	2000.01.31	261	MD-83	Mexico—San Francisco	Crashing into the Pacific Ocean	horizontal stabilizer trim system getting stuck	00	88 people killed
53	2000.07.25	4590	Concorde	Charles de Gaulle Airport, France—Kennedy Airport, US	Near the airport	fragments of debris cutting a tyre	Communication suspended, radar disappearing	113 people killed
54	2000.10.31	006	747	Chinese Taipei—LA	Taiwan Taoyuan International Airport	entering a wrong take-off runway, exploding	0	83 people killed
55	2001.10.08	686	MD-87	Milan, Italy—Copenhagen, Denmark	Near Milan Airport	Crashing into a civil plane	No ground radar installed	110 people killed
56	2001.11.12	587	A300B4	Kennedy International Airport—the Dominican Republic	Queens County	stabilizer going off the aircraft, the plane out of control	Null	265 people killed
57	2001.11.24	3597	AVRO–146	Berlin, Germany—Zürich, Switzerland	Near Zürich Airport	Pilots' driving fault	0	24 people killed, 9 people injured
58	2002.05.25	611	747	Chinese Taipei International Airport—Hong Kong	Taiwan Strait	Fatigue of skin metal	Communication suspended/Null	225 people killed
59	2002.07.01	2937	Tu–154M	Moscow, Russia—Barcelona, Spain	Uberlingen, Germany	Colliding with Flight 611	Air traffic control radar in the maintenance	71 people killed
60	2003.01.08	5481	1900D	Charlotte—Greenville, US	Charlotte/Douglas International Airport	Turnbuckles controlling tension on the cables to the elevators incorrectly set	0	21 people killed
61	2004.01.03	604	737	Sharm El Sheikh International Airport, Egypt—Charles de Gaulle Airport, France	Red Sea near Sharm El Sheikh International Airport	pilot suffering spatial disorientation or the spoilers getting stuck	0	148 people killed
62	2005.08.06	1153	ATR–72	Bari, Italy—Djerba - Zarzis International Airport, Tunisia	Mediterranean sea	Fault in oil quantity indicator	0	16 people killed, 23 people injured
63	2005.08.14	522	737	Cyprus—Athens, Greece	Hills in Greece	Loss of pressure in the cabin	0	121 people killed
64	2005.08.16	708	MD-82	Panama—Martinique	Mountains in Venezuela	Pilots operating fault	Null	160 people killed
65	2005.08.23	204	737–200	Pucalipa—Iquitos, Peru	Near Pucallpa Airport	Flying into storms	0	40 people killed, 58 people injured
66	2006.09.29	1907	737	Manaus—Rio de Janeiro, Brazil	Mato Grosso	colliding with an Embraer Legacy 600 business jet over	Communication suspended, radar disappearing	156 people killed
67	2007.01.01	574	737-400	Surabaya—Manado, Indonesia	Sulawesi	Thunderstorm and misoperation	Null/radar disappearing	102 people killed
68	2007.07.17	3054	A320–233	Porto Alegre—Sao Paulo, Brazil	Near Sao Paulo Airports	Heavy rain, airport not closed and misoperation	0	199 people killed
69	2007.08.09	1121	DHC–6	Moorea Island in French Polynesia—Tahiti	Near Moorea Island	Control cable broken	0	20 people killed
70	2008.02.21	518	ATR-42	Merida—Caracas, Venezuela	Crashing into mountains near the airport	Captain getting lost	Communication out of touch/Null	46 people killed
71	2008.11.27	888T	A320–232	Perpignan - Rivesaltes Airport flying training	Crashing into the sea near the airport	Faults in the detectors	0	7 people killed
72	2009.02.12	3407	Q400	Newark—Buffalo, US	Near Clarence Airport	Fatigue driving, loss of speed	Communication out of touch, radar disappearing	50 people killed, 4 people injured
73	2009.06.01	447	A330–203	Capital of Brazil—Capital of France	Crashing into the Atlantic Ocean	Loss of speed after entering an aerodynamic stall	Communication out of touch, radar disappearing	228 people killed

Number	Time	Flight number	Type	Departure—destination	Crash site	Causes	Communication and radar	Casualties
74	2010.01.25	409	737	Beirut, Lebanon—Addis Ababa	Mediterranean sea	The crew tired	Communication out of touch/Null	90 people killed
75	2010.04.10	special plane	Tu-154M	Warsaw, Poland—Smolensk, Russia	Near the Smolensk airport	Errors in operation	0	97 people killed
76	2011.09.07	9633	Yak-42D	Yaroslavl, Russia—Mensk, Belarus	Crashing into the river near the airport	Mistakenly hitting the brake	0	45 people killed
77	2013.07.06	214	777	Incheon International Airport, Korea—San Francisco, US	San Francisco Airport	Autothrottle turned off	0	3 people killed, 181 people injured
78	2014.03.08	MH370	777-200	Kuala Lumpur—Beijing	the South China Sea	Judged as an accident	Communication out of touch, radar disappearing	239 people killed
79	2014.07.17	MH17	777-200	Amsterdam—Kuala Lumpur	Ukraine	Attacked by missiles	Communication suspended, radar disappearing	298 people killed
80	2014.7.24	AH5017	MD-83	Ouagadougou—Algiers, Africa	Gossi, Mali	Mistakenly entering the eye of the storm	Communication suspended, radar disappearing	118 people killed
81	2014.12.28	QZ8501	A320-200	Surabaya, Indonesia—Chang Airport, Singapore	Java Sea	Human error in operation	Communication suspended, radar disappearing	162 people killed
合计						84 aircraft crashed	21 cases of dispearance of both communication and radar	10765 people killed, 1034 people injured

The second incident, on July 24, 2014, the Algerian flight AH5017, an MD 83 aircraft, took off at 01:00 GMT and was on its way from Waqu Du Gu, the capital of Burkina Faso in Africa to Algiers. It disappeared at 01:47 and vanished from the radar three minutes later, at 01:50. Flight AH5017 was proved to have crashed under where its radar signal disappeared, in the Marigosi area (see below)

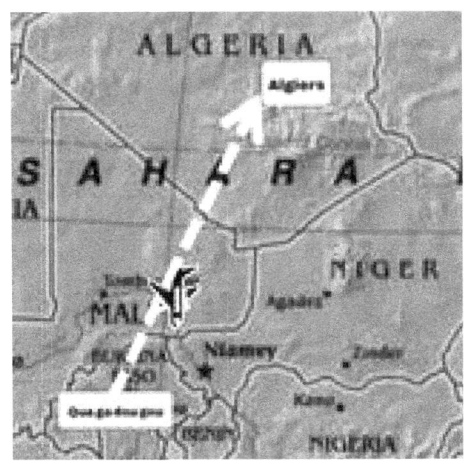

Diagram of the flight route of AH5017
(Drawn by Yang Jun)

Investigation revealed that flight AH5017 encountered bad weather and flew into the eye of a storm. Three minutes later, it was thrown to the ground and crashed into pieces, resulting in the deaths of all 118 people on board. The plane disintegrated when it hit the ground, and the splash range of the crashed flight was rather concentrated with a narrow drift range, unlike Flight MH17, which was shot down by a missile in Ukrainian air space and whose drift range was rather wide (see photo).

This case strongly suggests that Flight MH370, which vanished within three minutes, would not, no matter what happened, have crashed in the Southern Indian Ocean waters west of Perth. Instead, the main body would have splashed down in the South China Sea, Scene 1.

Pictures of the scene where AH5017 crashed

Pictures of the scene where MH17 crashed

In summary, as the author has repeatedly advocated, the search for the whereabouts of Flight MH370 should be based on the facts, guided by evidence, and adhering to the principle of searching where the disappearance happened. Therefore, I strongly appeal:

First, immediately restart searches at the Scene 1, exhausting every possible means.

Second, follow the search strategy of promoting wider range, for those suspected positions with coordinates, search them by exhausting all possible means and available detection equipment in an all-directional, three-dimensional way, and exclude them one by one, arranging appropriate forces to search the surrounding surface.

Third, on March 8, 2010, a New Zealand worker on an oil drilling platform in the South China Sea witnessed a plane on fire crashing into the South China Sea. The same day, a British woman sailing from India to Phuket, Thailand, also saw a smoking plane crashing into sea and other planes flying in different directions at the same time in the same area. The intersection spot of the two witnesses was in the same direction where the radar signals of the three countries disappeared.

Fourth, within the 24 hours from 0:00 March 8, 2014 to 0:00 March 9, 2014, there were no reports worldwide of any flights missing, crashed, or caught on fire or smoke except MH370.

Fifth, Thailand's Suratthani military radar station, which had been monitoring MH370 that day, had been tracking the flight of MH370 on March 8, 2014, and reported the plane's sudden disappearance from their radar at 1:22 the same day. Six minutes later, at 1:28, their radar detected a plane, but they said it was impossible to determine whether the plane was Flight MH370 ; in other words, during the same period of time at the same place there were at least two planes. The aircraft that appeared six minutes later, had different identifiers on their radar, which proves from another perspective that Flight MH370 went missing before 1:28! If it was still in the scope of their surveillance, it would be impossible for them not to recognize it. If it was Flight MH370, how could they not identify it only five or six minutes later?

Sixth, on March 8, 2014, the Earthquake Laboratory of the University of Science and Technology of China detected a "submarine event" at N7° 25 points, E104 ° 30 points, 116 kilometers northeast of Flight MH370's disappearance site. Within 24 hours of that time there were no earthquakes or other "submarine events" in the South China Sea. Therefore, this "submarine event" must be related to the missing Flight MH370.

In order to achieve an accurate search, positions with coordinates must be further corrected to decrease deviations. According to the current detection equipment capabilities in the world, search the key submarine sites and gradually expand the search by a radius of 5 km at a time.

At present, there are five target coordinate points at Scene 1:

1. N7° 25', E103° 55' (my first suspected site)
2. N8° 41', E104° 48' (my second suspected site)
3. N6° 55'15', E103° 34'43' (the disappearance site)
4. N6° 59' E117° 1'59" (crash site in the opinion of the Malaysian army)
5. N6° 06' E104° 36' (crash site according to USA NASA satellite).

In addition to the above five coordinate points, the rest include the Vietnam-Cambodia border, the Vietnam-China border, the Gulf of Thailand and so on, which have the direction but no coordinates.

Third, as a concerned country in the event, Vietnam should be absorbed as a search command and an identification member, so as to hear more of its opinion in this event. Vietnam has the strongest air defence force in this region and has made the most prompt and accurate response to this event, so it is a big mistake to ignore its views.

Fourth, governments or MAS should place a reward advertisement as soon as possible and offer a handsome reward to those who help find the missing aircraft or missing persons.

In summary, it was a major mistake to give up so easily and ignore the need to search at Scene 1.

CHAPTER NINE

Why were there no clues to MH370 at Scene 2, the Indian Ocean west of Perth?

The search teams left the South China Sea to search in the Southern Indian Ocean west of Perth. Why wasn't even a piece of wreckage found in the west of Perth despite the investment of large quantities of people, finance and materials? To find out the reasons, it is necessary to know about the search first.

ONE – THE SEARCH IN THE SOUTHERN INDIAN OCEAN

The search in the Southern Indian Ocean from March 15, 2014 was generally divided into three phases:

Phase One: March 14 to May 29

1. Duration: 26 countries participated, 75 days
2. Search spot: the Southern Indian Ocean waters, west of Perth, Australia.
3. Search Range: 62,023 square km
4. Search equipment: warships, planes, merchant ships, scientific research ships, submarines etc.
5. Search method: omnidirectional and three-dimensional search
6. Cost: about $100 million
7. Search Results: Nil

Phase Two: from August 4, 2014 to July 3, 2015

1. Duration: 300 days
2. Search location: 1,800 km off the Australian west coast
3. Search Range: 60,000 square km
4. Search Equipment: selected according to need by professional organisations
5. Search method: deep sea mapping by professional search organisation
6. Cost: about $55,910
7. Search Results: No findings

Phase Three: from August, 2015 to January 17, 2017

1. Duration: 500 days
2. Search location: On the seventh arc from the west coast of Australia.
3. Search Range: 60,000 square km
4. Search Equipment: Four search ships working in turn
5. Search Method: Fugro searching with the most advanced deep-sea detection equipment
6. Cost: Over one hundred million US dollars
7. Search Results: No findings

Phase Four: from January 10, 2018 to June 9, 2018
1. Duration: 120 days
2. Search location: Waters on the north of the Seventh Arc in the Southern Indian Ocean
3. Search range: over 112,000 square km
4. Search equipment: eight autonomous underwater vehicles working in turn
5. Search method: deep-sea mapping by the US corporation Ocean Infinity
6. Cost: expected to be about 70 million US dollars (nothing to be paid to Ocean Infinity if it fails to find the aircraft).
7. Search results: the aircraft not found

Since the disappearance of MH370, the search has been going on. From around 9 o'clock March 8 to noon on the 14th, 10 countries participated in the search, mainly in the 70,000 square kilometre area of Scene 1 in the South China Sea waters around the core N6° 55', E103° 34'. The search used the naked eye as well as electronic scanning, only to find no useful clues to MH370.

After noon on March 14th, all search teams were transferred to the Indian Ocean. On the afternoon of April 5, 2014, news came from the search in the Indian Ocean west of Perth: Australia's 'Ocean Shield' detected suspected black box pulsing signals at the frequency of 33.3KHz, 550 kilometres away from S25° E101°. On the same day, a Chinese coastguard ship detected a suspected black box signal at the frequency of 37.5KHz per second near S25°, E101°.

Australia's general coordinator happily announced: 'Because the sonar transmitting power of the black box is small, the pulse signal transmission range is only tens of kilometres, which indicates that the search boat was close enough to the black box to have the chance to occasionally listen to the pulse signal, which narrows the search range to only tens of square kilometres... we are searching in the right area and are very close to the target. However, further confirmation of the signal is still in progress'.

At present, the deep-sea search, mainly relies on unmanned underwater vehicles which can work up to 6000 metres deep. To search for sunken objects, unmanned underwater vehicles mainly rely on the high-resolution imaging of side scan sonar with a working high frequency at around 100KHz; in addition, unmanned underwater vehicles are equipped with optical cameras which can take close-up shots of seabed objects with a higher confirmation ratio than side scan sonar. As the unmanned underwater vehicles work at a very slow speed of only about 5 km per hour, and of a scan width of only about 1 km, it is not an overnight job to find the wreckage even the search area is greatly reduced. If the unmanned submarine finds the suspected aircraft wreckage, the manned submarine will be sent to determine whether the object is the crashed plane.

1. MH370'S BLACK BOX SIGNAL CONFIRMED BY AUSTRALIA

On the morning of April 12, 2014, Australian Prime Minister Tony Abbott, who was paying a state visit to China, said that a signal detected in the search in the Southern Indian Ocean was definitely from Flight MH370's black box. At a press conference held by China's foreign ministry, a reporter asked Mr Abbott what evidence he had. Abbott responded that the relevant conclusion was drawn by a very complex search of highly advanced equipment and through rigorous research. So Australia was very sure: the signal was from the black box on Flight MH370.

Mr Abbott said that the biggest achievement was to have narrowed the scope of search as much as possible. Meanwhile,

The Bluefin 21

the Australian Joint Coordinating Centre released the latest arrangements for the search of MAS Flight MH370. The *Ocean Shield* would continue to be search with a towed acoustic locator and try to locate further signals related to the lost black box. In addition, an Orion aircraft would aid the *Ocean Shield* in the search; the British Navy ship HMS *Echo* would also search in the same area. These search actions would continue to shrink the underwater search area.

On April 12, 2014, nine military aircraft, one civilian aircraft and 14 vessels were participating in the search. The Australian Maritime Safety Authority planned to search a total area of 41393 square kilometres. The centre of the search area was about 2331 km north-west of Perth. Nothing was found.

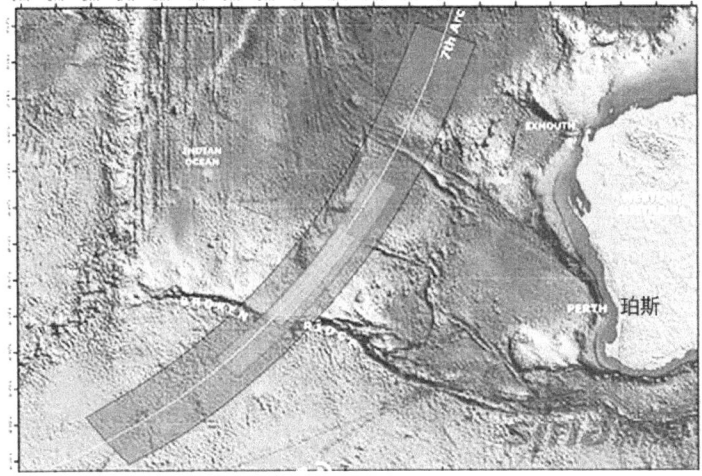

Diagram of MH370's suspected location in the
Southern Indian Ocean, west of Perth

2. SEARCH WITH ADVANCED 'BLUEFIN' UNDERWATER VEHICLES

The US military also sent a professional underwater search device – a Bluefin 21 autonomous underwater vehicle, specializing in short-distance positioning under water. This search device looks similar to a submarine and is 493 cm in length, 53 cm in diameter and weighs 750 kg. It can five to 4500 metres and travel at 4 knots, with 25 hours of endurance capacity. It can be loaded with a variety of detection equipment according to need. In the configuration of the relevant sonar, it can identify underwater objects down to 7.5 cm in size. Unlike the towed sound locator used by China in this search, it can travel underwater and communicate with the controller in a wireless manner without cable towing. The Bluefin 21 found no useful clues.

3. SEARCH CONDUCTED BY A SPECIALIZED UNDERSEA EXPLORATION COMPANY

From March 14, 2014 to May 29, 26 countries conducted a continuous search of more than 60,000 square kilometres in 'the prior search area' confirmed by authorities with various types of aircraft, ships, satellites, merchant ships and other advanced detection equipment without even finding a single fragment of MH370.

On June 10, 2014, led by the Australian Transport Safety Bureau, an undersea exploration contract was signed with Holland's Fugro Surveying Ltd., hoping to find the whereabouts of MH370 through submarine exploration of sea areas west of Perth (referring to the diagram below) in the Southern Indian Ocean.

The contract stipulates that the company can detect with any equipment. The probe was conducted from August 4, 2014 to January 17, 2017. Fugro tried all methods and obtained many underwater images – extinct volcanoes, depressions on the sea floor, four sunken ships, a 200-litre gas container and some smaller articles like anchors were found; the sea bed was studied, and many clear pictures were taken, but MH370 was not seen.

On October 3, 2017, the Australian Transport Safety Bureau (ATSB) issued an MH370 search-related final summative report which extended to more than 400 pages. It clearly stated that the aircraft had not been found in the Southern Indian Ocean. The search team felt 'very sorry' for that.

On January 10, 2018, Ocean Infinity, a US undersea mapping corporation, and the Malaysian government signed a contract with regard to the search. Ocean Infinity would send multiple underwater vehicles including Seabed Constructor to search, and go to the Indian Ocean to search the Seventh Arc for 90 days, with coverage of 25,000 square kilometres. If nothing was found, Ocean Infinity would not be paid; if it was successful, the Malaysian government would pay it 70 million US dollars.

By the time Ocean Infinity had searched for 90 days, the search coverage had extended to 100 thousand square kilometres, far more than 25 thousand square kilometres, and there was still no sign of the plane. Ocean Infinity asked for an extension, and the government agreed to give them 30 more days. By the deadline on June 9, 2018, the coverage had reached more than 112 thousand square kilometres, five times the area planned. An Ocean Infinity said that it was with a heavy heart they had to end the search.

Why were there no clues to MH370 in the Southern Indian Ocean?

The search in the Southern Indian Ocean started from Malacca 2° N and went southward to 40° south and eastward to 110°. It covered an area of nearly 9 million square kilometres. Why wasn't there any sign of MH370 when such a specialized team made such great efforts to search with such advanced equipment? The key point is the lack of a clear judgement about the MH370 event.

MH370 took off from Kuala Lumpur at 0:42 on March 8. At 01:19:29, the last conversation took place. At 1:37, the ground control centre should have been receiving signals from the ACARS system every half a minute, but it did not.

1. It is a mistake to define 01:20 as the disappearance time. 01:20 was neither the time of disappearance nor the time the plane went missing. It was the time when the pilots' verbal communication stopped. So the addressing signals and the Pacific satellite's signals didn't disappear; the satellites over the Indian Ocean were still 'shaking hands'. Back then, the flight was still in cruise; the communication was still going on. The time of disappearance should be 01:38 or 08:19. After that, the communications stopped.

2. The disappearance of telecommunications does not mean the disappearance of the plane. One of the overlooked facts is that the co-pilot said, 'OK, good night'. After that, there was no further verbal communication. Later, the radar signals directly reflecting the plane's existing state in the air disappeared at the same time within 3 minutes, from 01:22 to 01:25, from three different directions (Kuala Lumpur, Surat Thani and Ho Chi Minh City) as well as the monitoring devices in three or even four different countries. The flight altitude dropped from FL350 to 0. The plane's addressing signal disappeared at 01:37; after 02:03, it failed to log in to the satellite over the Pacific Ocean. The plane had disappeared. The chain of events indicate that the flight went missing before it disappeared. We should determine the whereabouts of the missing plane according to the time of disappearance.

If policymakers respected the objective facts, they would not be so determined to search the Southern Indian Ocean west of Perth. It seems that the time of disappearance, the radar signals and communication signals mentioned above were not taken into consideration. Instead, they moved to the west of Perth, the Southern Indian Ocean mainly according to the presumed 'handshake' data. What's more, they estimated the area where the plane disappeared on the basis that the last 'handshake' time was 8:19, so they inferred that March 8 was the time of disappearance and the plane must have disappeared in the waters of the Southern Indian Ocean.

This was ridiculous. It was wrong! If the definition of nature and the positioning are correct, all means should be taken to find out the truth according to the time and location of disappearance, however long it took. That's the basic principle.

You can compare MH370 to a human being at this moment. Its signals were like a person's pulse. They were gone at 1:37, meaning the pulse was gone. Vocal communications were like a person's speech. They were gone after 1:37, as if it had stopped 'speaking'. Satellite communication signals were like a person's ears. The signals stopped after 1:37, meaning it could no longer hear. Radar signals stopped, like eyes being 'closed', at 1:25, without reopening for the following few hours. If a person's four vital signs are all gone, the person is undoubtedly dead.

Was there any need, over an hour later, to take out the Indian Ocean satellite data from after 02:25? In fact, it was about continuing to try to solve the problem of the missing flight to take out the Indian Ocean satellite data, to artificially graft relevant data and to mathematically process it. When the Pacific Ocean satellite data were gone, could they be transferred to the Indian Ocean satellites covering the same area? As a coincidence, at 01:37 the addressing signals were gone; the Pacific Ocean satellite didn't log in at 02:03. That was where all should stop!

At 2:25, 47 minutes after the addressing signals disappeared, the 'handshake' data of a plane were found from Indian Ocean satellites. There were many flaws in the data, but some so-called experts thought they most closely matched those of MH370, so they continued to assume that the fuel had run out at 8:19. Because of human factors, the flight time of Flight MH370 had been extended for seven hours, extending thousands of kilometres, and the flight naturally went beyond the South China Sea and extended to the Indian Ocean. If there were no clues in the Pacific Ocean, then it was time to look in the Indian Ocean.

Among the seven handshake signals, four were from the Perth ground station, so naturally the search for MH370 was there. To the east is the land mass of Australia, and there are definitely no places for MH370 to hide there; to the west is the Southern Indian Ocean, and the only way to search there is to try to scoop the wreckage out.

'Disappearance of communication' and 'missing' are two

completely different concepts and lead to different consequences. Differences in nature bring different decisions, and consequently lead to different conclusions.

To find the causes is always the priority when a break-off in communication occurs. Is it because of a frequency shift, pauses in frequency, frequency hopping or faults in wires, transmission, mechanism, or power supply? It is desirable to apply a suitable way and try to get back in touch with the plane. To find the missing passengers is always the priority when a 'missing' occurs!

There might be various reasons, of which some are exceedingly strange. But the priority is to find its whereabouts. When the missing passengers are found, the reasons for the disappearance may come out.

When facing the disappearance of both the plane and the passengers, how do we judge whether it is an accidental disappearance or caused by human error? For an accidental disappearance, the reaction from all aspects is to search everywhere. For an accident caused by human error, which is usually related to politics, afterwards there will often be a claim that some organisation or individual is responsible. For one that is related to economy, a certain organisation or individual will ask the victims or their company for a ransom. Since MH370's disappearance, no country, no organisation or company has received political or economic demands, and no relative of the missing passengers has received similar demands. Therefore, the disappearance of MH370 should belong to the accidental category.

Don't let us complicate simple matters by making an ordinary security case into an abduction and murder case (including hijacking and terrorist attacks). Coping with accidental public security cases (including the disappearance caused by the evaporation and self-combusting of chemical substances), we should stick to the principle of searching where disappearance happens, and then try all means. If there is no gain out of it, then we take another way.

Not enough methods were adopted during the search in the South China Sea when the nature of the event was unclear. Moreover, the search equipment was not good enough; the search time was not long enough; the search area was not wide enough; and the search did not go deep enough. The sudden move in the search to the Southern Indian Ocean was against the common-sense principle of searching where disappearance happened. It was going in the opposite direction! A wrong judgement is the key to making the event a 'mystery'.

2. The preconceived ideas affected decision makers. The MH370 event happened unexpectedly and suddenly, and there were various opinions which all seemed to make sense, making it hard for the decision makers to distinguish. Some said the plane was hit by a missile; some said the passengers had been taken away by aliens; some said the captain or some criminals on board had hijacked the plane. From the reports following up, what prevailed was the opinion that the captain or someone on board hijacked the plane, and the communications system had shut off automatically, so the decision makers decided to believe this. That was why it was said at one time that the plane had flown to the Indian Andaman Sea, and then flew to the west of Perth. When someone signalled to the Southern Indian Ocean according to satellites' handshake signals, and when Australia's ADV Ocean Shield detected the supposed black box signals 2261 km north-west of Perth, the prejudgment that one kilometre around the signals was the final location of MH370 was more strongly believed.

After contact with the plane was lost, if it made a turn from north-east to north-west and continued to fly for more than another hour, it should have been within the surveillance range of the radar stations of Thailand, Ho Chi Minh City and Kuala Lumpur. Why couldn't the radar see it? The communication devices were artificially turned off, but for the radar outside, nobody on board was able to turn that off. Needless to say, the radar signals were different types from three different directions and different countries, and operated by different types of people.

As it turned out, to judge on the basis of the handshake signals was very similar to the judgment and decision-making based on the claim that Iraq had weapons of mass destruction. Subjective and preconceived thinking dominated the search and rescue planning. As a result, the idea that the captain hijacked the plane was invalid; there was no possibility of the other people on board carrying out a terrorist attack. Failing to search the place where the plane disappeared was against the principle of searching where the disappearance happened. The money spent on the search was wasted.

3. Some media misled decision makers. In the first three days after the disappearance of MH370, the search key areas were in the South China Sea and the gulf of Thailand, and the layout was relatively correct and reasonable. If we had continued to expand the scope of the search scope, intensify search efforts and improve the search mode, the mystery of MH370 would have been revealed.

Then some strange new information emerged. On March 14, 2014, US officials said that the plane had sent pulse signals several times to a satellite several hours after it had lost contact. Prompted by this new information, the US transferred its naval vessels from the South China Sea to the Indian Ocean. On March 15, the coordination centre, according to information from the US and the UK, began to adjust the deployment, and the search location was adjusted from the South China Sea to both the south and north of the Indian Ocean. On March 20, 2014, the Australian Prime Minister announced the discovery of two suspected MH370 objects in a satellite image obtained about 2,300 kilometres southwest of the western Australian city of Perth. On March 25, a British company used the Doppler effect to analyse the pulse signals from the plane, extrapolating the final location of the aircraft as in the Southern Indian Ocean.

In the face of so much information, how to get to the heart of the problem was a test of conscience, wisdom and decision-making ability of the directors in the search and coordination centre. As was proved through practice, some specious messages misled the decision makers, making it difficult for them to distinguish. Therefore, we should say that all kinds of methods have been tried. What has been achieved? Nothing. Not one piece of debris of MH370 has been found in these searches.

4. Having chosen the wrong clues, the search missed many opportunities. From March 9-14 2014, Malaysia's search leader organised forces to briefly search 70,000 square kilometres in the South China Sea on the basis of the time and area of disappearance. It is worth pointing out that before March 12th, the search team focused on the wreckage of the plane instead of on the black box. They didn't even pay attention to receiving any signal from an emergency locator transmitter (ELT) which is designed to eject from an aircraft and send out signals for 24 hours after a crash. How many opportunities were missed?

On March 15, according to the so-called satellite data, the search in the South China Sea where MH370 was most likely to be was abandoned, in the firm determination that the crash location was the waters west of Perth. The search there turned out to be fruitless.

We could use the satellite data. The problem was how to distinguish the real from the fake ones. It has been proved that

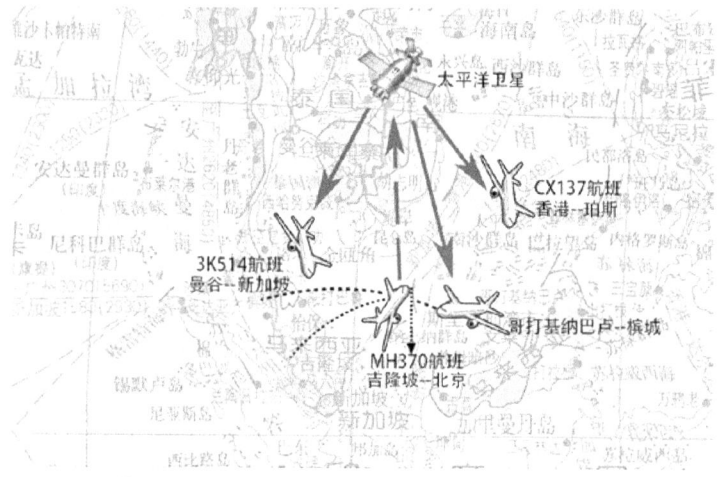

Four aircraft flying in different directions simultaneously
(Drawn by Yu Haibo)

without radar tracking and other types of satellite coordination, it is not accurate and scientific to use a synchronous satellite for aircraft positioning. Two or more satellites are required for location, but two satellites can only set a general direction, they can't specify the approximate location, let alone a precise one.

We could also use the 'handshake' signals. The key was whether the time matched and whether the one shaking hands with satellites was definitely MH370 with no other possibilities. Suppose at the same time, there appear two 'hands' and

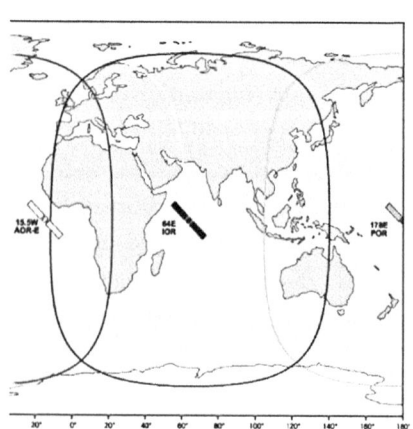

Diagram of area covered by the communication of International Maritime Satellite Organisation (Inmarsat)

世界交通 WORLD COMMUNICATIONS

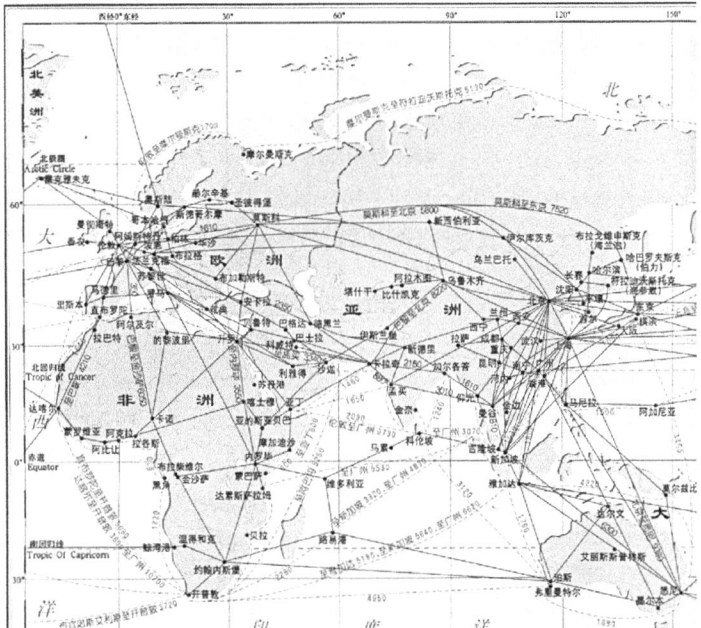

Four flights in the same area

only one 'handshake' signal, 1:2 or 2:1, can we tell which 'hand' the satellite shook, the first one or the second? For example, if MH370 was the first 'hand' and it disappeared, then the one the satellite shook hands with might be the second one which was in the same area during the same period, possibly Flight 3K514 or CX137; or before 1:25 on March 8, it was the Pacific's maritime satellite that was responsible for providing the channel's communications services, and after 1:25 that day, it was the Indian Ocean's satellite that was responsible for providing the channel's communications services. It is not rare to call white black when identification is not confirmed.

If there were three aircraft entering the space covered by

Malaysian Army's radars and renting maritime satellite communications, it might happen that one (presumably MH370) of the three planes smoked and disappeared, and at the same time, another of the three (presumably 3K514 or CX137 to and from Bangkok-Perth-Hongkong) to 'shake hands' in its place. Would it be strange to confuse one with another in such a situation? It was no wonder that the data was followed all the way to the Southern Indian Ocean, as shown in the following picture on p.112.

Moreover, in the same area of communication, a carrier at the same frequency is sometimes automatically converted, and only by timely measuring directions can it be found that the Pacific satellite and the Indian Ocean satellite are alternatively used without necessarily letting users know, and even the controller of communications may not be clear about that. If communication signals are not in the area covered by two satellites at the same time, the situation mentioned above won't occur.

In the same period when MH370 disappeared, four flights, MH370, CX137, 3K514 and a flight from Kota Kinabalu to Penang, were flying through the same area covered by the same synchronous satellite over the South China Sea. The satellite communication channel of MH370 happened to be under two

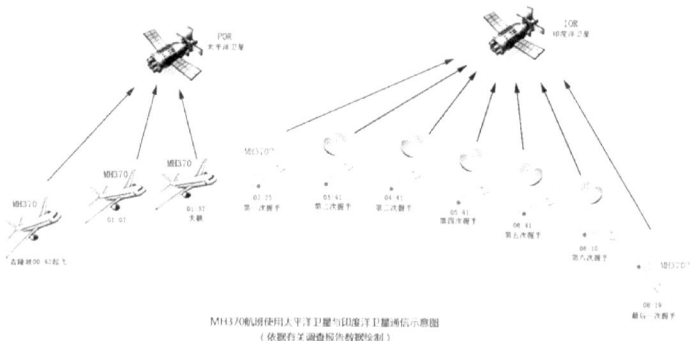

Diagram of MH370's use of the Pacific Ocean satellites and the Indian Ocean satellite to communicate (drawn by Yu Haibo according to relevant investigation report data)

maritime satellites' coverage. Without the support of direction-measuring and attention to ID code and sync. pulses, it is usually difficult to distinguish the instantaneous PING pulse signal and judge which satellite it belongs to with just instantaneous tracking signals. For satellites, there is no error in meeting the receiving threshold within the coverage area. Satellites will always take the signals as long as they are in their coverage area.

It is somewhat similar to tracking people. When someone appears who looks very like the real target, it is easy even for those specialized in tracking to follow the wrong target and miss the right one.

The safety investigation report on Malaysia airlines Flight MH370 afterwards showed that from 20:50 March 7 to 01:07 March 8, it used the Pacific Orbiting Region (POR); from 01:19:29, when the last conversation took place, to 02:03:41, all means of communication terminated, and POR data were never detected after that.

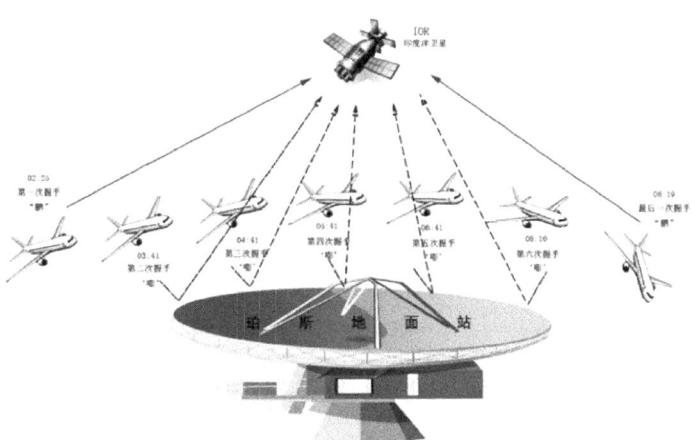

Diagram of "handshake" of the Indian Ocean satellite and the ground station
(Draw by Yu Haibo according to relevant investigation report data)

At 02:25:27 on March 8, 2014, the satellite communication logged again, but during the logging, the ground station did not receive the flight number, the satellite communication system register request or the synchronous pulse frequency of the request of the signal confirmation, recorded by the ground station. The satellite communication system registration request, as well as the synchronous pulse frequency of the request of the signal confirmation, recorded by the ground station, was abnormal. However, from the first handshake at 02:25 to 08:19 to the seventh and final handshake, all the data came from the Indian Ocean Region (IOR). These data include not only the login data of the aircraft directly linking to the satellite, but the login data of the Perth ground station connecting the satellite, illustrated on p.114.

Seven handshake signals appeared on the Indian Ocean satellite 'public channel', 'PENG', their time being irregular, the sources and frequencies being different. It was fine whether the time difference was one hour or nine minutes; it was fine whether it was the plane directly logging in or it was the ground station forward.

Was it a 'PPENG', a 'PEENG' , a 'PENNG', a 'PENGG'? Which was the PING from MH370? We have no clues, as illustrated below.

5. Lack of creativity influenced the search. Normal thinking says there must be plenty of floating objects; an air crash must mean the plane will break into pieces with wreckage spreading all over; more than 40 tons of fuel must cause a fire or oil stains whether it crashes into the sea or a forest. It is usually effective under regular circumstances to search for floating objects, floating fuel or wreckage. However, none of the methods above worked during the search for MH370 in the searched areas.

For one thing, the searched areas were not where MH370

crashed, or the real crash location has not been spotted, so the search has not covered the exact location. For another thing, the MH370 event is a special case in which the plane did not break up or explode. Or even though it broke up the moment it hit the ground or the water, there wouldn't be many pieces and the pieces might not spread out too much.

Since there were no big areas with floating objects, I think that was because when the flight hit the water, it was not a hard collision—the waves helped to cushion the aircraft and send it under the water, and it did not disintegrate. None of the cabin doors was open when the plane went into the sea. Therefore, there should only be a small number of pieces.

There were no signs of large areas of fuel or fire. That was probably because part of the fuel had been consumed after 30 minutes' flight, so there was some room in the fuel tank; when the plane hit the ground or the water, the impact force from outside the tank offset the overflowing force from inside, so the fuel tank did not explode and there was no leakage of fuel, which was enclosed in the tank as it had been before the crash.

Hence, it was not satisfactory to search for MH370 by looking for floating objects and floating fuel. And when conventional thinking cannot solve a problem, it is time to change the way of thinking.

6. Wrong data analyses & orientation and self-willed decision of conduct. How should we make a judgement of where MH370 was after its disappearance? Where to search became the focus of the event. There have so far been three major types of evidence:

First, what I call the satellite 'handshake type'. The main evidence was that it was presumed that the seven instantaneous 'PING' signals recorded by the maritime communications satellite over the Indian Ocean were sent by Flight MH370. It was combined with the data relating to fuel, time of flight and so on. A number of experts inferred, according to elements like elevation, intervals, distance and speed, that MH370 crashed into the 'Seventh Arc' in the Southern Indian Ocean, 1800 km west of Perth, Australia. The plane was estimated to have splashed down somewhere in an area of 60,000 square kilometres. Nothing was found after 75 days of search from March 14 to May 29 2014, despite the involvement of detection equipment from 26 countries. The equipment included satellites, aircraft, naval vessels, commercial ships, submarines and scientific expedition ships. In June 2014, Australia signed a contract with a Dutch company, Fugro NV, to explore an area of ocean floor in the Southern Indian Ocean. In April 2015, the search area was doubled to 120,000 square kilometres. By January 17, 2017, it had produced no clues closely related to MH370, although many clear images of extinct volcanoes, oceanic trenches etc were obtained and some articles were found, big and small, such as sunken ships, gas containers and anchors.

Second, disappearance evidence. This type inferred, based on the fact that the last words ('All right, good night') said by the co-pilot said were related to radar data when the last conversation took place, that MH370 crashed in the water around N06° 55'15', E103° 34'43', in the South China Sea. Between March 9-14 2014, Malaysia, China, Vietnam, the US and other countries sent aircraft and ships to search for five to six days, covering 70,000 square kilometers, only to find nothing.

Third, radar evidence. This type inferred, according to the time of MH370's disappearance from the radars of Vietnam, Malaysia and Thailand, the radar data, the plane's location, speed, flying direction and altitude, that MH370 had crashed, with all on board killed. Making some adjustments to the junction of the three azimuth angles, it can be determined that the splashdown area should be in the South China Sea, within a 50 km radius of N7° 25', E103° 55' under the set destination. It can't be ruled out that the crash site is in an oceanic trench, island or deep forest across the Vietnam-Cambodia or China-Vietnam border. I am a staunch supporter of this type of evidence.

Besides the three above, there are also suggestions, like the crash location was at S39.20, E88.36 on the US military base on Diego Garcia, or the crash was in Tajikistan and so on. Because these suggestions have little support, I won't talk about them in detail.

As for the 'handshake' advocates, I think the data they choose lack uniqueness, originality, certainty, consistency, regularity or coherence. There is no direct and convincing logical chain of evidence, and there was no supporting material or circumstantial evidence either. There are too many uncertain elements in their descriptions, too many probabilities, estimates, inferences, deductions and guesses. In addition, the handshake signals only had data from one IOR satellite, and no supportive GPS connection service. Therefore it is not possible, based on the data of this one satellite, to determine the crash location of MH370.

If the handshake signal had GPS service connection, the data presented were reliable and the conclusion should be accurate and reliable. There are dozens of GPS satellites monitoring results on the back of a geosynchronous satellite, so its data are reliable and can withstand tests. Putting it informally, when satellites watched MH370, there were dozens of 'eyes' rather than just one. Is it possible that the data were not accurate with so many 'eyes' watching it? The trouble is that there was no GPS as backup. Could it be inferred that the crash was in the Southern Indian Ocean, according to a small number of incoherent, irregular, unidentified data collected from only one Indian Ocean synchronous satellite and Perth ground station on one day (rather than many)? Such data make a great difference.

If the satellite's handshake signals' data were random, the

accuracy of the crash location of MH370 will be far greater than when a synchronous satellite was used.

When MH370 was flying, it was within the coverage area of two synchronous satellites in the Pacific Ocean and Indian Ocean. If there were two groups of matching data, or regular and frequent data, they might enable us to draw a more precise conclusion even if identification was not confirmed. Unfortunately, when the often-used Pacific satellite was abandoned and a small number of irregular data were taken from a satellite in the Indian Ocean, it turned out that the relevant data did not stand up to expert interpretation.

When some experts analysed the relevant data, the conclusion was that MH370 was travelling at 50 miles per hour at Kuala Lumpur International Airport before it was on the runway to get ready for take-off. If it had moved at such a speed, there would have been a serious accident.

There is no definite evidence that the seven PING signals were made by MH370. Moreover, no one can prove they were made during the flight. People who have monitored satellite signals know that communication signals in the same channel are not necessarily from the same transmitter; this uncertainty becomes even greater when the signals are inconsistent and irregular and last less than a second. In fact an accuracy of 50% is likely for this handshake. Since the handshake signal might have been from other aircraft, vehicles or ships, this evidence can only be used as a reference, not direct evidence.

The PING should be a pre-standby signal for the particular case of an aircraft, a car, ship, boat, and so on. As a pre-set standby signal, the transmission regulations and characteristics from the same transmitter should be standardized and consistent, instead of arbitrary and irregular.

Likewise, since the PINGs were made by the same plane, the

time intervals should be consistent. If the homogenous signals from the same transmitter are set to be sent every 5 minutes, then it is once every 5 minutes; if every hour, then once an hour. It should be like the "addressing signal" which is sent once every 30 minutes when it is set to be like that, with no variation. Flight MH370 appeared once at 01:07 and was supposed to appear at 01:37 for a second time, which didn't happen. This suggests that the addressing signal was stopped, cut off or out of order, as is called 'out of touch' at 01:37 in terminology. There was no disorder.

Under the same conditions, since the PINGs were released from the same plane, the length of the signals should be consistent. If the signals don't include actual information, they cannot be long at one time and short at another. If the beacon signal length was set to 50 milliseconds, they all should be 50 milliseconds. Although the transmission process will be subjected to some unpredictable factors, the deviation will not exceed 10%. when the same transmitter sends out signals of the same kind, there will never be a situation where the signal length is 50 milliseconds one time and the next time 500 milliseconds.

Under the same conditions, the frequency of the PING signals from the same transmitter in the same state should be the same. Even if there is a deviation, it should be regular, within a small range.

The seven PING signals, being just 'beacon' signals with no actual information, from the Malaysian medium-term safety survey report and the Australian survey report fell into four kinds based on time intervals, which were 76 minutes between the first and the second interval; 60 minutes between the second and fifth; 89 minutes between the fifth and sixth; and 9 minutes between the sixth and seventh. Judging from these time intervals there must have been four transmitters instead of one. So if the PINGs were from planes, they were certainly not from one plane, but three or four. Judging from the signal path, the first and seventh were signals directly from the plane to the satellite, while the second to the sixth were via the ground station at Perth. Since both end signals from the plane could log and be registered in the satellite through the public channel directly, how come the middle signals travelled thousands of kilometres to the ground station to be retransmitted to the satellite? This means that the two were not the same thing at all.

When frequency differences and time differences are classified, it is also clearly seen that the seven handshake signals cannot be grouped together. The second to the fifth were obviously similar, while the other two belonged to another.

According to frequency response speed and time difference response distance, the analysis of the seven handshake signals reveals that the cruising speed of MH370 over the Indian Ocean was quite unsteady, now fast and then slow, like a car driving on an expressway. Assume its cruise speed from 03:41-06:41 was 270 to 360 kph (according to the Indian Ocean satellite data frequency difference (if 1HZ = 10 km), its cruise speed at 02:25 reached 1100 km per hour. This speed is close to the aircraft cruise and endurance speed and consistent with the aircraft's log in and register speed.

The speed of 270-360 km per hour is similar to that of some top sports cars such as Porsches, Ferraris or Bugattis, and helicopters. If a Boeing 777 aircraft like MH370 cruised at 270 km per hour for three or four hours, I am afraid it must have run out of fuel long before. The three hours from 03:41 to 06:41 should be 09: 41-12: 41 in Australia, which is in line with daily routines of the local rich children.

Judging from the analysis of the seven handshake signals, if the two or three signals at both ends were assumed to be the pre-standby signals from an aircraft (including civil aircraft, helicopters and small passenger aircraft) and the middle four were from a car or ship's standby signals with message path for the former as aircraft > satellite and for the latter as ground station > satellite, then the messages might be matched up. If we suppose the pilot had been controlling the flight from 01:37-08:19, how come he operated for seven whole hours without saying a word, and how come more than 230 crew were indifferent to this situation and let themselves be at his mercy? If the pilot operated the plane like a zombie, why did the data change so suddenly? It seems quite puzzling that some parties just ignored the difference in these data.

Besides, the once-per-hour PING signal does not fully reflect the dynamics of the aircraft, and it is able to send out signals even when staying on the apron. Therefore, the conclusion that MH370 flew to the Southern Indian Ocean, over 6,000 kilometres away from Kuala Lumpur, may sound quite inconsistent with or even irrelevant to the reality if it is derived from multiplying the number of PING signals by the cruising speed of the plane.

It is not impossible to infer the whereabouts of MH370 using the mobile data of its handshake signal frequency and the satellite elevation data. But the key point is that with data only from the recipient side but without a third-party reference like data from the transmitter side and GPS data, the conclusion is surely wishful thinking.

As mentioned earlier, a geosynchronous satellite is not a star. It orbits more than 30,000 kilometres above the earth, subject to various factors. Although it is called a static satellite, in fact it is not fixed but drifts and swings all the time. The small changes resulting from communication frequency and pitch angle are always an objective phenomenon. The incomplete stripping of these factor data may render any conclusion based on these data unreliable.

Coming back to the last handshakes at 8:11 and 8:19 on March

8, we should treat them the same as those handshake signals at 7:11, 7:19; 6:11, 6:19; 5: 11, 5:19 pm and so on, but these signals were not reflected in the data. Assuming that the handshake really contacted MH370, then the aircraft could have been in one of two states – either still cruising, or it had splashed down somewhere. If it was in the cruise state, another PING should have appeared at 9:11, but it did not. One possible reason is that the transmitter might have powered off or broken down. Another possible reason is that the transmitter did sent out a signal, but the satellite failed to receive it. In the latter case, that means MH370 flew on for 800-1000 kilometres. Where would we find it?

If it splashed down somewhere and remained there, it is reasonable that the transmitter might send out signals until it ran out of power. PENG signals can be issued during flight as well as when stationary. 8:19 is not the time when MH370 lost contact, nor the time it totally disappeared, but the time when the satellite received a registered login signal from a transmitting station. Handshake advocates use this time as the time of MH370's final resting place, 1800 kilometres west of Perth. If so, according to the cruising speed of 900 km, MH370 should have started from Kuala Lumpur at about 03:11

So there is much to do when analysing the radar signal data 24° - 333°, the pre-set unchangeable addressing signals with half-minute intervals and the satellite handshake data. Searching for MH370 guided by the data from the Indian Ocean satellite and Perth ground station, based on the assumption of hijacking or suicide, is certainly wrong. Any such effort will inevitably be in vain.

Timely measures should be adopted following this incident:

1) In communication, immediate measures should be taken to monitor the fixed frequency signals of the 37.5KC black box. A quick lock of all the monitoring, communication and radar

data in Kuala Lumpur and Ho Chi Minh stations relating to MH370 should be implemented. Military and civilian radar data of the neighbour countries like Thailand, Vietnam, Singapore, Indonesia and other relevant communication satellite data should be collected as soon as possible.

2) Announcements should be quickly made to mobilize all the civilian and military radar in the neighbourhood to join in the search.

3). A large number of submarines and fishermen's trawls should be used to carry out underwater detection of the waters around the suspected splashdown. A large number of people and animals should be mobilized to search the suspected crash areas on land.

The Malaysian authorities, claiming that the flight was taking the Cambodian route, were totally ignorant about MH370 from 01:20 to around 03:00. Even when the air controller of the Vietnamese District reminded them, they still seemed indifferent. It was not until 05:30, when MH370 failed to appear in Beijing (06:30), that they finally rushed to respond.

The searches in the South China Sea for the first five days were mainly electronic scanning and lookout searches with safety ropes on the waist and binoculars in the hands, which can only scan what is exposed on the surface (sea or earth) and cannot detect what is hidden on the sea bed or in a forest. The visibility of a telescope extends only to 10-20 km. A reconnaissance plane may scan tens of square kilometres at a time.

Seabed scanning is not easy. The current best scanning equipment in the world may reach a vertical detection range of up to 1.5 km and a horizontal detection range of about 20-30 km through seawater. Any detection equipment that is unable to reach the seabed sediments basically cannot tell us where MH370 lies.

Although the search teams covered, from March 8 to March 14 2014, 70,000 square kilometres of the South China Sea, the actual effective detection range is insignificant, and perhaps not even near the supposed crash site. Perhaps they were distracted by 'new information' just as they were about to find it. On March 14 the US warships left for the Indian Ocean on this excuse, and Vietnam quietly closed the door as well. The search of the South China Sea and the nearby mountains, did not exhaust available means and cover all the suspected areas. Who would dare to be sure that MH370 does not lie in the South China Sea or in southern Vietnam?

7. POLITICIZATION OF THE SEARCH AND RESCUE MISSION

Over the past four years, many millions of people around the world have been deeply concerned about the progress of the search. I also keep a close eye on every development in the search, regularly adjusting my perspective in observing, analysing, problem-solving and judging. During the four days after the aircraft disappeared, everyone did their utmost to find MH370 and the 239 people on board. The Malaysian government, though in chaos, made every effort to find the plane and save those on board. Even though all the searching was in vain, everyone's efforts should be fully appreciated.

On March 12, a message from the Malaysian Air Force said that the radar data had shown that the aircraft, for unknown reasons, had flown in the direction of the Malacca Strait, a departure of hundreds of miles from the scheduled route. British media reported that the flight had kept flying for another seven hours after it lost contact.

On March 14, before all available means of search were exhausted, US warships searched the seas west of Perth in the Southern Indian Ocean based on the new intelligence. Subsequently, various similar reports came in, resulting in the suspension of the search in the South China Sea. The search was suddenly moved to Scene 2 – the Southern Indian Ocean.

On March 15, the Vietnamese National Search and Rescue Committee took the lead in announcing that Vietnam would stop searching for the Malaysia Airline in Vietnamese waters and demanded a termination of any foreign teams' searching in Vietnamese waters. I think this is like a guilty person giving himself away by unnecessarily protesting his innocence – the plane fell here, but I don't want you to look for it.

When the Chinese rescue ships, on March 11, went to Scene 1, especially the Vietnamese waters where the plane most probably crashed, Vietnam announced that it would restrict other countries' search there from then on. After searching in the joint area of Malaysia and Vietnam for only about three days, all teams hastily abandoned Scene 1 and moved five to six thousand kilometres away to Scene 2. So far, nearly four years has passed and it has been confirmed that there is no sign of MH370 in these waters. In the absence of new evidence, it is not surprising that the search yielded no results.

Looking back on the search and rescue operation, we feel, after a careful analysis of the performance of all parties, that the organisation and leadership of these operations is obviously effective in addition to the above technical reason. We leave this for later discussion. It is worth noting that from March 12, 2014, there seemed to be an 'invisible manipulating hand' in the dark. When the 'hand' played a role in and gradually controlled the search and rescue operations. This 'traffic safety accident' search in the first stage developed into something else. The search developed into a diplomatic, political and military game which some claimed was embarrassing. The *New York Times* revealed on March 14, 2014: 'The strange thing is that if a similar event happened in the United States, they would certainly collect information from all aspects and compile it into a progress report; but in this Malaysian event, at least for now, the Americans have not played such a role... Regardless of the official responsible for the air crash, no one can ignore the guiding role played by the United States... though we try not to let people feel that we (the United States) are in charge of the investigation, we are, to some extent, the ones who are truly in charge.'

Imagine that if all the searching teams had not moved to the Indian Ocean on March 14 and if following the idea of finding the missing plane where it disappeared, they had stuck to searching the South China Sea waters and gradually expanded their search. They might have now found the whereabouts of MH370, even if the field of the search scope was enlarged to 150 nautical miles from the assumed missing spot.

If MH370's wreckage had been found at the end of April 2014, what would have been the response to the anti-China chorus by the United States, Vietnam, Philippines and Japan at the Shangri-La Asian Security meeting in Singapore? What would have happened to the long-planned anti-China and anti-Chinese violence which took place nationwide in Vietnam in May with the smashing, robbing and burning of Chinese enterprises? Would the Philippines have dared to seize the beach and island and confront China?

Life is a stage play, and the same is true for a country. But we want the play of MH370 to end as soon as possible. We sincerely suggest that the leading search parties reorganise themselves and redeploy their resources and that as soon as possible they gather enough forces to search, focusing on the places where the communication and radar signals disappeared, the South China Sea waters from 300 to 800 km from Kuala Lumpur 24° north-east. Otherwise, it is like using a bamboo basket to carry water.

CHAPTER TEN

Was it wrong at the very beginning to move to the Indian Ocean?

After research, a specialist called Ari N. Schulman commented that the search for MH370 was done in the wrong way right from the first. He said that when the search personnel detected the suspected black box they had thought that finding MH370 would be only a matter of time. But now, with 154 square miles of undersea search for the signal they have not found any piece of the wreckage of the disappearing plane. Pessimism is spreading, and some even wonder if the signals were really related to Flight MH370. If not, the search will return to tens of thousands of square miles of ocean.

Before the black box salvage fails, observers have questioned whether the search area is correct. Based on a mathematical analysis of satellite signals, the survey concluded that Flight MH370 eventually crashed in the Indian Ocean waters west of

Australia. But other scientists and engineers have been testing the analysis, and many believe the official conclusions are unreliable.

ONE: THE GAME OF 'HIDE AND SEEK'

Inmarsat, a British satellite communications agency, provides flight communications services for Malaysia Airlines. At the beginning of the search, signals from Flight MH370 to a satellite of the organisation were used as key data for the investigation. The importance of these acoustic pulse (PING) signals is beyond doubt. After the aircraft had lost radar contact, only these signals could determine what happened to it. Without them, investigators could only search around the location data captured by radar. The flight radius of MH370 would be 3300 miles, depending on the remaining fuel at that time. That is to say, it could have disappeared at any point in that radius, which covers an area equivalent to 1/7 of the earth's surface area.

Inmarsat concluded that the plane ended in the Southern Indian Ocean. The agency's analysis has become the most important reference for MH370 search, and all other judgments are based on this analysis. According to its officials, this mathematical analysis has pioneering significance, but in fact it is based on a relatively simple geometric principle: from time to time (usually hourly), the satellites of this organisation will send a message to the aircraft's communications system, requiring the aircraft to respond briefly, confirming that there is still a link between the two. Although this response does not include the specific location of the aircraft or its flight direction, it does provide useful information that can narrow the scope of the search.

For this mathematical analysis of the acoustic pulse, we can imagine it as a game of hide and seek. The seeker asks: 'Have you hidden yourself?' and the hider answers: 'Yes'. Then the seeker judges the location of the hider according to the direction, the length and the volume of the hider's voice, and begins to seek. If the seeker finds the hider, the seeker 'wins'; if not, the seeker 'loses'. Children have their own rewards and punishment for both the winners and the losers.

This information is far from perfect. Each sound pulse signal will tell you how far the aircraft is from you, but they may come from any direction. You can determine whether the plane is flying towards you or away from you, but it may be on top of you or below you or on your left or on your right, because the speed sounds the same. For ATA engineers, their task is to rebuild possible flight routes that match the data through this fragmented information.

TWO: THE RELATIONSHIP BETWEEN TIME, DISTANCE AND FREQUENCY

Each acoustic pulse signal provides three related pieces of information. The first is the time it takes to travel from the plane to the satellite, the second is the distance travelled within that time, and the third is the radio frequency by which the signal is received. It is important to point out that the signal transmission time corresponds to the distance between the satellite and the aircraft, while the frequency corresponds to the relative velocity of the satellite and the aircraft. This is critical: the relative speed is not the actual speed of the aircraft, but the speed at which it is flying to or away from the satellite. The investigation authorities did not disclose too much distance-related information, but it published a lot of data on the frequency of the sound pulse and all this information is contained in one chart.

In the analysis of Inmarsat, this chart is the most important evidence. It shows the difference in the frequency of the signal, the so-called 'frequency shift', which is the difference between the normal pitch of the aircraft's sound (radio frequency) and the actual pitch that is heard. The chart also shows the frequency shift of two hypothetical flight routes (north and south). The frequency shift coincides with the south line, which convinced the agency that Flight MH370 flew south. Mathematically speaking, this is a very clear judgment.

So is this analysis correct? Some analysts who did not participate in the official surveys verified this, including Michael Exner, founder of the American Mobile Satellite Corporation and guest scientist at the NASA Ames Research Centre, physicist Duncan Steel, and Tim Farrar, a satellite technology consultant. They used the satellite toolkit (STK) and other flight and navigation software to draw charts and conduct accurate calculations on MH370's flight conditions, but seemed to fail to derive a definite conclusion.

THREE: BASIC BUT VITAL FLIGHT INFORMATION

Although satellite data provide the most important clues about the overall flight route of the Malaysian Airlines flight MH370, they are not the only clues. The investigation authorities also possess other basic but vital flight information.

First, the precise coordinates of the satellite. The Centre of Space Standards and Innovation(CSSI) provides public information about the orbit of MH370's satellite. The satellite receiving Flight MH370's signals is the IOR satellite of Inmarsat, located on the geostationary orbit above the Indian Ocean. That is to say, relative to the earth, this satellite should be stationary, but its orbit has some deviations. In fact, it has deviated slightly from its previous position.

Second, the departure time and coordinates of the flight. MH370 took off at 16:41 international standard time, from Kuala Lumpur airport. As for its route relative to the satellite, from the radar's tracking data, in the first 40 minutes after MH370 took off, it was flying away north-east from the satellite, but then changed the route (note: it does not seem that MH370 changed the route, but the tracking target was switched to another flight), flying west in relation to the satellite. 54 minutes later, it disappeared from the radar.

A spokesman for Inmarsat said that during the last five flight hours, the acoustic pulse signal showed a greater distance, which means that the aircraft was flying away from the satellite during that time.

Third, the two flight routes coincide with the sound pulse data. In addition to the frequency shift map, Inmarsat also provided two examples of flight routes in its report and assumed flight speeds of 400 nmh (nautical miles per hour) and 500 nmh respectively. These data will help us to carry out quantitative analyses.

Fourth, the frequency shift data should be negative. As the plane flew away from the satellite, the radio signals had to travel farther and farther, and the frequency decreased accordingly. This means that for most of the flight, the frequency shift data should be negative. From the beginning of the fortieth minute after take-off, the radar indicated that the aircraft flew westward for about an hour towards the satellite, but the Inmarsat chart shows that it did not send a sound pulse signal during this time. (one set of data shows the westward flight while another data shows no change, apparently contradictory. The latter with no sound pulse should be correct, and the former showing a westward flight should be false).

FOUR, CONFUSION OF LOGICAL RELATIONSHIP

Inmarsat's analysis chart conflicts with this information. It shows that Flight MH370 was moving very fast, even before it took off, and moved towards the satellite each time it sent a pulse signal (this signal had nothing to do with MH370). This explanation is not only inconsistent with the official conclusions, but conflicts with other evidence.

The frequency changes are not negative, probably because Inmarsat deliberately plotted them into positive values. For engineers, using the absolute value in the drawing is normal. For example, in the description of ocean depth, people will use positive rather than negative values. But the enormous frequency shift before take-off is hard to explain. The chart provided by Inmarsat shows that the first sound impulse signal was issued at 16:30 GMT, 11 minutes before the departure time. The frequency for this acoustic pulse signal shift in the chart is about -85 Hz. Public records show that the signal sent to the satellite by the aircraft uses a frequency of 1626~1660 MHz. Calculated by STK software, the satellite moved toward the airport at a speed of only 2 miles per hour. Considering the satellite's angle on the horizon, MH370 needed to reach at least 50 miles per hour on the ground to produce this frequency shift. For a plane 11 minutes before take-off, such a speed is not possible. Flight records showed that the plane had not started taxiing on the runway.

In addition, according to the frequency chart, the last sound pulse signal of Flight MH370 was given out at 00:11, GMT. The measured frequency was about -252 Hz. That is to say, the plane's flight speed relative to the satellite was only 103 miles per hour. But the south route diagram by Inmarsat shows that the aircraft was travelling at about 272 miles per hour away from the satellite. In other words, at the beginning of MH370's flight, frequency changes were much higher than they should be, but in the end, they were far below. Therefore, there must be other factors that affected the value the frequency shift.

FIVE: THE EFFECT OF FREQUENCY SHIFT

Will the signal transmission from the satellite to the ground station affect the measured frequency shift? Inmarsat did not give a clear answer to this (my answer is yes). But if there is an impact, then the actual frequency shift, too large at first and finally too small, can be explained by the influence of a ground station located in a remote area south of the satellite. Unsurprisingly, Inmarsat said in the analysis that there is a ground station which receives the transmission signal in Australia.

We can test this assumption in a more precise way. According to public records, Inmarsat in Australia has only one ground station, in Perth. The satellite toolkit software can accurately plot the satellite's moving speed relative to the ground station; the frequency of satellite-to-ground signals (about 3.6 GHz) can also remove satellite-to-ground motion from the frequency map. In this way, we can calculate the real 'satellite to the aircraft' speed value.

Calculated by this method, the result is almost perfect: for the first sound pulse signal before take-off, the speed of the satellite relative to the aircraft is about one mile per hour, which is in good agreement with the plane's lack of movement in the 11 minutes before take-off.

SIX: WHO IS WRONG?

In attempting to understand the Inmarsat analyses, peripheral experts may make mistakes or miss some important details, but it is undeniable that the analysis of the organisation itself had some problems, which aroused their doubts.

Before the officials offer more information, any conclusions about MH370's flight along the southern route do not respect science, only the views of the authorities.

Inmarsat and the investigating authorities seem to be using mathematical analysis to establish their authority. By publishing various charts and declarations, they want the outside world to see their respect for mathematics and science, but at the same time they have refused to make a full explanation of the approach taken. In the course of the investigation, these institutions always give a variety of definitive conclusions, but quickly lapse into silence when these conclusions are overturned. In addition, the authorities affirmed, based on the seven handshakes, that MH370 had flown along the south route (the Seventh Arc in the Indian Ocean); also they firmly believed, according to some so-called MH370 fragments found on French-owned Réunion Island and the use of mathematical models by some ocean current experts, that MH370 crashed into the Southern Indian Ocean, and they spent much money expanding the search area there repeatedly. The search was fruitless, but they were unwilling to give up.

The biggest risk to the search for the lost aircraft is the stubbornness of the investigating authorities. They think they have found the ultimate resting place of Flight MH370, and ignore all other possibilities that are not in line with their beliefs. The truth is that there is no conclusive evidence that MH370 ended up in the waters they delineated; at least, no piece of the wreck has yet been salvaged there. Thus it can be concluded that the decision to move the search from the South China to the Southern Indian Ocean was wrong at the outset. (Note by the author: this passage is an adaption from an online comment, translated by Hu Qi, by Ari. N. Shulman.)

CHAPTER ELEVEN

Guesses about the debris of BB670

By July 28, 2015, more than a year had passed and there was no news about the whereabouts of MH370. Families of the 239 people on the plane were waiting desperately for a definite conclusion.

On July 29, 2015, someone posted a video online which showed a 2-metre-long piece of aircraft debris found on Réunion Island off the east coast of Africa, suspected of being a component from MH370. Based on a picture of the wreckage, the aviation safety investigators were confident that it was from a Boeing 777 like MH370. The investigators determined that the component was a flaperon from the trailing edge of a Boeing 777 wing. Suddenly, everyone started to talk about the crash again and give their various opinions.

ONE: CLUES

On July 30, 2015, the day after this report, the French media revealed the details of this piece of wreckage. It was reported that a few months before a cleaner named Johnny Berger from Réunion's city hall was sweeping the beach along the coastline of San Andre City in the north-eastern part of Réunion when he found a strange object, so he invited his colleagues to take a look. One of them recognized that it was a part of the plane. The piece was partly buried in the sand, so they brought it ashore to prevent it being swept away by the tide, and then reported it to the police. In the same area they also found other wreckage, such as suitcases and seats. The component bore the number BB670 and was covered with the shells of sea creatures. It seemed to have been in the sea for a long time.

After watching the news, French aviation security expert Ghazavi Tytelman pointed out in a professional blog that the number was not a plane licence plate number, nor a production serial number. The wreckage lay a few hundred metres from the coast. It would take big waves to push such a heavy object inshore for a few hundred metres.

On July 30, the local cleaners found a bottle of Chinese-made mineral water with four Chinese words 'Nongfushangquan' and a washing liquid bottle from Jakarta, Indonesia. On August 1, when a local lawyer walked on the beach, he found three bottles of mineral water, two of which were from Malaysia. He said he often took a walk along the seashore here. Usually 99% of the waste found was from Réunion, but recently he had found a lot of foreign items, including some ointment from China.

On August 1, France sent the piece of wreckage to the French Civil Aviation Safety Investigation and Analysis Bureau's Toulouse office for identification. They could zoom in 10,000 times using an electron microscope to read the numbers on the flaperon and compare them with the coding, design, manufacturing materials and processing technology and other technical information from Boeing to determine whether this piece of wreckage came from

MH370. On March 2, the wreckage was confirmed as coming from a Boeing 777.

On August 5, representatives from five parties, Malaysia, the United States, China, France and Boeing, participated in the identification of the flaps in Toulouse, France. British media reported on August 1 that the cleaner who had found the flaperon said he had also found on the beach in May a blue seat and a few suitcases which were full of stuff. But he did not pay special attention to them and burned them as garbage in the usual way. The seat and the flaperon were found on the same beach. On July 29, he realised that the wreck was probably part of MH370 and reported it. He said he had first noticed the flaperon as early as May when he had sat fishing there, but thought it was a desk.

According to reports, on May 10, 2015, a local woman named Isabel with her 10-year-old son had seen the same flaperon. The son said after the discovery, 'Mom, that looks like a wing.'

It is reported that the Boeing 777 flaperon is of sandwich structure and the interior is filled with air, enabling it to float on the sea; the marine organisms attached to it could help to determine the crash site. From the photos, the attached shells look like barnacles. The discovery of this flaperon was an exciting moment, as many people thought it was a very promising clue to what had happened to Flight MH370.

TWO: CONFIRMATION

On the morning of August 6, 2015, the day after the meeting of the five parties, the Malaysian Prime Minister held a press conference in Kuala Lumpur. He said: 'I must tell you that an international panel of experts has affirmed the confirmation of the aircraft wreck found in Réunion Island from MH370. We now have physical evidence to prove that Flight MH370 tragically ended in the Southern Indian Ocean'. However, a few minutes later, the French Deputy Prosecutor, Purcell Markovik, issued a statement in Paris: 'According to the preliminary identification of experts, the aircraft wreckage found on July 29 in French Réunion Island, is likely to come from the Malaysia Airlines Flight MH370. Comparing the technical data provided by Boeing and Malaysia Airlines, they could confirm the aircraft wreckage came from a Boeing 777 passenger aircraft, and that the wreckage shared many commonalities with the technical data provided by MAS, so the wreck is 'very likely 'from the MAS Flight MH370, but the final identification results still need further professional analysis and may take a few more days'.

EFE commented that this statement showed that no credible evidence had been found to prove that the wreckage belonged to MH370. On the same day, Associated Press reported that a US official familiar with the investigation had said that a team of experts in France had not yet been able to find any clues explicitly linking it to the missing aircraft. So the conclusions of several experts are inconsistent.

CNN reported that a group of independent observers said the damage to the flanker indicated that parts of the aircraft had fallen during the flight. After the suspected debris was exposed, the French authorities dispatched, from August 6, military transport aircraft, helicopters, boats and manpower, etc, to search the surrounding coasts and sea waters near Réunion Island for a week. Mauritius, the Maldives and other countries in the vicinity also mobilized their police helicopters, coastguards and coastal police to conduct a three- dimensional search for seven or eight days, but they found no more clues.

About a month later, the assessment results came out. On September 3, 2015, the French prosecutor released a press announcement that stated: 'Today we can say with certainty that the flaperon found in Réunion on July 29 was confirmed to be part of the MAS Flight MH370 after technical identification by the US Boeing Spanish subcontractor. Careful studies by the Spanish subcontractor against the order and production information catalogue of the aircraft parts and through the endoscopy discovered, on the flaperon, three numbers. The investigation judge confirmed that one of numbers on the flaperon matched the series of MH370.'

In view of the above confirmed information, German experts inferred, through computer simulation, that the crash site of Malaysia Airlines Flight MH370 was in the eastern equatorial Indian Ocean, rather than the Southern Indian Ocean. That seemed to be the end of the matter. The media went quiet.

Since the flaperon was exposed to the world on July 29, 2015, it has undergone tests and examination, and it has again been confirmed as from a Boeing 777 aircraft. However, is it really from Flight MH370? Many people doubt it.

THREE: DOUBTS

Then the Boeing 777 type flaperon with the number "BB670" from French Reunion Island was revealed to the public on July 29. But Malaysia officially confirmed it as the flaperon from Flight MH370 even before the experts released their conclusions of their technical appraisal!

The reasons for rushing this premature confirmation could have been for the following possible reasons. First, perhaps Malaysia had secured reliable intelligence from other sources, confirming that the flaperon was from MH370. The second possibility was that someone or some group had previously purchased the piece of debris and then buried it on Réunion island in accordance with some plan. Note that the beaches of small countries like Mauritius and Madagascar were not chosen, but this French beach. Perhaps local French people believed to have relatively high credibility found it 'accidentally'. The media would then hype it up and the authorities could take the opportunity to announce the discovery of some of MH370's wreckage, so the crash would become an accepted fact. It would then be self- evident that those on board were dead. Thus, a serious problem troubling the Malaysian government would be solved. Compensation for the 239 people, insurance payouts and reforms to Malaysia Airlines, as well as the layoff of the airline's staff, could be easily and smoothly dealt with, thus relieving the Malaysian government of the enormous pressure on it since the disappearance of MH370. It would also reduce the suspicions of various countries and institutions and clear up many contradictions. It would also enable them to say with confidence that MH370 crashed in the southern hemisphere rather than the northern hemisphere, that the $200 million spent in searching in the Southern Indian Ocean was worthwhile, and that their search decision was correct. The fact that the plane has not been found is not because they made a mistake – they just haven't found the exact spot. Truly, this is a wonderful trick to kill three birds with one stone.

The third possibility is that Malaysia made the mistake of over-generalization. They think there is only one Boeing 777 aircraft missing, so if any fragments are found that match a Boeing 777, they must belong to Flight MH370.

The discovery of the numbered flaperon is seemingly a solid clue to the fate of MH370. But we should remember that the discovery site is definitely not at Scene 1 The news of the flaperon was released on July 29, 2015, but it was first found more than two months earlier, on May 10, 14 months after MH370 went missing. This piece of debris was found on Réunion Island, but everyone who is interested in this matter would admit that this is not where MH370 crashed.

One piece of reasoning is enough. MH370 was loaded with 55 tons of jet fuel. From its take off at Kuala Lumpur, it had flown for 40 minutes when it disappeared. Assuming a flight of 1000 km consumes 10 tons of fuel, MH370, with its remaining fuel, could in no way cover the distance of over 6,000 km from where it disappeared to Réunion. So, Réunion Island is definitely not the crash site of MH370, nor is it Scene 1 of its disappearance.

Second, did the flaperon drift from the Southern Indian Ocean or the Eastern Indian Ocean? Or did someone bury it there? Each sticks to his own argument.

After the discovery of the flaperon on Réunion Island, many marine experts speculated that it had drifted there on ocean currents. The shells of sea creatures on it are cited as evidence. Those who hold this view found that its starting point would be west of Perth, in the Southern Indian Ocean, the same as the search area. So they would say their decision to keep searching in the Southern Indian Ocean was correct, and that shortly after MH370 disappeared, it crashed west of Perth, pieces of wreckage later drifting to Réunion. But how?

A German expert holds another view. According to the position of this fragment on Réunion Island, by use of computer simulation of the ocean currents, he inferred that it had crashed on the equator in the Eastern Indian Ocean, not in the Southern Indian Ocean. Non-experts simply argued that it may have been deliberately buried there! Is this another trick?

FOUR. GUESSES

The flaperon was confirmed as being from Flight MH370 by relevant institutions and state heads, but it left many doubts and certainly would invite a number of guesses. Guess one – this fragment did not drift on the ocean currents from the starting point of the search range 1,800 km west of Perth in the Southern

Indian Ocean to Réunion. In my understanding, there are two possibilities.

First, it was deliberately transported by ocean currents near to Réunion Island and then buried on the San Andre coast there, or directly buried on the beach.

Second, an ocean liner had snagged the flaperon and dragged it along for a few days until it arrived in the vicinity of Réunion. When the boat stopped, the debris fell off and was swept onto the shore.

The reason for this conjecture is very simple. After the disappearance of MH370, aircraft, satellites, warships and submarines from 26 nations conducted a three-dimensional search for several months and found more than 400 floating objects of possible interest. If they could find other debris of less than two metres in length, why did they not detect a buoyant flaperon of two or three metres in length? Therefore it can be reasoned that its starting point was not in the Indian Ocean, let alone the Southern Indian Ocean.

On August 6, careful studies by the Spanish subcontractor of the order and production information catalogue of aircraft parts and through endoscopy discovered three numbers on the flaperon, one of which matched that of a flaperon on MH370s and hence confirmed fragment BB670 was from MH370. This conclusion is too far-fetched, because of three numbers compared, only one matches.

Identification is a very rigorous scientific process, and does not allow the slightest sloppiness. It must be 100% matching, and 99% will not do. If only one of the three figures matches, the confirmation is only a 33% match. To change a 33% probability into 100% is exaggerating.

Guess two, this piece numbered BB670 has nothing to do with MH370. From March 8, 2014 to July 28, 2015, within 15 months, there were two crashes involving Boeing 777s, not just

Flight MH370. Remember flight MH17, which was shot down by a missile in Ukraine on July 17, 2014. Its flaperons and Flight MH370's should be exactly the same. After MH17 was shot down, the wreckage was collected and sent to the Netherlands for identification. You could find information released online about the wreckage of Flight MH17, and there is a piece of debris with a length and thickness very similar to the Réunion flaperon but of a slightly different colour. Now it cannot be found on the Internet!

If someone disguised this flaperon as one from MH370, would there be the same result? The flaperon numbered BB670 is a standard component of the Boeing 777. If a flaperon from any 777 flight is transported to the island of Réunion, and is identified by the same method, what will the conclusion be? If we use an endoscope to inspect this fragment, we will certainly find 3 digits in it, and of the three figures, one or two or even three figures will be in agreement with those of MH370.

During flight, it is not unusual for parts to drop off a plane, and more than 400 777s are still flying around the world every day. According to the Xinhua news agency on April 17, 2017, a Boeing 777 passenger aircraft of Canadian Airlines flying from Montreal Airport to Britain dropped a rear wheel after take-off. The plane landed safely. When the airport staff told the captain, he was shocked. Luckily, no one was injured.

More than one media channel hypothesised that this piece of debris found on Réunion fell from a cruising plane. If so, it is not possible to predict which aircraft's flaperon fell into the Indian Ocean. In addition, on October 13, 2015, a survey report issued by the Holland Committee of the aviation safety investigation into MH17 enclosed with it an MH17 mechanical recovery plan. There was no wing display in this recovery plan, let alone a demonstration of the flaperon part. Where did the flaperons go?

As the currently published information about the flaperon

numbered BB670 does not have a unique prerequisite, the conclusions of identification are not strongly exclusive.

It reminds me of two influential criminal cases in China. One is the case of Mr She, who killed his wife, which shocked the whole of China in 2014. Mr She, born on March 7, 1966, came from a village in China, and was a security patrolman in the local police station before he was arrested. On January 20, 1994, Mr She had a quarrel with his wife over a family issue. The night after the quarrel, the wife suddenly disappeared. Mr She and his relatives searched hard but without success. On April 11 the same year, a rotting female corpse was found in a pond in a village near Mr She's home. The police station sent for the wife's immediate family to identify it. As the figure, hair, age and head size of this corpse were almost the same as the wife's and even the mole next to her breast and a scar from childbearing were also identical, the corpse was confirmed as the missing wife. The wife's friends and relatives suspected that Mr She had killed her and thrown the corpse into the pond. At that time, more than 200 local villagers signed a letter strongly urging the political and legal authorities to execute Mr She – a life for a life. Public security bodies investigated, and on April 22, 1994, Mr She was detained on suspicion of intentional homicide. After being questioned under torture, Mr She finally 'confessed'.

In June 1998, the People's Court of the county and the Intermediate Court of the city successively sentenced Mr She to the death penalty for intentional homicide and deprived him of political rights for life. Despite repeated protests, it was of no avail, and Mr She was found guilty and imprisoned.

But then on March 28, 2005, ten years later, his wife returned home. Everyone was shocked. To be certain, the authorities carried out DNA identification, and confirmed that she was undoubtedly the supposedly 'murdered' wife.

In view of this, on March 30, 2005, the Intermediate Court of the city had to revoke its first verdict on Mr She, who had been imprisoned for 11 years. He was acquitted and paid more than 700,000 yuan in state compensation. The case had been declared a deliberate murder, based on the evidence offered by the security department: the forensic identification, autopsy photos, on-site survey transcripts, the crime 'road map' and the record that Mr She showed the scene of the crime to the police.

So prosecutors and judges, when confirming the evidence, may be too confident of the findings of the investigating authorities. The lack of further investigation, analysis and verification of possible evidence derived from torture and inducement led to the misuse of evidence. Courts have too much confidence in evidence provided by official organisations, and find it difficult to believe that an innocent person would confess under torture (this is a common area of malpractice in the world at present). A confession despite lack of evidence led to a miscarriage of justice that shocked the nation.

The then High Court of the province had raised at least five major doubts about the case:

1. The killing process to which Mr She confessed was contradictory; indirect evidence cannot form an evidence chain.
2. There was no reason why he should kill his wife in as many as four or five ways.
3. The murder weapon was confirmed as a stone based only on oral confession.
4. What happened to the clothes the wife took off remained unknown – were they lost?
5. Trial transcripts, an important basis for conviction and sentencing, were inconsistent with the facts according to the investigation of the case officers, so the possibility of the 'dead' woman running away was not ruled out.

Even though the Provincial High Court pointed out the five doubts in the case in June, 1998, the County Court still sentenced Mr She to 15 years' imprisonment on a judgement of intentional homicide. Mr She refused to accept the decision and appealed, but in September 1998, the City Intermediate Court ruled to uphold the original verdict and dismissed the appeal. Fortunately, the Provincial High Court did not behead him at the Meridian Gate (a case of the same type in Inner Mongolia also shocked the country. The wrong man was executed, to great regret).

The resurrection of the 'deceased' woman led to a national review of many major homicide cases, and the state Supreme Court therefore recalled the right to review the death penalty, which had been delegated for many years.

Another case occurred in the forefront of China's reform and opening up of the world-famous Shenzhen Special Economic Zone. Mr Xu was born in 1958 and at the age of 37 he worked in Shenzhen as a government civil servant. At that time, Xu's work performance was excellent every year, his career was booming and his promotion prospects were very good. A woman of twenty-four years old, Ruan Ming (a pseudonym) contacted him through business and fell in love with him at first sight. Her hot pursuit and persistence made Xu very unhappy. Although he repeatedly told Ruan Ming that he had a wife and children, that he would handle her business as that of a good friend but would not date her, she would still visit his office from time to time because she was so infatuated by him that she dreamed about him day and night and the very sight of him would make her sweet and passionate. Whenever she found him at his office, she would stay there on any excuse, which made Xu extremely annoyed and made him suffer greatly. Ruan's constant visits made Xu look bad, with gossiping about him everywhere. Of course, her behaviour aroused the hatred of many better-informed colleagues.

One day when Ms Ruan came to Xu's office, she would not leave and said to Xu, 'You just concentrate on your work. I won't speak, can't I sit here a little longer?'

By four o'clock in the afternoon, Ms Ruan had been sitting there for more than an hour, and still showed no sign of leaving. Mr Xu, furious and at breaking point, sternly warned her: 'if you don't leave, I will call the police!' But she stayed where she was.

Mr Xu became so angry that he stopped work and walked out. When he left his office building, he ran into four of his team, officers who had just returned from their routine patrol. Xu told them without thinking, 'That annoying woman has come again, and won't leave. You help me teach her a lesson. Warn her not to visit me any more!'

The four officers came into Mr Xu's office, chatted with Ms Ruan for a while and persuaded her to go home early and not to pursue Xu any more, for her passionate pursuit was bringing trouble and humiliation to him. 'You love him, but you don't want to suffocate him with your love, right?' they reasoned with her.

Half an hour passed, then an hour passed, but she still had no intention of leaving. After discussion, the four patrol officers lied to her that Xu had called and invited her to dinner, and he had asked them to send her over. Excited, Ms. Ruan left Xu's office with them and got into a waiting van. They took her to a remote and deserted place and told her to get out and go home. 'Xu didn't invite you', they told her. They warned her not to visit their office again and not to interfere with their work any more. But she would not agree. A heated quarrel broke out, then they began fighting. Long annoyed by her behaviour and attitude, now suffering her shrewish abuse and crazy kicking, the four impetuous young men could withstand no longer. In anger and resentment, they beat Ms Ruan and she foamed at the mouth and fell to the ground dying. Seeing her motionless, the four young men panicked, and rushed to report back to Xu. 'M. Xu, didn't you tell us to give the bitch a lesson? We persuaded her, but she wouldn't listen. Even worse, she abused and kicked us. She is lying there motionless and pretending to be dead. What shall we do?'

When Mr Xu hurried to the scene and found Ms Ruan lying motionless on the grass, he also started to panic. He said, 'We must take her to the hospital and save her!' One of the officers said that since she was dead, if they sent her to the hospital, they would be asking for trouble and would have no way to escape. All of them would end up in jail.

They finally came up with a perfect plan. They drove her body to a remote lane in Shekou, Shenzhen, 7 km away, early in the morning when there were few people around, so it would look like a hit and run accident. They put her body in the fast lane, drove their van over her and then drove away. Early next morning, someone taking a morning run found Ruan's body. He called the emergency services. 'A young woman was killed by a car at Shekou Road,' he said. 'The car didn't stop. Please send the traffic police over as soon as possible to deal with it.'

Traffic police rushed to the scene, conducted a scene investigation and found tyre marks on the body. A forensic doctor arrived. After careful examination, he announced that this was not a traffic accident but a murder, and the body had been brought to the scene. He explained, 'You see, the deceased's clothing is relatively complete, without the tearing traces of being dragged along after being knocked down; look here, no blood splashing, no blood flowing. The woman was killed before she was run over. This is not a hit and run traffic accident but a murder case. It should be handed over for criminal investigation.'

Xu was charged with intentional homicide and executed.

When comparing the above two criminal cases with the reported identification procedures and conclusions over the Réunion flaperon, one can't help thinking whether it really came from Flight MH370, where it came from and when it arrived there.

According to my research conclusions, Flight MH370 crashed in the South China Sea. Although the world's oceans flow together, it is unlikely for a fragment, in 14 months, to pass the Strait of Malacca, cross the sea, or sail around the Pacific, and beach itself on the island of Réunion.

Although one of the three numbers found through endoscopy coincides with that of Flight MH370, is still not enough to be sure that it is MH370's flaperon. Malaysia rushed to announce that the component was one of the flaperons from Flight MH370 even before conclusive identification. Remember the announcement on March 24, 2014, in the absence of evidence, that 'MH370 flew along the southern corridor, and its final position should be west of Perth, Australia, in the middle of the Indian Ocean'. How similar are these remarks to the assumption that Mr She killed his wife!

If one day Flight MH370 is fished up, no matter from where, with its flaperons intact, who will judge the rights and wrongs as well as the responsibility of Malaysia's firm conclusion stated on August 6 2015? In addition, a technician from the Spanish subcontractor confirmed on September 3 that the flaperon was from Flight MH370 based on only one of the three numbers matching. How similar is this conclusion to Ms. Ruan's case, a murdered woman disguised as a hit and run traffic accident!

Since it is not possible to rule out the possibility that the flaperon from Réunion Island was from Flight MH17 or from another 777 aircraft, and since it cannot be ruled out that Flight MH370 crashed in the South China Sea, the official Malaysian 'confirmation' on August 6, or Spain's technical appraisal on September 3, are far-fetched. There will be many other doubting voices. Only when the component numbered BB670 found on

Réunion Island is shown to be one hundred percent consistent with MH370 can we say it is 'confirmed'. Otherwise, there inevitably will emerge a lot of guesses.

FIVE. THE STORY OF LITTLE FISH

Little Fish told a remarkable story in the Kampuchea WeChat group on October 5, 2015. She said that on March 5, 2014, her girlfriend, 'Big Fish', and Big Fish's lover, 'Prawn', decided to have a secret date in Singapore. In advance, they both lied to their partners that they were going to attend a meeting in Singapore for three days in Singapore, actually two days in Singapore, and one day in Kuala Lumpur, Malaysia, and would return to Beijing from Kuala Lumpur by Flight MH370 on March 8, 2014 according to the schedule. Late on the night of March 7, Big Fish called her husband Erlong in Beijing from a five-star hotel in Kuala Lumpur, saying she was about to board MH370 to Beijing. She said that if it was on time it would arrive in Beijing at 6:30 the following morning. She said 'It's too early, you do not have to pick me up. Sleep for a while and I will take a taxi home'. After the call, Erlong went happily to sleep. Big Fish went back to her lover's embrace. She did not board MH370 but stayed with him.

Unfortunately, at 6:30 on March 8, MH370 did not appear at Beijing Airport. When they heard this, Big Fish and Prawn considered themselves very lucky. 'Honey, it's a good thing we are not on MH370,' said Prawn to Big Fish.

At 7:30 am, Big Fish saw the first of a series of messages on her phone: 'Beijing mobile reminds you: user 1867673 x x x call you once at 06:31 March 8, you can press the call key or option key directly dial back.'

More messages followed:

'Beijing mobile remind you: user 1867673 x x x call you once at 06:40 March 8, you can press the call key or option key directly dial back.'

'Beijing mobile remind you: user 1867673 x x x call you once at 07:00 March 8, you can press the call key or option key directly dial back.'

'Beijing mobile remind you: user 1867673 x x x call you once at 07:20 March 8, you can press the call key or option key directly dial back.'

'Beijing mobile remind you: user 1867673 x x x call you once at 07:30 March 8, you can press the call key or option key directly dial back.'

Big Fish did not dare look any further. She turned off the mobile phone immediately. What if Erlong dialled her mobile phone now? She didn't know how to answer, how to face him.

Prawn felt happy: 'Honey, hurry up, stop watching, switch it off. Change the number. It's a godsend. Let's just stay here for a few days and not think about how to get back to Beijing until we get some news about the plane.'

Big Fish and Prawn tightly nestled together, and went off to sleep. The days passed.

Erlong waited eagerly for his wife. Big Fish became upset in the hotel. Prawn enjoyed his life in a foreign country. Then the police told Erlong his wife was missing on MH370. Big Fish said to Prawn, 'What shall we do?' Prawn told Big Fish that they should move to Thailand, change their names and make a life there. Two more weeks passed, and Erlong waited desperately for news. Big Fish missed her husband so much that she could not sleep day or night, and was looking haggard. Prawn also became upset.

Big Fish said: 'Prawn, we have been here more than a month,

but it is not a permanent solution. You still have to think of a way to send me back to Beijing. I want to go home!'

'If you decide to go back to Beijing, that shows you miss Erlong and still love him deeply,' replied Prawn. 'I also value your friendship and love. So long as we live together, I will feel happy if you are happy. Your smile gives me warmth; when you are upset, I will feel upset. For you, I will do anything and everything.'

'Prawn, I know you love me, but this secret life is not a permanent solution. When the aircraft is found, they will not find my DNA so they will know I was not on board. How can Erlong let that go? MH370, which has been missing for more than a month, has become a mystery of the world; for my family, my disappearance, will become another mystery. No, if you really love me, like me, you have to find a way to send me back to Beijing as soon as possible.'

Prawn knew very clearly what kind of a person Big Fish was, so he began to plot her return to Beijing. Four months later, on July 17, came a golden opportunity. He heard that another Boeing 777, also from Malaysia Airlines, had been shot down by a missile when flying over the Ukraine. The wreckage of the plane was scattered over an area of more than 180 square kilometres in the eastern part of Ukraine, bordering Russia. The new that the plane had been shot down once again caused a sensation around the world. The eyes of the world moved away from searching for MH370 to finding the murderers who had shot down MH17. An investigation committee was immediately set up. As the majority of the plane passengers were Dutch, the Netherlands presided over the investigation.

The remnants of MH17 were collected by the Commission of Investigation and shipped from Ukraine to the Netherlands for identification and to determine what type of missile it was hit by, who issued the order to shoot it down and who would bear the political, economic and legal responsibility for this indiscriminate killing.

Prawn had been keeping a close eye on any news about this event. He took MH17's crash as a golden opportunity to arrange Big Fish's return journey to Beijing. Prawn had a friend, Jiesi, a truck guard who was responsible for MH17's wreckage being shipped from Ukraine to Holland. He asked Jiesi to help solve the problem. From December 7 to December 14, 2014, Jiesi escorted the MH17 wreckage all the way west from the eastern part of the Donetsk region. When the vehicles arrived at a place near Munich, Germany, he arranged a rest. Deep into the night, he substituted 777 aircraft's flaperon with one from the Munich International Airport repair shop, which he had arranged in advance. He delivered one of the flaperons to a German friend, Ker. After Ker got the flaperon, he sent it, in early December 2014, to Port Louis in Mauritius, Africa. On May 1, 2015, Prawn and Big Fish arrived at Port Louis as planned and collected the flaperon. With the help of a local friend, they hired a local trawler, fixed the flaperon on the trawl, and sailed the boat all the way to Réunion Island. When they got to San Andre beach in the northeast of the island, they pulled in the trawler to shore. They hired two local men, dug a pit in the beach about 300 metres from the sea, and buried the flaperon horizontally, half exposed and half in the ground, waiting for it to be discovered by accident.

The flaperon waited peacefully on beach – and waited. People seldom visit this beach. On July 29 2015, the flaperon was finally 'discovered by accident', and was quickly reported on the Internet, to the world, and linked to MH370 as quickly as possible. It seemed there was finally a physical clue to the MH370 mystery.

The local police quickly sent the flaperon to the Lutzburg Aviation Safety Identification Laboratory for identification. On August 5, 2015, Malaysia issued a statement saying that it had been confirmed as one of MH370's flaperons before the identification conclusion was released. This announcement smoothly solved all the problems that troubled Malaysian government for a year and four months.

Big Fish's problem was also smoothly solved. She returned to Beijing on July 28, 2015 and met her family, telling them about the 'shocking experience' she had endured for the past year. She told them that at 23:30 on March 7, 2014, after she had called and messaged Erlong, she had boarded the plane, turned off her mobile phone and sat in the cabin, eyes closed, waiting for take-off. Flight MH370 had taken off from Kuala Lumpur International Airport safely and punctually, and soon began to cruise. She then went to sleep.

When she was awakened at an unknown time, she found herself drifting in the sea, and clutching the wing of the plane in her hand. She shouted, but no one answered. She looked around to see that she was surrounded by ocean. She was left alone in the wreckage, on which she vaguely detected the words 'Boeing' and 'BB670'. She realised that the plane had crashed and everybody else was dead. She had congratulated herself on surviving. She had drifted for a long time until she had seen an island and seen a group of black people whose language she couldn't understand. Finally she was rescued and was able to return home.

Her description is vivid and logical and everything seemed to happen before your eyes as she spoke. She was a wonderful storyteller. Her parents congratulated her, while Erlong was sorry he had not been able to help her and was feeling sorry and ashamed.

On July 29, 2014, the day after Big Fish returned to Beijing, the news that a suspected piece of wreckage had been found was published to the world. Big Fish's family were more convinced of her story. To her parents, she is still their beloved daughter; to her friends, she became a goddess, a hero able to overcome all difficulties; to Erlong, she was strong and tall and straight. The more he gazed at her, the more adored her.

Big Fish came back to Beijing. Prawn fulfilled his commitment and became an eternal idol, hero and god in Big Fish's heart.

On September 3, 2015, the flaperon found in French Réunion Island was identified by a Spanish manufacturer's technician with an endoscope as being from a Boeing 777. Of the three numbers on the flaperon, one was in agreement with that of MH370, so their identification also confirmed the debris as a piece of flank on Flight MH370. After a few months' examination of MH17's wreckage, on October 12 2015, the Dutch Security Council Committee released a survey report to the world: flight MH17 was shot down by a Russian System Buk missile on July 17, 2014 when flying over the province of Donetsk in eastern Ukraine. The report didn't mention whether the missile was launched by West-sponsored Ukrainian government forces or Russian-supported Eastern rebels. In other words, who shot down flight MH17 is still a mystery.

Whether the flaperon found on Réunion Island is really from Flight MH370 will have to wait until the aircraft is found and salvaged.

When Big Fish chatted with others, she told the following provocative story. She heard from a friend that when they were sailing in the South China Sea on May 1, 2015, they met a man who looked like a fisherman who had something to sell to them: they thought they had caught a big fish in the South China Sea, but when it was fished out, it turned out to be something looking like a component from an aircraft, and it carried the number BB670. They had had a French friend with them who showed strong interest and bought it. Later, this Frenchman sent the part to a mechanic in Réunion Island for collection.

The world is big, and nothing is too strange. Magical stories evolve with each passing day. But we must respect science – the truth will come out.

Flaps on the plane found in the French Réunion Island

Debris from MH17's wings

CHAPTER TWELVE

Why the search policy for MH370 should be changed

The omnidirectional, three-dimensional search in the South China Sea and the Southern Indian Ocean had got into a very difficult situation since the MH370 event happened, so the decision to suspend the search was inevitable. When we look back on the 1046 days of search in the Southern Indian Ocean, it can be vividly described in a Chinese folk art form 'San Ju Ban' – three sentences plus a half. San Ju Ban, also a kind of Chinese traditional rap art, is a rhyme-style musical performance. It originated in a canal chant in west Taoguan, Yi county, Shandong province in Jiaqing years, the Qing Dynasty. This folk art is generally performed by four players, the first three each uttering a full sentence while the last one speaks a half sentence of two words. It is characterized by rhyme, coherence, humor and comedy.

Here is the 'San Ju Ban' to describe the search for Flight MH370 in the Southern Indian Ocean:

Search time delayed once and again; Search area expanded once and again;

Search funds allocated again and again; (search results) no gains.

1: THE EVER-DELAYING SEARCH TIME

After MH370 went missing, the search in the South China Sea took less than six days, and was then abruptly suspended. The United States investigation agency claimed that at 13:06 on March 13, 2014, the aircraft had flown on for another four hours and repeatedly sent pulse signals to the satellite after its disappearance. Influenced by this new information, US warships and scouts stopped the search in the central waters in the South China Sea and moved to the Indian Ocean. From March 14, led by the United States, all search teams in the South China Sea left the most likely area in the South China Sea for the Indian Ocean. By May 29, 26 countries had sent various military or civilian types of aircraft, submarines, warships, satellites and so on to launch an all directional, three- dimensional 'disaster-relief' search in the vast waters of the Indian Ocean west of Australia.

The first phase of the search lasted 75 days, with a coverage area of 4.5 million square kilometres. 334 aircraft were called out, but no valuable clues were found. On May 29 2014, the search was suspended. It resumed on August 4. This time, the search changed to a commercial search. Through bidding, the search command selected the Holland Fugro Mapping Company to search for the whereabouts of MH370 through the seabed mapping approach. The contract stipulated that the search should be completed within 300 days in the 60,000 square kilometre area on the 'Seventh Arc', west of Perth, Australia. By July 2015, the search was completed as planned, with no findings.

After August 2015, the Transport Ministers of Australia, Malaysia and China decided at a meeting to extend the search time to the end of June 2016 and expand the search scope to 120,000 square kilometres on both sides of the Seventh Arc. By June 30 2016, the search was still fruitless. But this search was not completed as scheduled, for weather reasons. 110,000 square kilometres, 90% of the planned area, was completed, leaving 10,000 square kilometres to be searched at the end of August 2016.

After August 31 2016, the search and command coordination agency announced that only 50% of the 10,000 square kilometres had been searched, and the remaining half would be delayed until October 2016. When October 2016 passed, the remaining search area was supposed to be covered by the end of 2016. On November 2, Australia's transport minister announced again that the remaining 5,000 square kilometres would be searched by January 2017. The fruitless search in the Southern Indian Ocean was delayed time and time again.

2: THE EXPANDING SEARCH RANGE

After the search team moved from the South China Sea to the Southern Indian Ocean on March 14, 2014, some countries searched north-to-south in the Indian Ocean, from the Malacca Strait to the 1500 square kilometres west of Perth to the 1680 kilometres north-west of Perth, then to 2170 kilometres, then to 2261 kilometres. On April 11 2014, the Prime Minister of Australia announced in Shanghai: 'We know that the black box is within one kilometre of the 2261 km west of Perth'. So the warships, submarines, satellites, reconnaissance equipment and so on all rushed there. However, no clues were found after many days of searching, even after the coverage of 220,000 square kilometres, not to mention the one-kilometre range.

On April 15 2014, the search area was redefined with a total area of 62,023 square kilometres. After August 2015, a priority search area was identified: 60,000 square kilometres on both sides of the seventh section line, thus a total search area of 120,000 square kilometres.

By the end of October 2016, when the established search area of 120,000 square kilometres in the Southern Indian Ocean was near completion, Australia, which was leading the search, announced that it would be expanded to 34 degrees north of the line. On April 22 2017, investigators responsible for the search said the most likely location of the missing aircraft had been found. The wreckage of the aircraft should be located to the north of the original search area of 120,000 square kilometres, to a new search area of 25,000 square kilometres. In a word, everybody is confused. Nobody knows how far the search may go. But the blind search in the Southern Indian Ocean is expanding and expanding...

3: EVER-INCREASING SEARCH FUNDS

The search for the missing aircraft requires money. It is reported that from March 8 2014 to April 2014 alone, it consumed hundreds of millions of dollars, twice the search cost for Air France Flight 447, which went down in the Atlantic in 2009. After the search moved to the Indian Ocean in May, 2015, the search contract signed with Holland's Fugro Surveying and Mapping Company amounted to 60 million Australian dollars, about 55,910,000 US dollars; later on when the money was not enough, China added 20 million Australian dollars in November, 2015. Further money contributed by Malaysia, Australia, the United States and other countries is unknown. At November 2 2016, it was reported that more money was still needed for the search. Therefore, the

Australian transport minister issued a statement in the hope of increasing the funding by another 30 million Australian dollars (about 155 million Chinese yuan) to continue the search.

In summary, the search in the Southern Indian Ocean has been like casino gambling, where the stakes keep rising while the hope of winning fades.

4: SEARCH RESULTS – NO RELIABILITY

Official leaders were convinced that MH370 had crashed on either side of the Seventh Arc in the Southern Indian Ocean, based only on the data and analysis provided by the British satellite communications company Inmarsat, and with no conclusive evidence. Many believed that it had crashed beneath the established route in the central waters of the South China Sea, while others argued that it had crashed or was hidden somewhere inland, denying that the crash site was in the Southern Indian Ocean. Of course, the official decision makers have the final say.

5: WHY A NEW APPROACH IS NECESSARY

What should be done? How should we continue the search? I offer a suggestion – change the approach to the search!

In the light of the failure of the search in the Seventh Arc, we have to decide whether we should go on searching in the future, and where. We still have to solve the mystery. It seems that the original programme of increasing search funds and enlarging the search range in the Southern Indian Ocean is not a good way to solve the problem, for those delaying or indecisive actions cannot solve the mystery of where MH370 is. New ways of thinking are needed.

The guiding ideology before 2016 was always to search for the missing persons by looking for the missing aircraft, but it has not worked. Although oil and gas fields were discovered through seabed mapping and exploration, no sign was found of MH370. In view of this, I think it is imperative to change our way of thinking. But in what way?

It's simple – change the nature of the event. Instead of calling it an aircraft disappearance, call it a missing persons case. Instead of trying to find objects, let's try to find people.

When the guiding ideology has been changed, the strategy must follow. Searching for people is very different from searching for objects. There is a legal difference, and a change in jurisdiction. Based on ICAO principles on aircraft original hunt for the aircraft was led by Malaysia and executed by its transport management department, for the search had to start from MH370's departure port, Kuala Lumpur. If the object is now changed to finding people, on the basis of the fact that the entrance port of the on-board passengers was Beijing, the relatives of the 239 people on board should report them missing to the Beijing Public Security Bureau Airport Branch so that it can file a case for investigation. This will change the jurisdiction from Kuala Lumpur, Malaysia to Beijing, China. The host country is changed from Malaysia or Australia to China, and the leading department is also changed, from the transportation department to public security department.

The third change must be in the search strategy. The search for an aircraft is led by the transport sectors of various countries in accordance with traffic accident procedures and methods. Now the public security departments will search for the missing people in accordance with the relevant procedures and methods. A public security department is much better qualified to look for missing people, and will do so in a relatively short period of time. If this missing persons case can be reported, registered, filed and investigated by the Beijing Municipal Public Security Bureau, it will inevitably appear in the supervision list of China's Ministry of Public Security because of the large number of people involved in this case; also because the event involves 14 countries and has huge international influence. The Ministry of Public Security will inevitably ask the International Criminal Police Organisation and its member states to help investigate the case. After the judicial process starts, the leading search organisation will be changed, the investigation and search team will be re-established, a new search investigation plan will be made, the search area will be redetermined and the search methods will be changed.

First, changing the search structure. The current search and command coordination members are: leader, China; assistant, Malaysia; participants, Vietnam, Kampuchea, Thailand, Philippines, Singapore, Interpol, and ICAO.

Second, the reorganisation of the investigation and search teams. The command and coordination organisation is the leading body. The leadership and the searching and detecting teams should be reorganised. The team should not only have personnel at national level, but personnel with has strong technical ability who are familiar with detection, investigation, research, analysis, salvage and so on, using the right equipment and search animals.

Third, we need a new investigation plan. After the members of the organisation are selected, they should draw up new search plans. The scheme should fully incorporate the experience and lessons of the original programme, take in its strong points and avoid its weak points. At every step, the rights, obligations and responsibilities of every individual and the allocation and use of financial and material objects should be as detailed and comprehensive as possible, for the sake of easy handling.

Fourth – redefining the search area. There is much controversy over where MH370 crashed. According to some experts, the Southern Indian Ocean has been repeatedly searched despite the opposition and disagreement of many experts. As the latter have no power of decision, their objections have had no effect. The new organising and coordinating structure should take into account all parties and experts and have full verification so as to re-establish the search area.

No matter whether the future search area is the South China Sea, the Southern Indian Ocean or Jaliman Dan Sea and no matter how the search area is divided, we should, first of all, prioritise the target areas according to the opinions of experts and then exclude them one by one according to the searching situation.

Fifth – revising the search methods. After the search plan has been determined, a special panel consisting of verification experts and relevant organisations should gathered to vote on the following:

The search scope: according to the above identified search areas, determine the specific scope of the search.

The search agencies: whether to continue to use Fugro Mapping Company or choose other agencies.

The search means: whether to favour a combination of investigation and search, or human beings and animals, or humans and computers, or an integration of air, land and sea, or military and civilian forces....

The search equipment: boats, sonar detection equipment, Deep Sea Warrior, deep-sea vehicles, animals, and so on.

After the above changes are made, with the close cooperation and strong support of the families of the missing passengers, I believe that everything will change. I believe we will soon know the exact whereabouts of the Flight MH370 and all the passengers on board.

CHAPTER THIRTEEN

What will happen next?

Is MH370 going to be the mystery of the ages? No! I believe it will not be hard to find. To be sure, MH370 did not ascend into the heavens or fly away to another planet. MH370 is still on the earth, somewhere in the Asian region. Its whereabouts will be found sooner or later – it is only a matter of time.

I will now try to predict when the answer will be revealed, and how.

1: WE SHOULD RETURN TO THE SOUTH CHINA SEA

On March 8, 2004, a Malaysian aircraft took off at 0:42 local time from Kuala Lumpur International Airport and flew northwest at an angle of 24° all the way to Beijing in accordance with its established route. Eight minutes after take-off, the aircraft adopted normal cruise flight, and 30 minutes later it shifted to night cruise mode. At 1:19:29 the co-pilot finished his communication with Kuala Lumpur airport control tower by saying, 'good night'. The aircraft continued to cruise until at 01:21, it suddenly disappeared from the Kuala Lumpur Aviation Control Centre radar, and at 1:22 it disappeared from Thai radar. In accordance with the rules of international air navigation, the next stop of the navigational relay was Ho Chi Minh Air Control Centre in Vietnam. At 1:25, they should have received the plane according to the normal regulations and taken responsibility for sending the aircraft to the next air control area. However, not only did Ho Chi Minh ATC not receive the aircraft, but the signal from it disappeared from its radar.

Kuala Lumpur ATC, which was responsible for sending the plane, should have connected with the next station after the delivery, but it did not. One side sent it off, but the other did not receive it. Both ATC personnel called the plane for a long time without any response. That was when MH370 disappeared. From 7 am on March 8, Malaysia, Vietnam and China's aviation sectors all started an emergency response process, sending their respective aircraft and ships to the disappearance position to search for Flight MH370. On March 9, the United States, Singapore and other countries sent warships and aircraft to join the search team, starting, in the South China Sea, a non-stop 24-hour-per-day search.

The search went on till March 12, without result. Then an informal Malaysian military spokesman released the news that they had found that MH370 had changed its route and flown west at 1 am on March 8. Satellite organisations also said that the satellite signals showed that the flight had changed its direction from where it had lost contact, and had continued in 'zombie flight' for six to seven hours.

As a result, on March 14th, the US warships quit their search in the South China Sea and left for the Indian Ocean without saying goodbye. On March 15, Vietnam announced it was closing its territory and airspace and refused to allow outsiders to search. That was when the search in the South China Sea for MH370 came to an end.

After March 14, news emerged that floating objects had been found in the Southern Indian Ocean. All the search teams in the South China Sea rushed to the Southern Indian Ocean, like army forces mustering for a fight. From March 14 to May 29, 26 countries sent warships, submarines, aircraft, satellites and other advanced equipment to scan the sea floor west of Perth. 75 days later, all parties had exhausted all their skills without finding a single fragment from MH370.

When the searches yielded no results, the search and rescue director had an idea, announcing on May 29, 2014 that following over two months of searching for MH370 without result, they were suspending the current search by teams from various countries and would try another way. I have already described the resources that went into the subsequent search. The fact that all that searching had not yielded a single clue deeply puzzled the director of the coordination centre.

The director of the event was not puzzled at all. On October 24, 2014, the British media announced that the wreckage might have drifted to Indonesia. The search authorities carried out an assessment and then recommended that Indonesia should pay attention to aircraft debris. This message overjoyed the author because the news pulled the crash site from the Seventh Arc to a point 4000 km closer to the crash site advanced by the author.

On March 14 2014, the United States led a search of the Southern Indian Ocean. This was like luring one's enemy away from an advantageous position, or in chess, to give up a pawn to save the king. This plan was a big conspiracy, like a play called 'Storms in the South China Sea'. Because that is what it was – a play, directed by America, with Vietnam and the Philippines as the protagonists, Australia and Malaysia as supporting roles and Japan as the clown. It was a three-act play consisting of confrontation, driving relatives away and siege and attack.

We might as well look at what happened before. Wrecked Philippine warships have lain on the beach of Second Thomas Shoal, a reef in Chinese territory in the South China Sea, for 15 years. In March 2014, China once again sent a marine police vessel to patrol there. The Philippines abruptly sent warships and soldiers to the reef and confronted the Chinese army, seemingly to start a fight. They were, in response to the needs of the United States' Asian re-balancing strategy, deliberately provoking international tensions and complaining that China was bullying small countries, and even drafting complaints to the International Court of Arbitration. The Philippines out, Vietnam in!

Between May 13-16 2014, China's original 'comrades plus brother' Vietnam provoked a number of so-called 'militants', creating waves of anti-China activities. They broke into Chinese enterprises in Ha Tinh and other provinces, smashing and burning wantonly, resulting in more than 300 casualties. More than 4000 Chinese were forced to withdraw from Vietnam to China. Vietnam played at martial arts. The third act was 'siege and attack'.

On May 30 2014, the Singapore Asian Security Council met as scheduled. US Defence Minister Hagel said loudly at the meeting that China 'posed a threat to the prosperity of Southeast Asia.' Vietnam and the Philippines desperately applauded his speech and viciously attacked China for being a threat to Southeast Asia. At this meeting, the Japanese clowns put on their best performance, intimidating some small countries in Southeast Asia.

Just imagine, for such a large-scale drama as 'Storm in the South China Sea', how could the directing team not plan it six months in advance as the Chinese people do with their Spring Festival? The 'programme' and the lead and supporting 'actors' should have been set by the end of 2013. March 2014 should have been their 'rehearsal period'. Unfortunately, the weather was unpredictable. Then on March 8 2014, MH370 suddenly disappeared in the South China sea. A human tragedy shocked the world, and it became a big task to find a plane and rescue people in the South China Sea. The disappearance of MH370 interfered with the US plan to restrain China, seeing that its long-prepared farce in the South China Sea soon seemed to have been ruined.

On March 12, a person who was not a spokesman for the Malaysian military released a formal message that at 2:40 on March 8, aircraft MH370 had appeared on military radar and flown over the Malacca strait. The next day, a Malaysian official came out to clarify this, saying that yesterday's spokesman was not a formal spokesman, and the news he had announced was 'not verified'. At such a critical moment, what is the purpose of having an unofficial speaker publish unconfirmed information?

After that, the British media released the news that the lost MH370 aircraft might have flown to Andaman Island in the Indian Ocean. The US media also said that new intelligence showed that the lost aircraft had conducted 'tactical operations' trying to avoid radar monitoring. On March 14, the US warships took the liberty to give up their search and rescue in the South China Sea and headed for the Indian Ocean. On March 15, Malaysia also suggested that MH370 had turned off the communication system, and was believed to have turned to the west, flying to the south of the Indian Ocean. Maritime satellite headquarters also sent a message that after the aircraft had disappeared from ATC screen in the east coast of Malaysia, it was tracked by the satellite over the Indian Ocean for nearly six hours.

On March 15, all searches in the South China Sea were suspended; All search teams moved to the Southern Indian

Ocean for an omni-directional all -dimension search. On March 14 Vietnam degraded the rescue and search operation level from 'emergency' to 'normal', and on 15th it issued an announcement to close its territory, refusing to allow other countries' aircraft and ships to enter Vietnam. It is not difficult for experts to see that from March 14 to 15, the director of 'Storms in the South China Sea' was clearing the stage before the official performance. As soon as the action ended, the show would begin.

First act Confrontation
Time: Mid-March, 2014
Setting: China's Ren'ai Reef, in the South China Sea

Scene: China's Ren'ai Reef, which had never been noticed by the world in the past, became a hot topic of public discussion. On March 29, the Philippines military force in fishing boats fiercely confronted Chinese maritime police near the Ren'ai Reef in the name of protecting broken warships which had lain abandoned on the beach for 15 years. The Philippines soldiers broke through the Chinese interception and boarded the Ren'ai reef, which intensified the conflict between China and Philippines. The peaceful relationship between China and the Philippines became hostile.

China-Philippines confrontation at Huangyan Island

Second Act: Drive the relatives away
Time: May 13 to May 16, 2014
Setting: many Chinese enterprises in Ha Tinh, Vietnam.

Scene: in Vietnam, more and more so-called 'militants' undertook anti-China activities. They broke into Chinese enterprises in Ha Tinh and other provinces, smashing and burning wantonly, resulting in more than 300 casualties. More than 4,000 Chinese were forced to evacuate from Vietnam to China. Since then, the 'Comrade brothers' relationship between China and Vietnam has almost dropped to freezing point.

Attack on Chinese property in Vietnam

Some of the burned properties

Chinese workers' evacuation

Third Act: Siege and Attack
Time: May 30, 2014
Setting: Shangri-La Hotel, Singapore

Scene: The 13th 'Shangri-La Dialogue' officially opened in Singapore. US Defence Minister Hagel actively involved himself in the South China Sea dispute and unreasonably accused China of provoking Vietnam there. Vietnam and the Philippines, in their best cooperation, tried to besiege and attack China and on the other hand sang its praises for strengthening the Asia-Pacific regional alliance and cooperation with the United States. They spread a 'China threat' theory.

If all the aircraft, warships, civilian ships and personnel from 26 countries had not moved to the Indian Ocean but continued to search in the South China Sea, on the same scale, in the same way and with the same equipment, in an omni-directional, three-dimensional manner, the mystery of Flight MH370 would have long since been solved. Could the anti-China farce 'Storm in the South China Sea', written and directed by the USA, have been staged as scheduled? Even if it was staged reluctantly, there would be few who would welcome it or show interest in it. Some people worry that if the Indian Ocean submarine exploration contract expires but MH370 has still not been found, what will they do? How will they handle it? We should not worry. With the passage of time, someone will appear to make up for it; there will be news. I believe that those countries who were fooled by someone but still thanked him would, under the pressure of the families of the missing passengers and the pressure of international public opinion, withdraw from the Southern Indian Ocean and resume the search in the South China Sea near where MH370 lost contact.

Wait and see. I believe this day will soon come.

1: A STRANDED WHALE

The various theories about the whereabouts of MH370 mainly fall into three kinds of conclusions based on three pieces of evidence.

One, based on the time of the last 'handshake' signal with the satellite, MH370 rests 1800 kilometres west of Perth on 'the Seventh Arc' in the Southern Indian Ocean.

Two, the aircraft crashed into the sea at N6° 55'15', E103° 34'43' according to the time of disconnection.

Three, it crashed in the waters or deep forests south of Nam Can, Vietnam, around N7° 25', E103° 55' according to the time when the radar signal disappeared.

The author holds a negative attitude towards the first conclusion and a reserved attitude towards the second conclusion, but firmly supports the third conclusion. Although no organised teams searched or explored in depth the areas inferred by the third conclusion, it does not mean that this area is not the resting place of MH370.

Perhaps one morning, on a beach somewhere along the coast of the South China Sea, someone will find a whale or other marine animal stranded on the shore, and in its huge belly will be neither its eggs, young nor daily food but human remains. The discoverers may abandon these items in the wilderness and take their meat away; perhaps a passer-by may send these unknown human items to the officials for inspection and identification, or release pictures on the Internet. This may shock the world. They will be items from the missing MH370, things belonging to the plane, the passengers and crew. Experts may then be able to determine the whereabouts of MH370 in accordance with the habits of cruising marine animals, thus finally uncovering the veil of MH370.

2: HOW EXPLORATION OR FISHING COULD FIND AIRCRAFT WRECKAGE

In this modern information age, many people who have knowledge and culture know about the tragedy of the disappearance of Flight MH370. It is well known that MH370 went missing in the South China Sea. Those who are fond of adventure in the deep seas or high mountains may inadvertently find in their adventures the clues to MH370's whereabouts. It may happen to fishermen or divers, who encounter strange objects which they cannot pull up, or when they are wandering along the beach they may find a piece of aircraft wreckage. It is quite possible that we could find fragments from MH370 in such a way, thus unveiling the mystery.

3: DEEP SEA FISHING AND SUBMARINE EXPLORATION

As mentioned in the previous chapters, MH370 went missing within three minutes. As no floating objects were found, people believe that the flight did not break up in the air. Some parts of the plane might have disintegrated at the moment of the crash due to the great impact force. The failure to find any floating debris indicates that when MH370 crashed, the fuel tank did not burst or explode and the cabin door remained closed. Otherwise, floating objects would have long since been found. The outcome is likely to have been similar to the crash of the Algerian aircraft AH5017, with scattered debris concentrated in a very narrow area. According to photographic data, the scattered area is less than one square kilometre. The scene is shown in this picture.

Malaysia Airlines flight MH17 was different. MH17 disintegrated in the sky after being hit at an altitude of 10,000 metres, with assorted objects and bodies scattered over 180 square kilometres, as shown in this picture of part of the scene.

If MH370 lies in a small area of ocean, to find its whereabouts is like looking for a needle in a haystack. It is quite likely that a deep-sea fishing boat or seabed explorer could accidentally find part of a plane wreck with trawls, ropes and other simple equipment. The specialized search teams won't necessarily find clues first.

4: HERBS PICKLING, HUNTING, EXPLORATION, RESTLESS EAGLES AND DOGS...

After the disappearance of MH370, all kinds of information came in. Some reports and related data were not consistent; some were incomplete; some were contradictory and full of mistakes. In view of this, it is difficult for the author to avoid mistakes in selecting materials and using data. In order to minimize the errors caused by my selection of materials which may mislead my readers, I will point out some of the potential risks. My inference of the whereabouts of MH370 in Vietnamese waters below the established routes is one such case. A one-sided approach may lead to searching in the wrong place. Although according to the three radar signals, MH370 disappeared between 1:22 and 1:25; there are also reports that its disappearance time on Malaysia Kuala Lumpur radar was 1:30. Thailand Surat Thani military radar reported its disappearance first at 1:22, but 6 minutes later, its signal was restored before vanishing again. If so, MH370 disappeared in Thailand radar at 1:28; though it was only about 3 minutes from 1:28 to 1:30, the crash site, under the cruising speed of the aircraft, will vary from 120 to 150 km away, the former giving a landing place in the sea, the latter pointing to either water or land.

There is also a report that MH370 disappeared from the radar after flying for 54 minutes. if so, the whereabouts of MH370 would be 800-900 km from Kuala Lumpur and 200-300 km from Ho Chi Minh City, the area around the surrounding sea coast and islands in Nam Can, Vietnam. From the satellite map, the south of Nam Can Island is sparsely populated with few villages, dense forests and blocked roads. If MH370 fell into any of these inaccessible places, it will be difficult to find. There is a chance for climbers, herdsmen, hunting prospectors, herb gatherers, travellers and so on who may occasionally visit the place. Perhaps the activity of eagles or dogs will attract their attention and they will accidentally discover MH370's whereabouts.

5: IF THE REWARD OFFERED IS ATTRACTIVE ENOUGH, THERE WILL ALWAYS BE ONE WHO IS BRAVE ENOUGH TO TAKE THE RISK.

The documented cost for searching for Flight MH370 now amounts to nearly 200 million US dollars, all without finding even one piece of suspicious wreckage. It seems some fundamental changes must be made to achieve a breakthrough. If the reward offered is attractive enough, there will always be one who is brave enough to take the risk. It was revealed that the families of the missing persons had raised 5 million dollars to pay informants who provided valuable clues or hired private detectives to find MH370's whereabouts. This can be described as a coup, for it should turn up heroes who may come from the military forces, the aviation community or the navigation field, or satellite data analysts.

If we follow the energy the United States used in the pursuit of Osama Bin Laden, taking advantage of every possible means like widespread advertisement, handsome rewards and the like, we may likely come across another Snowden generation who dare to do anything. And the time when the mystery of MH370 is unveiled may be just around the corner.

6: ALTERNATIVE IDEAS

Every possible means has been tried, without result. In such a difficult situation, what shall we do? We might as well try some unconventional approaches. Who knows, they may work. I offer one or two here, hoping they may be of use.

Today, high technology is widely used, and the Internet, electronic monitoring and other advanced technologies emerge in an endless stream. In north-east China, in order to understand the living conditions of the Siberian tiger, wild animal protection people have abandoned the use of rangers to find pawprints and employed micro video surveillance equipment. They have clearly the tigers' trails. They not only obtained the image of the tiger but were able to discover his activities and diet. Why can't we use a similar approach to find the whereabouts of MH370? Since most experts agree that MH370 is likely to have crashed in the sea, it is only a question of whether to search the South China Sea or the Southern Indian Ocean. Aircraft and warships are effective tools for searching the vast expanse of the ocean, but on the seabed, these weapons will be useless, while equipment such as submarines, The Bluefin 21, Jiaolong (the Chinese submersible) and similar move as slowly as a snail climbs a tree, so progress is slow.

What dominates the bottom of the ocean floor? Sea creatures. Why not use them to search for MH370? Sea animals like dolphins, sea lions, turtles, sharks, whales and so on are as sensitive as hawks and dogs. If we use marine animals and equip them with suitable electronic equipment, we have many more opportunities to find MH370. It is not necessarily humans who will first find the whereabouts of Flight MH370. It is quite possible that animals will find it first. Then the mystery of MH370 s disappearance will be finally and completely uncovered after human confirmation.

The combination of electronic technology and animals, or the extensive collection, mining, analysis and interpretation of the data from weather satellites, monitoring satellites, remote sensing satellites and other random satellites from midnight on March 8 to midnight on March 9, combined with professional analysis, are good ways to find the crash site. We must interview possible witnesses, like fishermen, merchant seamen, travellers and so on. It's especially important to understand what the New Zealand oilman Mike McKay and the British sailor Catherine Tee saw. More attention should be paid to the British woman's GPS data, because the exact resting place of MH370 may be determined through its use. Eventually, MH370 will also rise to surface.

CHAPTER FOURTEEN

What will happen next?

The news surrounding Malaysia Airlines MH370 has always attracted the interest of readers. However, we should be wary of the many scams involving the aircraft.

On July 7 2014, there appeared a video entitled 'Malaysia Airlines Flight MH370 was discovered by sailors, mystery revealed'. The sailor was rewarded $5 million on the spot. The video is listed in the 'news' articles in which a picture is shown of an aircraft submerged in water. The picture was actually taken in January 2009, when an American airliner crashed into the Hudson River. Obviously the photo was copied from a legitimate news article. However, once the victim clicked on the link to the video, he was directed to a Facebook account, which popped up a window with an instruction saying, 'You must share this video with other friends to start watching.' But if you do this, you still will not see the video. After sharing it, you will be told that you have to complete a survey to verify your age. You will never see the video, as it does not exist.

The scam is a marketing plan designed to make money through Facebook. The more people share, the more victims they have, and they can amass more money. Often this video appears in the guise of 'the latest video,' 'shock video' or 'breaking news', with bold titles and lots of exclamation marks. Sometimes it comes in the form of controversial topics or tracking messages. At worst, the scam might require the victim to provide his or her mobile phone number, QQ number, email address, bank account number, full name, address and important contact details. This usually results in a shock for the victim. They subscribe to expensive text messaging services and end up paying high phone bills. Victims may also receive more promotional emails, as well as marketing phone calls and junk mail.

So whenever it comes to offers of money, rewards or prizes, never enter your bank account details, name, address or mobile phone number. Don't be cheated. Remember, if MH370 is found, it will be on the news immediately. You don't need to check yourself.

APPENDICES

APPENDIX 1

Details of Flight MH370, passengers and crew members

1. Model: Boeing 777-200ER
2. Length: 63.70 metres
3. Wingspan: 60.90 metres
4. Height: 18.50 metres
5. Cabin width: 5.86 metres
6. Maximum seat number: 440 Number of seats: 301
7. Cruising distance: 14260 km
8. Cruising speed: Mach 0.84
9. Maximum take-off weight: 297550kg
10. Motor: PW4090/RR Trent895/GE90
11. Registration number: 9M-MRO
12. Production number: 404
13. Engine: Rolls Royce engines

14. Cabin layout: 35 business class seats, 247 economy class seats

15. Flight number: MH370

16. Total flying time: 53465.21 hours

17. Route: Kuala Lumpur-Beijing

18. Flight time schedule: departure at 00:42, March 8, 2014, arrival at 06:30 March 8, 2014

19. Time missing: between around 01:21:30 and 01:01:25 on March 8, 2014

20. Time of disappearance: 01:37, March 8, 2014

The aircraft made its first fight on May 14, 2002 and was delivered to Malaysia Airlines on May 31 the same year. On August 9, 2012 on Malaysia Airlines flight 389 (Shanghai-Kuala Lumpur), in a collision with an Airbus A340-600 (No. B-6050) ready to fly to Los Angeles, the wing was damaged.

MH370 contained 239 people, including 227 passengers (2 infants) and 12 crew members, with passengers from 14 countries.

The passengers include: 154 Chinese (including a baby); 38 Malaysians; 7 Indonesians; 6 Australians; 5 Indians; 4 French; 3 Americans (including a baby); 2 New Zealanders; 2 Ukrainians; 2 Canadians; 1 Russian; 1 Italian; 1 Dutch; and 1 from Austria .

The Chinese passengers include 9 Chinese artists and three employees from Shenzhen (ZTE 1, HUAWEI 2).

Pilot: Zahari Ahmad Shah, 53 years old, had been with Malaysia Airlines for 33 years since 1981, with more than 18,000 hours flying time.

Co-pilot: Rick Abdel Hamid, 27 years old, had been with Malaysia Airlines for seven years since 2007, with more than 2,763 hours' flying time.

List of the 154 Chinese passengers

No.	English name	Chinese name	Gender	Date of birth	age
1	AN/WENLAN	安文兰	女	1949-10-20	65
2	BAO/YUANHUA	鲍媛华	女	1951-10-21	63
3	BIAN/MAOQIN	边茂勤	女	1947-7-19	67
4	BIAN/LIANGJING	边亮京	男	1987-6-6	27
5	CAO/RUI	曹蕊	女	1982-2-19	32
6	CHE/JUNZHANG	车俊章	女	1946-3-20	68
7	CHEN/JIAN (SHE)	陈建设	男	1956-3-7	58
8	CHEN/CHANGJUN	陈长军	男	1979-6-6	35
9	CHEN/YUNMS	陈昀	女	1957-8-11	57
10	DAI/SHULING	戴淑玲	女	1956-12-7	58
11	DI/JIABIN	邸佳彬	男	1978-6-5	36
12	DING/YING	丁莹		1952-4-25	62
13	DING/LIJUN	丁立军	男	1971-4-6	43
14	DING/YINGMS	丁颖	女	1986-10-24	28
15	DONG/GUOWEI	董国伟	男	1966-10-26	48
16	DOU/YUNSHAN	窦运山	男	1953-10-10	61
17	DU/WENZHONG	杜文忠	男	1964-6-7	47
18	FENG/DONG	冯栋	男	1993-3-9	21
19	FENG/JIXIN	冯纪新	男	1944-1-6	70
20	FU/BAOFENG	付宝峰	男	1986-12-6	28
21	GAN/TAO	甘涛	男	1970-1-29	44
22	GAN/FUXIANG	甘福祥	男	1965-11-21	49
23	GAO/GE	高歌	女	1987-11-16	27
24	GUAN/WENJIE	管文杰	男	1979-10-3	35
25	HAN/JING	韩静	女	1961-5-28	53

No.	English name	Chinese name	Gender	Date of birth	age
26	HOU/AIQINMS	侯爱琴	女	1969-6-24	45
27	HOU/BO	侯波	男	1979-5-15	35
28	HU/SIWANCHD	胡偲馆(婴儿)	女	2011-2-25	3
29	HU/XIAONING	胡效宁	男	1980-1-1	34
30	HUANG/YIMS	黄毅	女	1984-6-18	30
31	HUANG/TIANHUI	HuangTianhui	男	1948-5-28	66
32	JIA/PING	贾平	男	1982	32
33	JIANG/CUIYUN	姜翠云	女	1952-3-27	62
34	JIANG/XUEREN	姜学仁	男	1952	62
35	JIANG/YINGMS	姜颖	女	1987-4-13	27
36	JIAO/WEIWEI	焦微微	女	1983-5-9	32
37	JIAO/WENXUE	焦文学	男	1956-12-17	58
38	JU/KUN	鞠坤	男	1982-11-7	32
39	KANG/XU	康旭	男	1980-8-9	34
40	LI/YANLIN	栗延林	男	1985-10-26	29
41	LI/ZHI	李智	男	1973-5-5	41
42	LI/GUOHUI	李国辉	男	1958-5-18	56
43	LI/HONGJING	李红晶	女	1994-12-9	20
44	LI/JIE	李洁	女	1987-2-6	27
45	LI/MINGZHONG	黎明中	男	1945-12-19	69
46	LI/WENBO	李文博	女	1985-7-16	29
47	LI/YAN	李燕	女	1983-7-19	31
48	LI/YUCHEN	李宇辰	男	1987-11-6	27
49	LI/ZHIJIN	李志锦	男	1984-4-14	30
50	LI/ZHIXIN	李志欣	男	1979-5-22	35
51	LI/LE	李乐	男	1982-12-3	36

No.	English name	Chinese name	Gender	Date of birth	age
52	LIANG/LUYANG	梁路阳	男	1954-3-26	60
53	LIANG/XUYANG	梁旭阳	男	1984-11-12	30
54	LIN/ANNAN	林安南	男	1987-3-27	27
55	LIN/MINGFENG	林明蜂	男	1980-5-25	34
56	LIU/FENGYING	刘凤英	女	1949-5-10	65
57	LIU/JINPENG	刘金鹏	男	1981-12-26	33
58	LIU/QIANG	刘强	男	1974-8-13	40
59	LIU/RUSHENG	刘如生	男	1938/01/22	76
60	LIU/SHUNCHAO	刘顺超	男	1968-2-29	46
61	LIU/ZHONGFU	柳忠福	男	1942-5-22	72
62	LOU/BAOTANG	楼宝棠	男	1935-4-21	79
63	LU/JIANHUA	鹿建华	男	1957-3-28	57
64	LU/XIANCHU	卢先初	男	1981-10-14	33
65	LUI/CHING	LuiChing	女	1969-8-2	45
66	LUO/WEI	罗伟	男	1985-8-20	29
67	MA/WENZHI	马文芝	女	1957-8-1	57
68	MA/JUN	马骏	男	1981-12-25	33
69	MAIMAITIJIANG/ABULA	买买提江·阿布拉	男	1979-7-10	35
70	MAO/TUGUI	毛土贵	男	1942-8-2	72
71	MENG/BING	孟兵	男	1974-4-26	40
72	MENG/FANQUAN	孟凡全（余）	男	1944-8-23	70
73	MENG/GAOSHENG	蒙高生	男	1950-1-1	64
74	OUYANG/XIN	欧阳欣	女	1976-10-12	38
75	SHI/XIANWEN	石贤文	男	1988-1-18	26
76	SONG/FEIFEI	宋飞飞	男	1982-3-1	32
77	SONG/CHUNLINGMS	宋春玲	女	1954-4-6	60

No.	English name	Chinese name	Gender	Date of birth	age
78	SONG/KUN	宋坤	男	1989-12-15	25
79	SU/QIANGGUO	苏强国	男	1943-3-5	71
80	TANG/XUDONG	唐旭东	男	1983-8-3	31
81	TANG/XUEZHUMS	汤雪竹	女	1957-2-6	57
82	TIAN/JUNWEI	田军伟	男	1985-9-7	29
83	TIAN/QINGJUN	田清君	男	1963-3-1	51
84	WANG/SHOUXIAN	王守宪	男	1945-3-17	69
85	WANG/SHUMIN?	王淑敏	女	1953-7-9	61
86	WANG/XIANJUN	王献军	男	1953-1-16	61
87	WANG/CHUNHUA	王纯华	男	1980-1-13	34
88	WANG/CHUNYONG	王春勇	男	1971-4-22	43
89	WANG/DAN	王丹	女	1960-3-21	54
90	WANG/HAITAO	王海涛	男	1988-1-4	26
91	WANG/HOUBIN	汪厚彬	男	1986-10-6	28
92	WANG/LINSHI	王林诗	男	1945-11-11	69
93	WANG/YONGGANG	王永刚	男	1987-7-1	27
94	WANG/YONGHUI	王永辉	男	1981-4-12	33
95	WANG/YONGQIANG	王永强	男	1984-6-18	30
96	WANG/LIJUN	王利军	男	1956-6-1	58
97	WANG/RUI	王睿	男	1979-8-5	35
98	WANG/MOHENG	王墨恒(婴儿)	男	2012-5-25	2
99	WEN/YONGSHENG	文永胜	男	1980-3-17	34
100	WEN/HAO（DONG）	温浩东	男	1982-3-14	32
101	WENG/MEI(LING)	翁美玲	女	1975-9-16	39
102	XIE/LIPING	谢莉萍	女	1963-11-7	51
103	XIN/XIXIMS	辛曦曦	女	1982-5-24	32

No.	English name	Chinese name	Gender	Date of birth	age
104	XING/FENGTAO	邢锋涛	男	1978-9-22	36
105	XING/QIAO	邢桥	女	1987-4-15	27
106	XIONG/DEMING	熊德明	女	1951-9-9	63
107	XU/CHUANE	许传娥	女	1947-10-10	67
108	YA/NA	娅娜	女	1988-9-11	26
109	YAN/LING	燕岭	男	1985-7-20	29
110	YAN/PENG	闫鹏	男	1985-1-17	29
111	YAN/XIAO	严笑	男	1987	27
112	YANG/LI	杨丽	女	1979-11-4	35
113	YANG/AILINGMS	杨爱玲	女	1954-6-9	60
114	YANG/JIABAO	YangJiabao	女	1988-8-25	26
115	YANG/MEIHUA	杨美华	女	1949-12-12	65
116	YANG/QINGYUAN	杨庆元	男	1957-1-1	57
117	YANG/XIAOMINGMS	杨晓明	女	1955-11-17	59
118	YAO/JIANFENG	姚建锋	男	1944-4-28	70
119	YAO/LIFEI	么立飞	男	1983-6-15	31
120	YIN/BOYAN	殷博岩	男	1981-9-1	33
121	YIN/YUEWANG	尹月旺	男	1993-9-13	21
122	YUAN/JIN	袁进	女	1951-8-10	63
123	YUE/GUIJUMS	岳桂菊	女	1963-9-13	51
124	YUE/WENCHAO	岳文超	男	1988-8-31	26
125	ZANG/LINGDI	臧领弟	女	1956-1-2	58
126	ZHANG/CHI	张弛	女	1956-7-15	58
127	ZHANG/LIQIN	张立勤	男	1971	43
128	ZHANG/QIMS	张琪	女	1983-1-28	31
129	ZHANG/YAN	张妍	女	1978-4-28	45

No.	English name	Chinese name	Gender	Date of birth	age
130	ZHANG/HUA	章华	男	1971-1-28	43
131	ZHANG/LIJUANMS	张丽娟	女	1953-4-17	61
132	ZHANG/NAMS	张娜	女	1980/07/27	34
133	ZHANG/SIMING	张四明	女	1943-8-21	71
134	ZHANG/XIAOLEIMS	张晓蕾	女	1982-10-3	32
135	ZHANG/HUALIAN	张华莲	女	1972-10-30	42
136	ZHANG/JIANWU	张建武	男	1983-10-11	31
137	ZHANG/JINQUAN	张金权	男	1942-1-25	72
138	ZHANG/MENG	张梦	女	1985-5-3	29
139	ZHANG/XUEWEN	张学文	男	1953-8-1	61
140	ZHANG/YAN	张岩	女	1969-3-21	45
141	ZHANG/YANHUI	张晏珲	女	1970-1-8	44
142	ZHANG/ZHONGHAI	张忠海	男	1971-5-3	43
143	ZHANG/SHAOHUA	张少华	女	1982-4-27	32
144	ZHAO/GANG	赵刚	男	1968-6-29	46
145	ZHAO/QIWEI	赵琪威	男	1977	37
146	ZHAO/YINGXINCHD	赵滢心	女	2011-6-22	3
147	ZHAO/PENG	赵朋	男	1989-8-10	25
148	ZHAO/ZHAOFANG	赵兆芳	女	1941-12-18	73
149	ZHENG/RUIXIAN	郑瑞仙	女	1972-3-8	42
150	ZHOU/FENG	周枫	女	1958-3-12	56
151	ZHOU/JINLING	周金陵	男	1953-11-18	61
152	ZHOU/SHIJIE	周仕杰	男	1950-10-9	64
153	ZHOU/JUNYAN	朱军燕	女	1973-9-14	41
154	CHUANGHSIULINGMS	康秀玲		1969	45

List of the 73 passengers from other countries

(sorted by the number of passengers):

No.	English name	Nation/Region	Age
1	BIBYNAZLI/MOHDHASSIM	Malaysia	62
2	CHAN/HUANPEEN	Malaysia	46
3	CHEN/WEI	Malaysia	43
4	CHEW/KARMOOIMS	Malaysia	31
5	CHNG/MEI	Malaysia	33
6	DAISY/ANNE	Malaysia	56
7	DINA/MOHAMEDYUNUSRAMLI	Malaysia	30
8	GUAN/HUAJINMS	Malaysia	34
9	HASHIM/NOORIDA	Malaysia	57
10	HUE/PUIHENG	Malaysia	66
11	JINGHANG/JEE	Malaysia	41
12	KOH/TIONGMENG	Malaysia	40
13	LEE/KAHKIN	Malaysia	32
14	LEE/SEWCHUMDM	Malaysia	55
15	LIM/POWCHUAMS	Malaysia	43
16	MARIA/MOHAMEDYUNUSRAMLI	Malaysia	52
17	MATRAHIM/NORFADZILLAHMISS	Malaysia	39
18	MOHDKHAIRULAMRI/SELAMAT	Malaysia	29
19	MOHAMADSOFUAN/IBRAHIM	Malaysia	33
20	MUHAMMADRAZAHAN/ZAMANI	Malaysia	24
21	MUSTAFA/SUHAILIMISS	Malaysia	31
22	NG/MAYLIMS	Malaysia	37
23	NORLIAKMAR/HAMIDMDM	Malaysia	33
24	PUSPANATHAN/SUBRAMANIAN	Malaysia	34
25	RAMLAN/SAFUAN	Malaysia	32
26	SIM/KENGWEI	Malaysia	53

No.	English name	Nation/Region	Age
27	TAN/TEIKHIN	Malaysia	32
28	TAN/AHMENG	Malaysia	46
29	TAN/WEICHEW	Malaysia	19
30	TAN/CHONGLING	Malaysia	48
31	TAN/SIOH	Malaysia	42
32	TEE/LINKEONG	Malaysia	50
33	TEOH/KIMLUN	Malaysia	36
34	TONG/SOONLEE	Malaysia	31
35	WAN/HOCKKHOON	Malaysia	42
36	WONG/SAISANG	Malaysia	53
37	YAP/CHEEMENG	Malaysia	39
38	YUSOP/MUZI	Malaysia	50
39	SIREGAR/FIRMAN	Indonesia	25
40	SUADAYA/FERRYINDRA	Indonesia	42
41	SUADAYA/HERRYINDRA	Indonesia	35
42	SUGIANTO/LO	Indonesia	47
43	TANURISAM/INDRASURIA	Indonesia	57
44	VINNY/CHYNTHYATIOMRS	Indonesia	47
45	WANG/WILLYSURIJANTTO	Indonesia	53
46	BURROWS/RODNEY	Australia	59
47	BURROWS/MARYMRS	Australia	54
48	GU/NAIJUN	Australia	31
49	LAWTON/CATHERINERINEMRS	Australia	54
50	LAWTON/ROBERT	Australia	58
51	LI/YUAN	Australia	33
52	KOLEKAR/CHETANA	India	55
53	KOLEKAR/SWANAND	India	23
54	KOLEKAR/VINOD	India	59

No.	English name	Nation/Region	Age
55	SHARMA/CHANDRIKAMS	India	51
56	SHIRSATH/KRANTI	India	44
57	WATTRELOS/AMBRE	France	14
58	WATTRELOS/HADRIEN	France	17
59	WATTRELOS/LAURENCE	France	52
60	ZHAO/YAN	France	18
61	MENG/NICOLECHD	USA	4
62	WOOD/PHILIP	USA	51
63	ZHANG/YAN	USA	2
64	WANG/XIMIN	New Zealand	50
65	WEEKS/PAUL	New Zealand	39
66	CHUSTRAK/OLEG	Ukraine	45
67	DEINEKA/SERGII	Ukraine	45
68	BAI/XIAOMO	Canada	37
69	MUKHERJEE/MUKTESH	Canada	42
70	SURTIDAHLIA/MRS	The Netherlands	50
71	BRODSKII/NIKOLAI	Russia	43
72	KOZEL/CHRISTIAN	Austria	30
73	MARALDI/LUIGI	Italy	37

List of the crew members

(sorted by the number of passengers):

No.	Name	Nationality
1	ZAHARIE BIN AHMAD SHAH (TECH CREW)	Malaysia
2	FARIQ BIN AB HAMID (TECH CREW)	Malaysia
3	PATRICK FRANCIS GOMES	Malaysia
4	ANDREW NARI	Malaysia
5	GOH SOCK LAY	Malaysia
6	TAN SER KUIN	Malaysia
7	WAN SWAID BIN WAN ISMAIL	Malaysia
8	JUNAIDI BIN MOHD KASSIM	Malaysia
9	MOHD HAZRIN BIN MOHAMED HASNAN	Malaysia
10	NG YAR CHIEN	Malaysia
11	FOONG WAI YUENG	Malaysia
12	TAN SIZE HIANG Malaysian	Malaysia

Note that these lists come from Malaysia Airlines.
There might be mistakes – be careful when using them.

APPENDIX 2

The communication and tracking systems of MH370

According to reports, the vanished aircraft should have been equipped with at least 10 communication systems, but it had not installed a satellite tracking system. The ten communication systems were:

1. Three VHF radiocommunication systems.
2. Two high frequency (HF) communication systems.
3. One selective call (SELCAL) system.
4. One audio synthesis (AIS) system.
5. Two aircraft communication addressing and reporting systems (ACARS).
6. One engine health management (EHM) system.

Of these, the audio synthesis system is mainly for internal communication, while the rest are for external contact. The VHF radio communication system, high frequency communication system, selective call system and audio integrated system are artificial communication systems, while the reporting system is an automated communication system; the engine health management system is for the engine, a system which has recently been mentioned by the engine manufacturer, Rolls-Royce and which can provide the engine data.

In addition to the above 10 systems, aircraft may also carry a set of airborne satellite phone. As shown below:

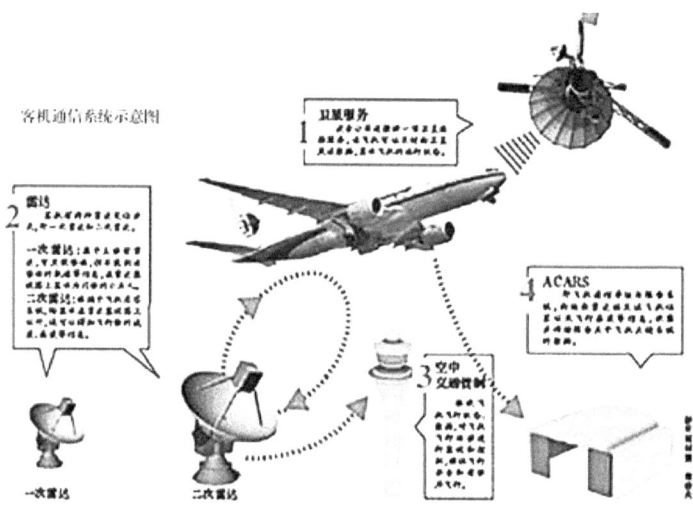

One, the 10 communication systems of Flight MH370

1: THE VERY HIGH FREQUENCY COMMUNICATION SYSTEM - 1 SET

The Very High Frequency communication system (VHF), uses VHF radio waves. Short as its effective range is, limited to the visual range, it varies as height changes. At a height of 300 metres its effective distance is 74 km. So VHF is the main communication tool for civilian aircraft. When an aircraft takes off, lands or passes into controlled airspace, the crew will use VHF to achieve two-way voice communication with the ground control personnel.

VHF consists of three parts: the transceiver unit, control box and antenna. The transceiver uses a frequency synthesizer to provide a stable reference frequency and then transmits the signal through the antenna. The receiver part receives signals through the antenna and the received signals, after amplification and detection, are converted into an audio signal and enter the driver's headphones. The knife-shaped antenna is usually fixed in the belly or back of the plane. Take-off and landing are the busiest time for the pilot to deal with problems and hence the times when the aircraft is most prone to accidents. Therefore, it is necessary to ensure that the VHF communication is highly reliable, so civil aircraft are generally equipped with more than one standby system.

2: THE HIGH FREQUENCY COMMUNICATION SYSTEM – 1 SET

The high-frequency communication system, HF (shortwave), is a long-distance communication system, with a range of thousands of kilometres. It is used to maintain contact with base and remote terminals during flight. The system consists of a transceiver unit, antenna coupler, control box and antenna; its output power is large and need a ventilation cooling device. The use of single sideband communication greatly helps to compress the occupied frequency band and save transmission power. The modern high-frequency communications antenna used in civil aircraft is usually buried within the aircraft skin or installed in the tail. Large aircraft are generally equipped with two high-frequency communications systems, but the system is rarely used.

3: THE SELECTIVE CALLING SYSTEM – 1 SET

The select call system, SELCAL, is also known as the answering machine system. When the ground calls a plane, the aircraft on SELCAL will prompt the crew to answer or make contact somehow so as to avoid a long wait by the pilot for a call or prevent them forgetting to make contact. The selective call on each aircraft must have a specific four-character identity, and the communication system on the machine is tuned to the specified frequency. When the ground's high-frequency or VHF system sends a call pulse containing the four-character code, the plane will input the impulse signal into the decoder after receiving it. If the call code matches the aircraft code, the decoder will connect the cockpit signal and the audio device to prompt the pilot to respond. For example, 'MAS is 5101, answering machine, 0363'. The pilot enters the answering machine code 0363 manually on the aircraft, after which the aircraft's radar screen will correctly display the aircraft's identity information.

4: THE AUDIO INTEGRATED SYSTEM - 4 SETS

The Audio Integrated System, AIS, basically the aircraft's internal call system, is divided into the flight internal speech system, the service internal speech system, the cabin broadcast and entertainment system, and the calling system.

The flight internal speech system's main function is for the pilot to send signals to the crew when he connects his microphone to the audio communication system he chooses and at the same time enables the signals in this system to enter the pilot's headphone or loudspeaker. The system can be used to pick up the audio signals from different types of navigation equipment or achieve inter-crew calls via the connected lines.

The service internal speech system refers to a call system composed of microphones or jacks installed at various service stations on the plane, including the cockpit, cabin and the service positions of flight attendants and ground maintenance personnel. With it, crew can communicate with ground personnel and each other. For example, the service stations for ground maintenance are generally installed in the front landing gear, and ground personnel can call by inserting the microphone into the jack.

The cabin broadcast and entertainment system broadcasts notifications to passengers and plays music.

The call system usually works with the internal speech system. It consists of call lights, tuners and call buttons on each service station. When a staff member wants to speak to a colleague, he or she presses the button that represents his service station, and then the loudspeaker of the service station will sound or flash, reminding him of the call. The call system also includes buttons on passenger seats calling the flight attendants and an indicator light on the attendant's station.

5: THE AIRCRAFT COMMUNICATION ADDRESSING AND REPORTING SYSTEM – 1 SET

The Aircraft Communications Addressing and Reporting System (ACARS) is a digital data link system for transmitting short messages between aircraft and ground stations via radio or satellite. The Boeing 777 has two sets of equipment, a set of ground stations to send aircraft location and flight height information, and another set of collection and transmission of data on several key systems on the aircraft. The station radio and transponder can be artificially switched off, but the pilot cannot turn off ACARS. After the shutdown of the VHF radio, the ACARS on the Boeing 777 automatically begins to attempt to transmit aircraft real-time status monitoring data (including engine status) to the ground via satellite communication systems. Because Malaysia Airlines did not order the ACARS satellite communications service, the satellite communications system has refused to provide links, even though the satellite communications system on Boeing 777 has issued a ping directive. This situation is like trying to link a WIFI hotspot with a login password on a mobile phone. If you don't have a password, you can't link to the WIFI hotspot.

6: ENGINE HEALTH MANAGEMENT SYSTEM – 1 SET

The engine health management system (abbreviated as EHM) mainly transfers engine monitoring data through airborne sensors and satellites. The system includes induction, acquisition, transmission and analysis. The engine can install up to 25 sensors, recording important technical parameters such as temperature, pressure, speed and so on, during each flight. Once EHM obtains these technical parameters, it will report to the aircraft condition monitoring system, which will collect these data when the plane takes off, climbs or enters level flight, and complete a full engine status report at the end of the flight.

7: AIRBORNE SATELLITE TELEPHONE – 1 SET

All aircraft are equipped with airborne satellite phones through which aircraft can keep in touch with the ground in real time. The aircraft uses the transmitter of the satellite communication system to transmit signals to high altitude communication satellites, which are then forwarded by the satellite to the ground receiving station, and then through a series of transmissions, telephone and image communication between the aircraft and the ground is achieved. The satellite communication network consists of four stationary synchronous communications satellites in the sky, and their coverage covers the whole world, with some coverage of the communication.

8: THERE IS NO SATELLITE TRACKING SYSTEM ON MH370

On November 13, 2015, the media reported that as there were no matching satellite tracking systems on MH370, the search became extremely difficult. After learning the lesson of the MH370 event, the World Radio communication Conference, convened by the International Telecommunication Union (ITU), decided that a new means of ascertaining the position of an aircraft through satellite communications would be introduced. The frequency used for aircraft and satellite communications would be set at 1087.7-1092.3 MHz. It will be therefore possible to track the location of cross-border aircraft at any time in the future.

ICAO is expected to release, by November 2016, a satellite-based Aircraft Tracing System Application Guide which will stipulate that an aircraft should report its place and altitude once every 15 minutes, and once every minute in an emergency.

APPENDIX 3

Major relevant events after the MH370's disappearance

Records of ground to air calls on March 8, 2014

Kuala Lumpur Tower

00:36:30

MH370: air traffic control, I am MH370, good morning.

ATC: Good morning, MH370, here is the Kuala Lumpur tower, please keep in the A10 32R position.

00:36:50

MH370: A10, MH370 understands.

00:38:43

ATC: MH370, please run from 32R A10.

MH370: 32R A10 on the runway, MH370 understands.

00:40:38

ATC: MH370, position 32R, the runway is ready to take off. good night. MH370: Location 32R, runway ready to take off. MH370 understand, thank you, goodbye.

Kuala Lumpur Station

00:42:05

MH370: MH370 Departure.

00:42:10

ATC: MH370 position confirmation, flight height 180, follow the instructions to the right, the target IGARI navigation point.

00:42:40

MH370: OK, height 180, direction IGARI navigation point, MH370 understand.

00:42:52

ATC: MH370, into the Kuala Lumpur radar 132.6, good night. MH370: 132.6, MH370 understand.

Kuala Lumpur Regional Radar

00:46:51

MH370: Kuala Lumpur Control Centre, this is MH370.

ATC: MH370, please climb to flight altitude 250.

00:46:54

MH370: MH370 will climb to flight altitude 250.

00:50:06

ATC: MH370, climb to flight altitude 350.

00:50:09

MH370: this is MH370, flight height 350.

01:01:14

MH370: MH370 Keep to flight altitude 350.

01:01:19

ATC: MH370.

01:07:55

MH370: MH370 Keep to flight altitude 350.

01:08:00

ATC: MH370.

01:19:24

ATC: MH370, please contact Ho Chi Minh 120.9, good night.

01:19:29

MH370: Good night, this is MH370.

After that, MH370 disappeared. At 01:20, the aircraft entered the Ho Chi Minh air traffic zone. It disappeared between 01:20-01:37.

March 8, 2014 timetable of Flight MH370

00:41

Take-off from Kuala Lumpur.

01:07

Last transmission signal. The aircraft had reached normal cruising height (Level 350, 35,000ft.)

01:19

MH370 last call with ATC.

01:20

Malaysian civil aviation control department lost contact with MH370.

01:21

MH370 disappeared from Malaysian civilian radar.

02:40

Subang Air Traffic Control Centre could not contact MH370.

06:30

When MH370 failed to appear in Beijing at the scheduled time.

March 8, 2014 - other events

01:20 loss of contact.

02:40 Malaysia confirmed.

06:30 Flight due in Beijing.

08:44 Malaysia Airlines official website released the first statement: Flight MH370 had lost contact with the tower at 2:40 on the 8th, Beijing time.

09:00 Malaysia Airlines officials said the fuel would be exhausted.

09:44 The Ministry of Foreign Affairs declared the start of the emergency mechanism; the second media statement from

Malaysia Airlines.

09:55 The Malaysia Airlines official website issued a second statement. They expressed their deep regret for the disappearance of Flight MH370 and updated the flight information, saying that the passengers were from 13 countries. The Malaysian government had launched a rescue mechanism and would work with MAS to locate the aircraft. Malaysia Airlines was informing the families of the passengers and crew members.

10:08 Beijing border check announced that there were 154 Chinese people on board.

10:30 China's Ministry of Transport started an emergency response.

11:10 The Malaysia Airlines official website released a third statement stating that the aircraft was a Boeing 777-200, which had taken off from Kuala Lumpur at 0:41 bound for Beijing and was scheduled to arrive at 6:30 am Beijing time at Beijing Capital International Airport. The flight carried a total of 239 people, including 227 passengers (including 2 babies) and 12 crew members. The passengers came from 13 countries.

12:00 Chinese Premier Li Keqiang gave instructions to immediately start the emergency response.

12:30 Vietnamese media claimed MH370 had crashed in the sea about 120 kilometres southwest of the Ca Mau province.

13:20 The Vietnamese naval general claimed that the plane had crashed 153 miles south of Fugu Island.

13:30 A China Sea police ship immediately rushed to the expected location.

13:36 A Vietnamese naval official said the plane had crashed 153 miles from the Tsugaru Island, Vietnam.

14:00 A Vietnamese naval official said the flight had crashed into the sea.

14:30 Malaysia Airlines defined the event as a disappearance at the first press conference.

15:10 The Malaysian Minister of Transport denied that Malaysia Airlines Flight MH370 had crashed.

15:52 China's specialist rescue vessel departed for the scene.

16:00 The original scheduled news conference of the Prime Minister was delayed.

16:33 Malaysia, Vietnam and Singapore started a joint search and rescue operation.

17:32 Vietnam said the plane may have crashed in the maritime waters on the Malaysia-Vietnam border (this statement is worthy of attention).

At 0:36:30 on March 8, 2014, MH370 moved into runway A10 32R ready to take off. At 0:42:05 it left the ground and climbed 35,000 feet (10,668 metres) to reach its cruising altitude 50 minutes 06 seconds later. Its communication frequency was 132.6MC. At 1:19:24 on March 8, air traffic control called: 'MH370, please contact Ho Chi Minh City', communication frequency 120.9 MC. At 1:19:29, MH370 responded: 'OK, good night.'

At 1:38, ATC officers at Ho Chi Minh City informed Kuala Lumpur officials that the flight has disappeared from Vietnam's civilian radar.

At 09:30, The VP of Malaysia Airlines told a CNN reporter that the last time MH370 had transmitted data to the ground, it had dropped more than 200 metres and turned its heading from 24° to 333°. It lost contact at 02:40 minutes, Vietnam time.

At 10:43 on the 8th, an iPad user from Flightradar 24 stated, 'We are monitoring the MH370 event all the time. The last data of our radar receiver were a change from FL350 to 0. Pray for peace!'

On March 8, Malaysia Airlines website issued a statement saying that the final position of Flight MH370 on radar was N06° 55'15 ', E103° 34'43'.

Associated Press reported that the Boeing 777 was the world's most popular and safest jet. In 19 years of service, there had been only one fatal crash, in July the previous year, when an Asian Airlines aircraft had crashed at San Francisco airport; of the 307 people on board, three were killed. Malaysia Airlines had suffered an accident in August 2005 when a 777 had flown from Perth, Australia to Kuala Lumpur. When the plane was cruising at 11580 metres above the Indian Ocean, its software calculated the speed and acceleration inaccurately, resulting in the aircraft suddenly rising 915 metres.

According to a German news agency, Fan Guixiao, Vice Minister of the Vietnam Transportation Ministry, announced that at 5:20 pm, two oil slicks had been discovered, one 150 km from Soil Pearl Island, Vietnam, the other 190 km from Cape Ca Mau. In accordance with the relevant provisions of the International Civil Aviation Organisation, once the flight had lost contact for more than 30 seconds, airlines need to start the relevant response, including releasing and updating public information as soon as possible. MH370 lost contact at 1.20 am, but Malaysia Airlines did not announce this information until 7 am.

According to the families gathered in the Beijing Lido Hotel, a delegation of about 100 people from MA headquarters had departed from Kuala Lumpur airport at 4 pm and were expected to arrive at 10 pm. Facing the media, family members were reluctant to express their views. They looked upset and some were panicking. At the news of the disappearance, some families became very excited; some collapsed on the spot, stamping and crying; many broke down in tears. A middle-aged woman said her daughter, son-in-law and grandchildren were on the flight.

The *New York Times* reported a US government official as saying that the Pentagon used a search system that could search for any flashes to analyse the preliminary monitoring data collected from the ticket counters, security areas and boarding areas related to the vanished aircraft, but failed to find any evidence that an explosion had occurred. Among the passengers, there was a tourist group consisting of 23 Chinese, on average 60 years old, who had just completed a holiday in Nepal and had chosen to transfer at Kuala Lumpur airport for their return journey to Beijing. Fortunately, 14 of them chose to transfer at Guangzhou Airport and hence escaped.

At 9:00 on March 8, the fuel loaded for seven hours of flight must have run out. At 12:28, Premier Li Keqiang gave important instructions on the disappearance of the flight from Kuala Lumpur to Beijing: please promptly start the emergency procedure to strengthen communication with the Malaysian civil aviation department, making sure to devote resources fully to the search and verify the specific situation of Chinese passengers on board. They must make joint preparations for an emergency rescue with the foreign parties under the framework of overseas Chinese citizens' protection mechanism, and would work with the local authorities to carry out communication with the passengers' families.

At 14:47 on March 8, the general secretary of the CPC Central Committee, state president and CMC Chairman Xi Jinping, gave important instructions. He asked the Ministry of Foreign Affairs and China's relevant embassies and consulates to strengthen contact with the relevant departments of the host country, to pay close attention to the progress of the search and rescue operation and to do their best for the emergency procedures and the care of Chinese citizens. The Ministry of Transport, Civil Aviation Authority and other relevant departments should immediately start the emergency procedures, actively cooperate in the relevant work and further strengthen the field of civil aviation security checks to ensure the absolute safety of civil aviation operations.

On March 9th Zulkifeli Mohd Zin, Commander-in-Chief of the Malaysian Armed Forces, said that a total of 22 aircraft and 40 ships from Malaysia, China, the Philippines, the United States and Singapore were searching in the South China Sea, as well as the unknown search ships and aircraft in Vietnam's territory. The Vietnamese aircraft found, in the waters between Malaysia and Vietnam, two 15-to-20-km long parallel oil traces, 500 metres apart, as well as other debris, suspected to be related to the plane.

The US Embassy in China revealed that an American base in Thailand had heard the SOS signal sent by China Southern Airlines flight CZ748, which shared its communication code with MH370. The embassy said the call from that aircraft's pilots showed the plane was in danger of disintegration and was ready for a forced landing.

The Commander of the Malaysian Air Force, General Rosari Daoud, said the change of direction of the aircraft had been confirmed by civilian radar. They were expanding the search for aircraft wreckage to the coast of Malaysia. On the 9th, the Chinese government took comprehensive measures involving the civil aviation, diplomatic, maritime rescue and maritime police. They could only pray for the survival of the people on board. On the afternoon of the 9th, Marine Police ship 3411 arrived in the area where MH370 was suspected of having disappeared. Two warships, *Jinggangshan* and *Mianyang*, were also on their way. The US military sent a missile destroyer, *Pinckney*, and a maritime patrol aircraft, *Orion*.

On the 9th, Hong Kong's 'Apple Daily' reported that a Malaysian passenger aircraft was missing in bizarre circumstance, the passengers in danger. But in dealing with the passenger list, the authorities were surprised to find that two of them, Italian Luigi Lardi and an Austrian, had not boarded the plane at all. They had claimed that their passports had been stolen in Thailand, so someone else must have boarded the plane with their passports. Interpol sources said that the details of the stolen Italian passport were in its database, but the details of the stolen Austrian passport were not. The Malaysian authorities apparently did not inquire about the Interpol database.

Hissam Ding Hussein, Malaysian Defence Minister and Minister of Transport, said that an attack was only one possibility, and other possibilities could not be excluded, including shooting. The airport authorities were investigating security checks on passengers and luggage. When someone asked if he suspected a terrorist attack, Mohammed Najib responded that all possibilities were being considered and it was too early to come to any conclusions.

At 11:30 on March 9, a Chinese Maritime police ship found two large oil slicks. One was 20 km long and 200 metres wide at longitude 103° 24 ', latitude 6°; the other was 13 kilometres long and 1 km wide, 119 kilometres from the search area. Floating oil stains were broken into separate pieces with large pieces of about 70 square metres and small areas of about 7 to 8 square metres. Samples were collected in cans and sent to the authorities for checking. The checking would take a day. However, as there were many drilling platforms there, many ships were moving to and fro and oil leaks were common.

MH370 had been loaded with enough fuel for 8 hours' flight. There should be 55 tons left minus forty minutes' worth of consumption. Aviation oil is much lighter than general fuel.

On the 10th, according to the NASA satellite pictures released, an accurate 250 square metre satellite image of the relevant sea shot by NASA satellite TERRA MODIS at 11:35 on March 9 Beijing time, seemed to show the crash site. The location was about E104° 36', N6° 06'.

On the same day, China dedicated nine ships to search and rescue. Fortunately, the weather was fine with sea visibility 5 to 10 km and waves only 1-2 metres high. There were now more than 40 ships from seven countries participating in the search and rescue operation. Xiong Jie, Deputy Director of China's Civil Aviation Authority Aviation Safety Office, explained that a sudden loss of the radar signal is very rare in the history of civil aviation, so it was hard to guess the specific reasons. According to international civil aviation practice, if an aircraft's wreckage is not found at the end of the search and rescue operation, it can be defined as a missing flight.

On March 10th, the Chinese Ministry of Transport, the State Oceanic Administration, the General Staff, the Chinese Maritime Police and the Navy jointly and developed a search and rescue programme. A number of satellites were mobilized to support the search on land and in the air, taking advantage of their high-resolution imaging of the ground, visible light photography and other technologies. Any relationship between a suspicious life-saving vest found by a Hong Kong business aircraft in the disappearance zone and the vanished flight was denied. Also denied was the claim that floating oil found about 100 nautical miles from Kelantan coast north-east of Malay Peninsula was connected to MH370.

The same day, the crew of a Thai aircraft reported, around 3 pm, finding debris near Vung Tau in south-east Vietnam. But the distribution of these fragments was not in line with the scheduled route of MH370, as it was 125 km to the south-east. Vietnamese border guards, naval and fishermen vessels searched the 60 kilometres southeast of Vung Tau without result. The debris discovered by US warships turned out to be some unrelated fragments.

Fake passports become the biggest threat. An Italian and an Austrian both looked like Asians, and neither of them boarded.

On the evening of October 10, the Chinese government sent, to Kuala Lumpur International Airport, a joint working group headed by Guo Shaochun, Deputy Director of the Ministry of Foreign Affairs, to work with the Malaysian government. The Chinese Ministry of Public Security also sent a working group to investigate who had stolen the two passports.

On the afternoon of March 11, the Malaysian officials promised to give each family member a special sum of condolence money of to 31,000 RMB, which must not be regarded as compensation.

On the same day, Interpol held a press conference in Lyon, France to say that one of the owners of the stolen passports was currently travelling in Thailand and the other was in Austria. Their passports had been stolen in Thailand two years before. Now the two who were using them were Iranians, one 19 years old and the other 29. They had first entered Malaysia with their own real passports, and then boarded MH370 with the fake passports. The two were not suspected terrorists. With more and more information available to Interpol, the possibility that terrorists had attached the plane was declining.

By 18:00 on March 11, a total of 6,000 square km had been covered by boats, aircraft and merchant ships with nothing suspicious found. Vietnam decided to extend the search to the waters north-west of Phu Quoc Island and north-east of Ca Mao port, all the way to the shore. The straight-line distance between Vietnam's southernmost point to Malaysia is about 360 km. If 3000 square kilometres was searched per day, 100,000 square kilometres would not take long to search.

Malaysia then indicated that if no clues were found in the current search areas, they were considering investigating the possibility that MH370 had flown back to Subang. The first Chinese families of the missing people arrived in Kuala Lumpur. Wang Mingcai, the Malaysia Airlines spokesman, said in Beijing at 6 o'clock on March 11 that the search and rescue had covered the eastern and western Malay Peninsula without success.

Then the Malaysian military announced that after the last contact with Civil Aviation Air Traffic Control at the country's east coast, MH370 had changed its heading and flown west for hundreds of kilometres. A senior officer told reporters: 'After Kota Bharu, the aircraft changed its route, reduced height and flew to the Malacca Strait.' This seems to rule out the possibility of a sudden major mechanical failure, for it had continued to fly for at least 500 km after its last contact. Malaysia now ruled out five possible causes for MH370's disappearance: hijacking, disintegration in the air, radar and electronic failure and others.

On the 11th, John Brennan, head of the US Central Intelligence Agency, said the possibility of terrorist attacks could not be ruled out.

On the 12th, a Malaysian government and military conference was filled with the smell of gunpowder. The Malaysian Air Force Commander, Rodzali Daoud, confirmed that at 2:15 am on the 8th, about 55 minutes after Flight MH370 lost both communication and radar signals in the ATC zone, Ho Chi Minh City, Malaysian Air Force radar detected a flying object about 320 km north-west of Penang. We did not know whether it was Flight MH370 as its identity was not confirmed. Hussein: "The flight may have turned around, although this is unlikely. We are still investigating and viewing radar data, but we have decided that it is necessary to extend the search to this area, the Malacca Strait.

A spokesman for the Premier's office said there had been no

notification from the military that the flight had flown across the Malaysian peninsula and arrived in the Malacca Strait.

An Indonesian Air Force official said Indonesia had received official information from the Malaysian authorities that the flight flew back, when it was about 20 kilometres east of Kota Bharu, Malaysia, to the Malacca Strait and then lost contact.

The feelings of the Malaysians changed from patience as they waited for the search for the lost flight to embarrassment and dissatisfaction over their failure to find it. The search and rescue personnel had previously focused on searching the waters between eastern Malaysia and Vietnam, but by that afternoon they had not found any clues to MH370. Vietnam had stopped aerial searching and narrowed its sea search. 'We informed Malaysia the day it disappeared that we had noticed that the flight had turned west, but we were not answered,' said Fan Xiao, on behalf of Vietnam.

On March 12th, at the request of the Malaysian side, Indonesia began to help with the search in the Andaman Sea in the Eastern Indian Ocean. China's war ship *Kunlun Mountains* arrived in Thailand Bay. The search area was adjusted, from the original 90 × 25 nautical miles to 60 × 60 nautical miles, a westward expansion. The Malaysian Ambassador to China said that a pilot had said 'Good, good night' as the aircraft flew from Malaysian airspace into Vietnamese airspace. Interpol Secretary General Noble said: 'The more information we have, the more we think this is not a terrorist attack.'

On the 12th, before the search and rescue operation became long and costly, teams were racing against time to find MH370's flight data recorder. The battery life of the location beacon was 30 days. If they could not find it within that time, they knew it would become much harder to locate it in the future. The other means of locating the missing aircraft had expired. Any signal from the emergency positioning transmitter (ELT) can only be received for the first 24 hours.

Many parts of the world are not covered by radar stations, and many others are covered by only one. Radar coverage at sea is particularly low because there is nowhere to place radar stations. Space radar is not used to track civilian aircraft. The navigation system on the plane knows the location of the plane – via GPS – but will not send this information back to Earth Station. If the plane crashed in the middle of the South China Sea, any emergency transmitter on the machine would send a signal that could spread far through the air, but it would not travel far in water.

On the 12th, senior US intelligence officials said the US spy satellites had not detected signs of an air explosion after Flight MH370 disappeared. By then China had been searching the waters for 100 hours, with a total coverage of 45,763 square kilometres. Chinese Premier Li Keqiang said: 'as long as there is a glimmer of hope, we will never give up search and rescue.'

'Malaysia should be criticized - they are very bad about it,' said Ernest Bower, an American expert on Southeast Asia. At 13:06 that day, the United States investigation agency said the aircraft had continued to fly for another four hours after it lost contact.

On March 13th, Xia Xinghua, deputy director of the China Civil Aviation Administration, made four suggestions to the Malaysian side: first, they hoped that the Malaysians would continue to expand the scope of the search and rescue, intensify efforts, and coordinate cooperation and information sharing between search and rescue parties; second was to allow the Civil Aviation Administration of China to send expert teams to assist in search and rescue, and to provide technical support; the third was to inform the Chinese side immediately of any developments; and the fourth was to ask Malaysia Airlines to send people in Beijing to look after the passengers' families.

By the morning of the 13th, Flight MH370 had been out of touch for more than five days and there was still no definite information. The multinational team of search and rescue personnel continued to search a vast area from Vietnam to the Andaman Sea, but the information about the final flight route and location of the flight was confusing. The Malaysian military had found an unknown signal received in Malacca.

Malaysian Civil Aviation said they thought the flight had turned around, but they were not sure. The Malaysian Prime Minister's office did not know. The Malaysian civil aviation authorities and the military said the aircraft might lose contact before re-entry, but re-entry direction and re-entry flight distance are different.

At a press conference on March 23, the Chinese Foreign Ministry spokesman, Qin Gang, talking about the rumours that MH370 had flown back on itself before its disappearance, told reporters that China had asked the Malaysian side through diplomatic channels to immediately check rumours about the re-entry and make appropriate arrangements to expand the scope of the search and rescue.

The US media quoted a US official as saying the aircraft had gone on sending a pulse signal to the satellite several hours after it had disappeared. Affected by this new information, the United States sent warships and reconnaissance planes to search the Indian Ocean. On March 13 and 14, Britain and America cooperated closely to bring the world's attention to the Indian Ocean.

On the 14th, Reuters quoted Malaysian military sources as saying that MH370 might have flown to the Andaman Islands in the Indian Ocean: 'We cannot rule out the possibility of sabotage or hijacking'.

From the South China Sea to the wider and deeper Indian Ocean, the search difficulty would undoubtedly increase greatly. 'It's like moving from a chessboard to a soccer field,' said Commander Marx, the seventh US Fleet Commander. Investigators in the United States believed that the aircraft data reporting system and radar transceiver shut off at different times, one 14 minutes after the other. This showed that it may have been done deliberately, but it also shows that the aircraft initially lost contact, and it might not be caused by a catastrophic accident to the fuselage. Reuters said officials were now focusing on suspicions that the missing aircraft was associated with malicious action. On March 14th, When the airliner is suspected of changing its course intentionally after turning from the IGARI navigation point between Malaysia and Vietnam, Reuters suggested that the plane had been guided by aviation professionals through multiple navigation points. Malaysian police senior officials confirmed that the Malaysian side had begun to focus on investigating the idea that the pilot had deliberately changed course.

On the 14th, Reuters and Associated Press from Washington, Kuala Lumpur and Paris, said that after the aircraft had disappeared from radar, more than one satellite had received a weak electronic pulse signal from it. However, it was hard to determine where it went and what happened to it. Associated Press said Boeing had offered a satellite connection service to enable the aircraft to send data to the satellite, but Malaysia Airlines had not registered for this service. As for the authenticity of the news, Boeing and the engine company declined to comment.

On the 14th at 17:00, Vietnam released the news that an An-26 aircraft had detected a 20-mile long patch of spilt fuel in the southwest corner of Ca Mau. At 18:00, Sea Patrol 31 sailed from the Gulf of Thailand to the designated sea waters of the Malacca Strait and started to search. The *New York Times* said that the United States experts had become the main investigation force. 'We try not to let people feel that we are in charge of the investigation, although to some extent, we are,' they said.

The Vietnamese search and rescue operation was downgraded from 'emergency' to 'normal' and they stopped the operation on March 15.

Aircraft engine manufacturer Rolls-Royce said that the argument that the aircraft had continued to fly several hours after it had disappeared from the radar screen was not correct. Indonesian airlines flight analyst Soja Terman said: 'How could the aircraft fly over so many radars without being found? If it did, how many people are going to lose their jobs in the army?'

On the 15th, Shenzhen Economic Daily quoted the China Daily as saying that at 2:55 pm on March 8 local time, the Wen Lianxing research group, Earthquake and Earth Physics Laboratory, University of Science and Technology of China had detected an undersea event in the sea waters between Malaysia and Vietnam at N7° 25', E104° 30', 116 km from where MH370 had disappeared. This latitude is consistent with the author's opinion. But the time difference between the two events is 1.5 hours, and the distance difference, shown on the map is about 100 km from the intersection point of disappearance of the radar signals. But that the two event could have been be the same thing can be explained.

On the 15th, The whole search and rescue work was shifted to the world's third ocean, the Indian Ocean, with an average water depth of nearly 3900 metres.

The American Broadcasting Company reported that because new information showed that the disappearing aircraft had carried out a 'tactical avoidance operation', trying to avoid radar surveillance, US intelligence officers tended to believe that MH370's pilots bore some responsibility and their behaviour seemed to be subjective and intentional. The disappearance of Flight MH370 was caused by its 'cockpit cabin crew'.

Malaysian Prime Minister Najib presided in person over a

press conference on March 15th. He said the communication system of MH370 was turned off, and the plane had deliberately turned to the west, but we cannot conclude that this implied a hijack. The last time the aircraft had sent out the satellite signal was at 8:11, March 8. He said that although the exact location of the airliner was still unknown, it was believed to be along one of two flight corridors based on new satellite data: one was the north side of northern Thailand to Kazakhstan and the other was to the south of Indonesia to Indian Ocean. He said the new satellite information would have a significant impact on search operations, and Malaysia would stop searching in the South China Sea and redeploy search operations. During the period, 13 countries participated in the search. By 18:00 on the 18th, China had searched for 150 hours in the suspected sea area, covered 89052 square kilometres and scanned and explored 8441.3 kilometres.

On the 15th, the Washington Post reported that the investigators believed that MH370 had departed from the established route. Maritime satellite headquarters said its satellite network received the 'conventional, automatic signal' sent by MH370. After the aircraft disappeared from the ATC's screen on the east coast of Malaysia, it was tracked by the satellite over the Indian Ocean for nearly six hours. After the last radar record, an automated system on the aircraft linked to the satellite five times. The plane stopped sending signals at 8 am March 8 local time. The aviation community and investigators were increasingly sceptical that the plane had been hijacked. The various communication systems on the plane seemed to have been artificially and gradually closed, including radar transponders that provide details such as aircraft identity, speed, altitude, and heading.

Since the 16th, the Malaysian side strengthened their investigation into the aircraft crew and passengers, with focus on the two pilots. It was said that the two pilots had not asked to fly together. It was also said that investigators had found a flight simulator in the pilot's house. From then on, suspicion began to be directed at Captain Zahari. These were the reasons:

1. The simulator in the home had been used to drill 'evasive action' (to avoid radar, or to avoid lightning?)

2. Several hours before the flight, he participated in a court hearing, and may have felt unhappy.

3. He may have received terrorist training.

4. His family moved away a day before the plane disappeared.

The Director of Malaysia Airlines said that when the aircraft had sent signals to the satellite, it may have been on land (I also think so).

On the 16th, A person in charge of the investigation had previously driven the same model of aircraft along the suspected flight route, and thus determined that MH370 had turned west. The plane also returned halfway, across the Malaysian peninsula, and then headed north.

By now 25 countries had sent more than 40 ships, 58 aircraft and search teams. On the 16th, India stopped searching in the bay of Bengal and Andaman Sea. Indian radar can detect at a range up to 200 nautical miles. The Andaman Sea can be surveyed.

After the disappearance of MH370, a Taiwan Buddhist charity, the Tzu Chi Charity Foundation, sent volunteers to Beijing to provide translation services, help families apply for passports and visas and resolve the contradictions between MAS and the passengers' families. On the 16th, Boeing revealed that Malaysia Airlines had not bought its aircraft status management (AHM) service. As long as an aircraft is still running, the communication device attached to AHM remains in 'standby' status. The communication device automatically transmits a pulse signal every hour, indicating that it is on standby. Then the signal used to analyse and calculate the track of the disappearing aircraft is intercepted by the same geostationary satellite, so the arc can only be of the same radius. If another synchronous satellite receives the signal at the same time, it can calculate another radius and its arc; the intersection of the two arcs is the position from which the plane is transmitting.

On the 17th, the US destroyer withdrew from the Southern Indian Ocean search. The number of countries participating in search and rescue increased to 26: China, Malaysia, Vietnam, Australia, Bangladesh, Brunei, France, the United States, the United Kingdom, New Zealand, South Korea, Singapore, Pakistan, India, Indonesia, Japan, Kazakhstan, Myanmar, Thailand, Turkmenistan, Russia, United Arab Emirates, Laos, Kyrgyzstan, Uzbekistan and the Philippines.

On the 17th, at a press conference, the Malaysian side disclosed some details. After the last contact with the satellite at 8:11 am on March 8, the fuel in the aircraft could support about 30 minutes' flight. (Note: in 30 minutes MH370 could have flown 400-500 kilometres. Can this contact be confirmed? Can it be identified as MH370's last contact?)

At this time, the Malaysian investigators were checking the background of the pilots, crew and associated ground crew. There was no problem with the boarding and security of the crew and passengers.

Australian sources said that almost all the Indian Ocean had no radar coverage. If a commercial airliner crashes, ships cannot find it; radar can hardly detect it; and satellites can scarcely help. In addition, Pakistan, Kazakhstan, India and other countries denied one after another the suspicion that the disappearing aircraft had entered their territory. The Malaysian side said that the internal security warning information was working very well and had found no aircraft heading for cities or other land destinations.

On the 17th, Ahmad Jauhuri Yahyain, Malaysia Airlines' CEO, said at a press conference that at 1:19 pm on the 8th co-pilot Hamid had completed the last call with the ground control centre with: 'Good, good night.' the last communication of ACARS system with the ground control centre was at 01:07. Since the system is linked to the ground control centre every 30 minutes, it may be artificially shut off at any time within 30 minutes. (Note: the aircraft crashed in this period!) In general, if military radar control personnel spot a UFO, they tend to contact the civil aviation radar control personnel to verify the target and see if it target has answered. If not, the control personnel will attempt to contact the aircraft via radio. If they still do not get a response, the ground will take the final action of deploying fighters. No action was seen to be taken by the Malaysian military.

At 17:30 on the 17th, at a Kuala Lumpur press conference, the MAS chief executive stated that there were no signs of fighting on MH379, nor was there any evidence that the passengers' phones had been used.

The Indian Foreign Minister, Hulshid, said intelligence information showed that there was no sign that the lost plane is trying to carry out a 9/11-style terrorist attack on India. According to New York public radio, MH370's landing runway requires a length of 1500 metres, and of the 634 runways in the 26 countries within the aircraft's cruising range, only four meet this requirement: Christmas Island, Cocos coral reefs, Mu Cloud Qom Desert and Kyzylkum Desert.

On the 17th, the UN said no explosion or plane crash had been detected on land or water that week. On the 18th, the Chinese Ambassador to Malaysia, Huang Huikang, confirmed that

China did not find any possible evidence for of terrorist attacks and other destructive activities through the investigation of passengers from China's mainland. This basically excluded the involvement of the Iranian passengers and the possibility of the aircraft having crashed in the Malacca sea area.

On the 18th, Laos civil aviation chief said the flight had not entered Laos airspace. The same day, the United States denied any reports of the disappearing aircraft landing on the Diego Garcia Island US military base in the Indian Ocean. A Thai Air Force spokesman said military radar had received Flight MH370's track and communications data normally until 1:22 March 8, when the aircraft disappeared from radar. Six minutes later, the military radar detected an unidentified object flying westward, seemingly MH370, filling the gap between the disappearance coordinates and the coordinates of the spot where the plane went missing. (Note: when I checked the flight information for that time, I found that an unidentified flying object at 1:28 should have been a civil aircraft of another airline, not MH370.) Commander Bazin said Suratthani radar station detected a flight from Kuala Lumpur to the north which had turned around and flown to Malacca via the Malaysian city of Butterworth. Both Malaysia and Thailand were investigating the information to see whether the aircraft was MH370. The Malaysia Airlines CEO confirmed that the plane changed its course westward after the final call of the deputy captain.

The *New York Times* quoted an unnamed senior US official as saying that the computer system (Flight Management System FMS) on the plane is likely to have been changed by someone who was in the cockpit and was familiar with the system. This person made 7-8 keystrokes on a computer to key in the instructions. (Author note: if this information is true, MH370's disappearance is due to a hacker's or passenger's interference.) Usually before the flight, the height, destination and other information are entered in to the system, and then the aircraft can fly automatically in accordance with the scheduled route. Pilots can manually enter a new waypoint to change the route (though it must be approved by the command centre), but this is rarely used, and the destination cannot be changed.

On the 19th, Chinese Defence Ministry spokesman Geng Yansheng said: 'There are no signs of the aircraft entering China.' The Malaysian police chief announced that the flight records of the MH370 captain's aircraft had been deleted on February 3. The police were restoring the data. Transport Minister Hossain denied the report that before the final call of the deputy captain the plane had turned back.

By now 6,300,000 participants had helped the satellite search for MH370 through this platform, of which the United States accounted for 29.5%, and China 9.4%.

On March 20th, The Australian government said the Australians had found two objects in satellite images of the Southern Indian Ocean which were 'extremely likely' to be associated with the missing aircraft. One was 24 metres long and could be the tail fin of the aircraft, the other was 5 metres long. The satellite image, with a resolution of about 0.5 metres, was obtained on March 16 by the Digital Earth Company, referred to as DGI, a United States listed company. Because meteorological and hydrological conditions were not conducive to positioning, the rough data of the target area could only be given as about 2,300 kilometres southwest of Perth. (Note: the data of the 5 satellites should be retrieved from 00:00, March 8 to 00:00, 9 for analysis, rather than after 9th, for detailed interpretation.)

On the 21st, five aircraft flew out to search the area identified. International Maritime Satellite Organisation Vice President Chris McLaughlin told Xinhua News Agency reporters that on the 11th they had submitted MH370's satellite data to the Swiss-based International Aviation Telecommunications Group. These data should have been be transferred to Malaysia on the 12th, but Malaysia had not released them until the 15th. (Author's note: three days is enough for those with ulterior motives to change or even forge the data to serve their purpose.) McLaughlin continued that the company did receive signals from the disappearing aircraft, a pulse signal similar to the phone 'standby signal' automatically sent out once every hour. The satellite received a total of six or seven pulse signals from the disappearing aircraft. From the general position of these signals, the aircraft appeared to be in motion. But he stressed that the analysis of relevant clues should be scientific and careful.

On the 23rd, a French Foreign Ministry spokesman said that a French satellite using radar echo had found a suspicious floating object in the Indian Ocean region about 2,300 kilometres from Perth. The Australian Prime Minister said that the past 24 hours had witnessed three major pieces of progress:

First, the latest satellite images provided by China (at 18:00 on the 18th), they had found U-shaped and at least one resembled satellite images issued by Australian government last week

Second, the civilian aircraft searching in the Australian areas found some small pieces searching with the naked eye.

Third, China's and Japan's reconnaissance aircraft joined the search operation. As radar scanning was not effective, the search mainly depended on the searchers' naked eye observation of the sea situation from the air.

On the 23rd, The 'Abyss' submarine was ready to search, the *Daily Telegraph* website reported. There are only three such submarine in the world. They can dive 6000 metres underwater and stay there for 24 hours. These submarines are equipped with special sensors, cameras and ultra-sensitive sonar systems, like torpedoes.

On April 24, Mohammad Najib Abdul Razak said that according to the new analysis, Inmarsat and the British Air Traffic Investigation Bureau has concluded that MH370 was flying along the southern corridor, and its final position is in the middle of the Indian Ocean, west of Perth, Australia.

On March 24, Inmarsat vice-president McLaughlin said that although MH370 had turned off its communication system, the satellite could still receive a pulse signal from the aircraft every hour. This signal, a simple sound pulse, does not contain information like a global positioning system (GPS) data, time or location. Based on the time and elevation of these signals from the aircraft to the satellite, the Maritime Satellite Organisation was able to extrapolate that Flight MH370 flew for at least five hours along one of the two corridors in the north or the south. According to the Doppler effect, the signal frequency would vary with the movement of the satellite in the orbit. 'We do not know whether the plane has been flying at a fixed speed, and we do not know whether or not it may change direction, so we assume that the aircraft was flying at an automatic cruising speed at about flight level 350. We also screened a large number of electronic signals based on the fuel and flight data. 'The Malaysia flight was not forced to send out location signals, so we guessed its position, which had never been done before.'

On the 24th, Vice Minister Xie Hangsheng of the Ministry of Foreign Affairs met with the Malaysian ambassador to China and asked the Malaysian side to provide all relevant information and evidence on the analysis of the satellite data in the Indian Ocean as soon as possible. The U.S. Seventh Fleet commander said that because of the position of the wreckage that may have been found, the U.S. military had decided to call a 'drag and drop' acoustic locator. This locator has a high ability to detect sound signals. If the position is correct, it can receive, within 6000 metres, signals from the black box .

On the 25th, Inmarsat inferred that the final position of the aircraft was in the Southern Indian Ocean by using Doppler analysis of the acoustic pulse signals (not including GPS data and other information like time and location) issued by Malaysia Airlines flight. MH370's last 'handshake' with the satellite was at 8:11, March 8, Beijing time, which is consistent with the maximum range of the aircraft.

On the 26th, an international working group on the task of analysing satellite data was set up, composed of relevant institutions from Malaysia, China, the United States and the United Kingdom, including Inmarsat, the British Air Traffic Investigation Service, the General Administration of Civil Aviation of China, the US National Security Transport Committee , Boeing and engine manufacturers. About 2,500 kilometres west of Perth, some 122 suspected floating objects (some up to 23 metres long) were identified over 400 square kilometres. Chris McLaughlin, Inmarsat' senior vice president for external affairs, said that the analysis on the 'ultimate ending' of the aircraft was 'not very accurate'.

On the 26th, the Australia Broadcasting Corporation website reported that now that MH370 had been determined to have disappeared in the Southern Indian Ocean, concerns had shifted to find the aircraft's black box. A US law firm said the families of the parties had reached an agreement to proceed with the prosecution of Malaysia Airlines and Boeing. The focus was on Boeing. They stated: 'We understand that equipment failure in the cockpit, resulting in loss of awareness of the crew, or body design defects led to loss of pressure in the cabin, resulting in two pilots losing consciousness.'

On the 29th, The Australian Department of Defence announced that the Australian Navy's rescue ship 'Ocean Shield', armed with black box positioning equipment provided by the United States, was expected to sail to the target area on the 30th. Hishamuddin Tun stated: 'There is little chance of life'. A British newspaper criticized the search as full of chaotic and wrong information.

On the 30th, a United States senator stated that no evidence had been found that showed the loss of the aircraft was associated with terrorism.

On the 31st, Nanfang Daily reported that 24 insurance companies had agreed to pay insurance claims to about 190 MH370 passengers, with an estimated claim of over 30 million yuan. An Australian Maritime Safety Bureau spokesman confirmed that the suspected objects were fishing equipment and other floating waste, definitely not associated with MH370.

April 2014

On April 2, Malaysia police chief Barkar said all passengers had been excluded from any suspicion of having personal or psychological problems that might have led to them being involved in hijacking or deliberately destroying an aircraft. The British nuclear power submarine 'Impeccable' arrived to participate in the search. The 22 million square kilometres of ocean 1500 km west of Perth became the focus of the search. On April 3, they searched 2.23 million square kilometres of sea 1,680 km north-west of Perth. On the 4th, Australia announced that the search key area would move north to the waters near latitude 20 degrees north, longitude 100 degrees east, an area the equivalent of China's Hunan province.

On the 4th, Battelle, the manufacturer of the acoustic transmitters in the black box, said they had been produced in 2005 and the second half of 2006 respectively, and should have been overhauled or replaced in 2012. Malaysia Airlines had not done so in recent years. If they had not got another company to replace them, the batteries for these acoustic transmitters had been in use for eight years. Battery life may have been reduced from 30 days to 20 or 25 days.

On the 5th, at 16:30, the ship Sea Patrol 01 detected, through its black box search instrument, a suspected pulse signal with a length of 90 seconds or so and a frequency of 37.5KHz per second in the Southern Indian Ocean waters near latitude 25 degrees, 101 degrees east. The signal had been heard but not recorded on April 4. On the 5th, 'Ocean Shield' intercepted the suspected signals at 16:45 and 21:27 respectively. The black box on a Boeing 777 carries an underwater locator beacon (ULB) which will be activated and send out a continuous pulse signal of 37.5KHZ for about 30 days once the aircraft sinks into the water. These signals can be detected by sonar and acoustic positioning device.

On the 6th, the Australian chief coordinator said that in addition to the suspicious pulse signal detected by China's ship Sea Patrol 01, another suspicious pulse signal was found by the Ocean Shield at a place about 550 km from where the Chinese side intercepted the signal. Search forces from many countries were making further efforts at these two different locations.

On the 8th, Houston said that they had detected the signals again respectively at 16:27 and 22:17on the 8th. The first the signal lasted for 5 minutes 32 seconds and the second 7 minutes. Of the four signals, the shortest distance between them was about 5 km minimum, the longest about 10 km. The frequency of these signals was 33.3 kHz, different from the 37.5 kHz of the black box. On the 9th, Houston told reporters: 'We are searching the right area, but we need to see the wreckage before we can fully confirm that this is the final resting place for MH370.'

The results of the satellite data analysis led the investigators to conclude that the Boeing 777 fell in a distant area in the Indian Ocean, about 2,260 kilometres north-west of Perth. On the 10th, the Australian Coordination Centre issued a statement confirming that an Australian patrol aircraft, 'Orion', had detected again the suspected black box's underwater pulse signal in the afternoon, near the location of 'Ocean Shield'.

A reporter from *21st Century Business Herald* interviewed people about Captain Zahari. According to his classmates and friends, he did not have any motivation or impulse to perform a terrorist action that would destroy his happy life, regardless of speculation by the outside world.

On the 11th, Australian Prime Minister Tony Abbott said in Shanghai that they knew the black box's location to within a kilometre range, but that did not mean they could find the wreckage.

On the 12th, the *New Straits Times*, Malaysia, reported that a member of the crew had used a cellphone to 'call for help' when the aircraft flew over Penang, the same day MH370 had disappeared. By investigation, the call had come from co-pilot Rachman's cell phone. Through the mobile phone application software inquiries, the last record of Rachman's mobile phone was at 23:30 March 7, that is, before he boarded MH370.

On the 14th, USA Today reported that as the black box had now gone silent, the hunt for MH370 turned to underwater searching. A US-made underwater search engine, 'Bluefin 21', would be deployed on the evening of the 14th to the Southern Indian Ocean for ocean floor detection. Britain's The Independent website reported that investigators had said the plane could have ascended to 45,000 feet (13,700 metres) before disappearing - 10,000 feet higher than the normal cruise altitude of 35,000 feet – then dropped to 5,000 feet.

On the 14th, the Australian Coordination Centre said they believed that the batteries of the two pulse transmitters on Flight MH370 had been exhausted. On the 15th, the search area was re-designated as a total area of 62023 square kilometres, 2170 kilometres north-west of Perth, slightly larger than the previous one. On the 17th, Agence France-Presse Washington reported that security experts had said that the security flaws of many satellite communications system would become the target of hackers, a potential threat to aviation, shipping, military and other areas. All satellite systems have multiple 'high-risk' vulnerabilities: 'These vulnerabilities may enable malicious attackers to intercept, manipulate, or block communications, and sometimes even remotely control physical devices.' For aircrafts and ships, attackers can 'cheat data' to block or interfere with emergency communications. Tampering with airliner communications is technically possible. Vulnerabilities mainly exist in ground equipment connected with satellites.

On the 20th, Mr Bizley, the Australian Ambassador to the United States, said that if the scanning of the Indian Ocean by the US Navy underwater unmanned aerial vehicle yielded no discovery, they would change the deployment and reconsider the search operation.

On the 20th, MAS began to discuss economic assistance with the families. On the 21st in Australia, The *Sydney Morning Herald* said that the military sensitivity and geopolitical environment reflected in the searches for MH370 offered 'a unique flavour' to the search. The *New Straits Times* reported that MH370 may have landed somewhere rather than ended up in the Southern Indian Ocean.

On the 22nd, the joint coordination centre stated that Bluefin 21 had completed its ninth underwater search task, covering 80% of the underwater core area, still without any discovery. On the 23rd, Reuters reported in Hong Kong that the search for the disappearing aircraft had exposed Chinese military shortcomings. At some point in the future, they must address the lack of secure access to ports. With the growth of the Chinese Navy, this would become a potential strategic dilemma. China's satellites lacked the capacity to monitor global aviation.

On the 24th, the coordination centre stated that there was still nothing found after searching more than 90% of underwater core area. On the 29th, the Malaysian Defence Minister said that India, Bangladesh and other countries in the north had announced that they had never, in their airspace, detected the aircraft. This jet had contacted an Inmarsat satellite a few hours after its disappearance. According to this data, it is concluded that this aircraft ended in the Southern Indian Ocean.

May 2014

On May 1, the preliminary investigation report was released; the air search was stopped and underwater searching would be stepped up. Malaysia would will issue a preliminary investigation report on the disappearance. It was understood that many countries' aircraft had stopped their search work. The search work had entered the deep-sea stage, which would require negotiations between many countries and organisations.

Bluefin 21 had now completed a search of about 314 square kilometres of the underwater core area and would continue to search the areas adjacent to the core area. The air search was called off.

After 52 days of intense but fruitless search, all the planes from various countries that had participated in the search for MH370 officially stopped the aerial search work. By April 28, a total of 10 civilian aircraft and 19 military aircraft, Including seven from the Australian Air Force, one from the New Zealand Air Force, two US aircraft, two Chinese Air Force aircraft, three Japanese military planes, two South Korean aircraft and two Malaysian Air Force aircraft had participated, as well as a total of 14 ships from Australia.

On May 1st, Malaysia released the first MH370 survey report, which mentioned the seven handshake signals, including the last one at 8:11 local time, transmitted by the plane's communications addressing and reporting system after the plane's normal communication stopped. The report also mentioned that the Malaysian transport minister had confirmed that its military aircraft had detected that a plane turned west and flew over the Malay Peninsula on the morning of March 8. (At 08:30 on the morning of March 8, Malaysian military played a military radar video and found an unidentified airliner flying westward towards the Indian Ocean, according to the *Wall Street Journal* website on May 2). The centre for the families of the passengers would be closed on the 7th, replaced by an SMS, telephone and network news service.

On the 2nd, the Xinhua News Agency published the first comprehensive comment on the disappearance of MH370, 'Common Adherence, Common Belief', summing up the search and rescue work by China after the event.

On the 3rd, the British *Daily Mail* reported that Malaysia had arrested 11 suspected terrorists related to the disappearance of MH370, but Malaysian police denied that Bada Te, a Muslim hidden in the UK, told the New York court via video that the event was plotted by Khaled Sheikh for Mohamed, the mastermind of 9/11, and that there were problems with the passengers' baggage, more than 4 tons of mangosteen and a number of lithium batteries. On the 5th, Malaysian police announced that the arrested 11 terrorists were not associated with the disappearance.

On the 5th, Australia, Malaysia and China held a trilateral meeting of ministers in Canberra to discuss the search for MH370. The three sides agreed to carry out the next phase of the search in the relevant areas of the Southern Indian Ocean, and invited all parties involved to bring in relevant professional equipment and companies and further improve their underwater search capacity and efficiency. The results of the search would be announced in time. An international panel of experts would reanalyse all data

More than 600 soldiers from at least seven countries involved in the search stood solemnly in front of their aircraft to have photos taken.

obtained so far to confirm again the correct search area.

The general coordinator, Mr Houston, said: 'We have come to a stage where a very sensible approach is to look back at all the data collected and all the analysis; make sure there are no bugs, confirm that the assumptions are correct and confirm that the analysis is correct, as well as the inference and the conclusion'. The Australian Deputy Prime Minister said: 'According to the information obtained, we believe that the search area is correct, but in fact, this confidence has not been translated into any traces of the discovery of the airliner. Unfortunately, all our efforts went nowhere.'

The Chinese Minister of Transport, Yang Chuan Tang, said that China would carry out four types of work: first, earnestly implement the search programme, sending three ships to participate. Second, actively support and use the business model and select a capable company for the search. Third, organise competitive Chinese companies to participate. Fourth, continue to send experts to participate in the search programme and accident investigation of the event.

On the 7th, the analysis of the data and information collected by the current search operation was started. It was estimated that the new search phase would cost Aus $60 million (US $55.91

million). To date, 334 aircraft had been involved in a search covering an range of about 4.5 million square kilometres.

On the 7th, the families of the lost passengers submitted an open letter to the Malaysian, Chinese and Australian governments, asking why the authorities were so sure that MH370 had crashed in the Indian Ocean. On the 9th, the French judiciary said that the French air gendarmerie would begin to investigate four Frenchmen on board, a criminal investigation on involuntary manslaughter. On the 13th, the 'Ocean Shield' returned to the search. The same afternoon Bluefin 21 encountered a communication failure after working in the waters for two hours and was brought on board. It was being debugged and would be sent for repair.

On May 18, Australia's *Sydney Morning Herald* reported that the Australian writer and journalist Nigel Cauthorn would be launching a book in Sydney on May 19 entitled *The Mystery of Flight MH370*, which supported the case for an accidental shootdown by Thailand and the United States during joint military exercises in the South China Sea. He believed the search and rescue teams may be headed in the wrong direction because the perpetrators wanted to cover up their mistakes. The party could spread misinformation through anonymous sources, causing people to search in the wrong place. He thinks Mike Mackay, the man who worked at a drilling platform in the Gulf of Thailand, had seen a burning plane before and after the 1:21 communication.

On the 18th, former Prime Minister of Malaysia Mr Mahathir said that the CIA and Boeing had deliberately concealed the facts in the disappearance of Flight MH370, so Malaysia Airlines and Malaysia should not become a scapegoat. He said that on the issue of the crash, it was very confusing that the international media did not doubt Boeing or the CIA.

On the 27th, the VOA radio website reported that MH370's raw satellite data released by Malaysia basically confirmed that it had crashed into the sea because of 'fuel exhaustion'. Malaysia Airlines released the original data of the disappearing aircraft, a document of 47 pages recording MH370's data and communications logs. With these logs, as well as related radar data and calculations of engine performance, international experts drew the conclusion that MH370 has ended in the Indian Ocean, that is, about 25 nautical miles from where the final pulse was transmitted. The fact that the last handshake between MH370 and the satellite is not consistent with the regular hourly signal transmissions may be because the fuel system was reset when the fuel was used up, said the transport bureau.

The Australian Transport Safety Authority also said for the first time that the search area intersected the only air route (route M641) across the Southern Indian Ocean. The route is from Cocos island to Perth, with four stops in the centre. Air lines are pre-set in aircraft computers, enabling automatic flight without human intervention, so the plane may fall when the crew are unconscious.

On the 29th, the Coordination Centre issued a statement that the search for the acoustic signal area had been completed and the region may not be the last resting place of Malaysia Airlines Flight 370. The search would continue by drawing a search area of 60,000 square kilometres along the southern part of the Indian Ocean, making a submarine map of the area through a deep sea survey, followed by a comprehensive seabed search by a professional service organisation. The first two steps were expected to take about 3 months; the underwater search was expected to start in August, taking 12 months.

June 2014

On June 3rd, at the request of the Malaysian government, Australia hosted the continued air search. The Australian government published tender documents, inviting contractors to search for Flight MH370. Requirements were time, 300 days; area: 60,000 square kilometres in the Southern Indian Ocean; demands: to draw 5000 square kilometres of the seabed map every 25 days, or deduct funds.

On the 4th, according to Agence France-Presse, Australia said the searchers had found a new clue. A 41-year-old British woman speedboat driver, Catherine Tee, reported that when she was sailing from Koch (India) to Phuket, Thailand in March, she saw a plane flying by with its tail trailing black smoke. She suspected the aircraft was on fire. At the same time, she also saw two other planes in the sky flying in another direction. (Note: there were three aircraft in the same area at the same time, confirming the results of my query.)

On the 4th, the Comprehensive Nuclear Test Ban Treaty Organisation Preparatory Committee announced that a special signal had been received from the Lu Yan Kok monitoring station in the West Bank of Australia at about 9:30 pm on March 8 (Beijing time). this special signal may have been due to earthquakes and other natural factors, but its time was so close to that when MH370 disappeared that it is worth the attention of the search team.

On the 7th, according to the Voice of Russia News, the families of the lost passengers from the United States, New Zealand, France and India were ready to raise $3 million as informant bonuses for anyone who provided important clues. The families of the Chinese and Malaysian passengers did not participate.

On the 8th, Singapore's Zaobao website reported that the families of the missing passengers were ready to publicly raise $5 million to search for the aircraft themselves. Of this money, $3 million would serve as an intelligence bonus to informants on the MH370 event, and the remaining $2 million would be the cost of hiring private investigators. The girlfriend of a 50-year-old missing man,

Philip Wood, told *USA Today*: 'they [the national search teams] spent $100 million and did not find anything in the end. Of course, we will not search by boat. We will use 'smart search'.'

On June 10th, the Australian Transport Safety Authority signed a contract with Fugro Mapping Co. Ltd. to entrust the company to carry out submarine mapping of the areas of seabed below where Flight MH370 may have crashed. Using a deep-sea multi-beam echo sounding search system, the latest data would be collected.

On the 26th, the Australian Deputy Prime Minister and Director of Transportation Safety announced at a joint press conference that MH370 was very likely to have been on autopilot, otherwise, the aircraft would not fly along the regular flight routes which can be detected by satellite. The new area was about 1,800 kilometres off the coast of Western Australia, and on the Seventh Arc, south of Bluefin 21' s search area. Underwater search would begin in August. 'We are convinced that it must have been be in an automatic flying mode when crossing the Indian Ocean until the fuel was exhausted,' said Martin Doran, Australian Transport Secretary.

July 2014

On July 6th, a Malaysian official said his country would send more equipment to the Southern Indian Ocean to participate in the search. Malaysian Defence Minister Hussein said a Malaysian naval vessel, equipped with a multi-beam echo detector, would be launched on August 4 in the search of the deep ocean away from Western Australia. The State Energy Corporation, the Malaysia National Petroleum Corporation, would deploy a drag and drop device called 'platform aperture sonar' to scan the seabed. The equipment is expected to be in place by mid-August.

On the 17th, a Malaysia Airlines Boeing 777 similar to MH370, on a flight from Amsterdam to Kuala Lumpur, was shot down by missiles when it flew over the eastern part of Ukraine.

August 2014

On August 20, news came that Chinese hackers had attacked the Malaysian government departments concerned with the search. The Malaysia network security chief said the malware, disguised as 'MH370 has been found' news reports, had been sent to Malaysian officials' emails on March 9.

On the 20th, Australian Prime Minister Tony Abbott said in an interview with the Australian Broadcasting Corporation that the underwater search for MH370 'had the opportunity to' find the aircraft, because the parties were using the latest technology, as long as the plane really had fallen into the Indian Ocean west of Australia.

On the 21st, the New Zealand air crash investigator and a New Zealand reporter co-authored a book called *Good Night, MH370*. The authors believed that Zahari had mental health problems. Forty minutes after the plane took off, he had cheated the deputy pilot into taking a rest and switched off the air-to-ground contact system. After breaking contact, he had pulled the plane up to 39,000 feet and decompressed the cabin, so that everyone in the cabin lost consciousness within 60 seconds.

On the 28th, The *Wall Street Journal* reported that the Australian government believed, according to a tentative telephone contact after the aircraft lost contact, that MH370 had turned south earlier than expected, which provided new clues for determining the aircraft's potential crash location in the Southern Indian Ocean. Investigators believed that it had sent out the last 'handshake' signal to the satellite at a point on the 7th arc.

September 2014

On September 27, 2014, the search teams released a detailed undersea image showing the sea floor features, including extinct volcanoes and 1,400-metre deep depressions.

October 2014

On October 5th, according to the Voice of China news, two vessels equipped with high-tech sonar devices and cameras, Phoenix and Exploration, would arrive in the Southern Indian Ocean to start a new phase in the search for Flight MH370.

On the 10th, the Australian Transportation Security Agency released the latest external aviation survey report — 'Analysis Progress on MH370's Flight Path'. The report, based on radar data and the signals received by the SATCOM satellite communication system, speculated that the aircraft may have spiralled down into the sea after its fuel was exhausted. The crash site is probably at a more southern position in the Seventh Arc.

On the 13th, *Reference News* reported that the President of Emirates Airlines questioned Malaysia Airlines' search operations. He believed that the aircraft may not have fallen into the Southern Indian Ocean. 'I'm sceptical about the so- called 'signal switching,' he said. On the 17th, *Reference News* reported that the second stage of the search had yielded no result. 670,000 square kilometres had now been searched without success.

On the 24th, the *Daily Telegraph* website reported that the wreckage of Flight MH370 may have drifted to Indonesia. After the search authorities had assessed that the wreckage was likely to drift westward from the crash site, Indonesia was advised to pay attention to the debris.

November 2014

On November 26th, according to Xinhua News Agency, Australian search staff said that Australia was studying a new ocean current model to expand the search range for the wreckage. Previous ocean current analyses showed that the aircraft could have drifted near the west coast of Sumatra, Indonesia, after 123 days since losing contact. (Is Flight MH370 made of wood? How could it drift 4,000 km to Sumatra?)

December 2014

In late December, this book, *MH370 Should Be Here* by Long Wen, was officially published by Hong Kong Kunpeng Publishing Co. Ltd. *Global Military* magazine ranked 'Where is MH370?' number two in the 2014 World Top Ten military suspense books.

January 2015

On January 29th, the Malaysia Civil Aviation Authority announced a formal farewell to Flight MH370. The official announcement that the aircraft had crashed cleared the way for the MSA to pay compensation to the families of the victims.
On the 30th, Malaysia Civil Aviation Bureau officials said at a technology conference held on Boutra Gaya that the underwater search for MH370 would be completed by May this year and about one-third of the search area had been covered so far.

February 2015

On February 22nd, someone mischievously spread the news on the Internet that Flight MH370 has been found, after clipping and editing a CCTV news broadcast on March 20, 2014. On the

24th, the British *Daily Mail* reported that an expert had said that Russia had hijacked Flight MH370, and secretly landed it in Kazakhstan.

On the 25th, the British Broadcasting Corporation website reported that air crash investigation expert Malcolm Brenner had pointed out that after MH370's last contact with the ground, it turned three times in the air. It turned left first and twice right, heading west and south to Antarctica.

March 2015

On March 1st, the *Sunday Times* reported that a British pilot had 'solved' MH370's mysterious disappearance. Simon Hardy, the captain of a Boeing 777, spent six months analysing the data and concluded that the actual location of the plane was about 100 nautical miles from where Australia was now searching. The plane had flown over Penang, Malaysia, and turned around the island three times; it did not crash into the sea, but landed on the surface and then sank into the water in one piece.

At the beginning of the month, this book, 'MH370 Should Be Here— Analyses of Its Disappearance and Whereabouts' had its second edition, which revised some fallacies in the first version and clearly put forth the theory that Flight MH370 did not fall into the Southern Indian Ocean, but had crashed into the ocean, mountains or forest south of Nam Can, Vietnam, in the range from N7° 25', E104° 30' to N8° 42', E104° 59' (later modified to around N7° 25', E103° 55').

On the 7th, the Malaysian Minister of Transport, Liow Tiong Lai, said that if the search yielded no result by the end of May, the three countries that led the search operation would re-examine the data and put forward a new plan.

On March 8th, the anniversary of the disappearance, the

Malaysian Prime Minister issued a statement cherishing and commemorating the 239 passengers, promising to continue to search and stating that he hoped the missing aircraft would eventually be found. The families of Flight MH370's missing passengers prayed at the Lama Temple in Beijing.

The Malaysian traffic safety investigation team and the Malaysia International Civil Aviation Organisation issued an interim survey report, 'Factual Information MH370's (9M-MRO) Security Investigation'. On March 8, 2014, between 01:19:30 to 02:02:41, all means of communication had been interrupted, and the Pacific satellite data were never seen again. Based on available data and relevant records analysis, no personnel or maintenance error related to the missing aircraft had been found.

On the 10th, the Australian Traffic Safety Bureau issued a message that a wet wipe 6 cm x by 8 cm and printed with the MSA logo had been found on July 2, 2014 on the shore at Thirsty Point, but it was difficult to determine whether it came from Flight MH370.

May 2015

On May 28th, Reuters reported that the search for MH370 led by Australia had found no clues and that the cost of the search was a record in the history of aviation, which incurred complaints and comments about reconsidering the search method.

A former French naval officer said that Ferguson was a big company, but they did not have any experience with such a search.' The Fugro Group denied that they were searching with inappropriate equipment.

June 2015

On June 1st, Malaysia Airlines released a comprehensive

restructuring plan to its employees stating that about 6,000 workers would be dismissed and that the number of employees would be reduced to 14,000. After the reorganisation, the new Malaysia Airlines would begin to operate on September 1.

July 2015

On July 29th, US media reported that cleaners on Réunion Island had found some wreckage on the beach of the eastern coastline. It was about two metres long and looked like a part of the wing which had been immersed in water for a long time. The piece of wreckage carried the number BB670, which was not the aircraft's number, nor the serial number. On the 30th, France sent the wreckage to the French Civil Aviation Safety Investigation and Analysis Bureau in Toulouse for identification.

August 2015

On August 2nd, the Malaysian Minister of Transport, Liow Tiong Lai, said the wreckage previously found on Réunion Island has been officially identified as a flaperon from a Boeing 777 aircraft, the same aircraft as the missing Flight MH370. On the 6th, the Malaysian Prime Minister said at a news conference that an international group of experts had confirmed that the wreckage found in Réunion Island was from Flight MH370.

On the 6th, the French Deputy Prosecutor said that the wreckage found had something in common with Flight MH370 and was very likely from the wreckage, but it needed further analysis. On the 7th, France, Mauritius and Madagascar searched the vicinity of the coast for a week, finding some suspect items such as a bottle of mineral water branded 'Farmer's Spring' and some Indonesian washing liquid.

On the 28th, German experts inferred by computer simulation that MH370 had crashed in the eastern equatorial Indian Ocean, the area of the Southern Indian Ocean now being searched.

September 2015

On September 3rd, the French prosecutor confirmed that the flaperon found on Réunion Island belonged to the Flight MH370, after careful studies by the Spanish subcontractor comparing it with the order and production information catalogue of aircraft parts and through endoscopy which discovered, on the flaperon, three numbers, one of which matched the series of the MSA Boeing 777 aircraft MH370.

In mid-September, 'A Survey of The World's Major Mysterious Crash— from the First Black Box to Flight MH370', compiled by Wan Zhongyi and published by the Chinese Yanshi Press, concluded that Flight MH370 had quite likely crashed in the Gulf of Thailand.

October 2015

On October 12th, the Philippine military said someone had told the Malaysian police that he had found a piece of aircraft wreckage with the Malaysian flag logo in the Ubian mountain jungles at Tawitawi in the southern Philippines. He suspected that it was from MH370. On the 13th, the Philippines denied that the wreckage of MH370 had been found.

On the 13th, the Dutch Security Council announced the final report of the air crash investigation into the loss of MH17, saying the aircraft had been shot down by a Buk missile. But it did not mention whether the plane was shot down by the government or anti-government armed forces.

November 2015

On November 1ˢᵗ, Malaysia News Agency reported that the search range in the Indian Ocean had been expanded to 120,000 square kilometres. The search funds were enough to keep it going until next May. The Vice Minister of the Ministry of Transport, Ahdu Aziz, was disappointed at the fruitless long search.

On the 16ᵗʰ, *Reference News* reported that in the light of the lessons learned from the disappearance of MH370, the World Radiocommunication Conference, convened by the International Telecommunication Union (ITU), had decided that the frequency used for aircraft and satellite communications would be set at 1087.7-1092.3 MHz. As a result of establishing this as an international frequency, it would be possible to track the location of cross-border aircraft at any time in the future.

ICAO was expected to release, by November 2016, a satellite-based Aircraft Tracing System Application Guide which would stipulate that aircraft should report their position and altitude once every 15 minutes, and every minute in an emergency.

On the 22ⁿᵈ, the Malaysian Transport Minister, Liow Tiong Lai, issued a statement expressing his sincere gratitude to Chinese Premier Li Keqiang and the People's Republic of China for providing 20 million Australian dollars to the ongoing search and rescue of Flight MH370. Malaysia, China and Australia pledged to complete the 120,000 square kilometre underwater search announced in April 2015.

December 2015

On the 3ʳᵈ, Australian Deputy Prime Minister Warren Trice held a press conference in the Federal Parliament Building to report the latest progress in the search for Flight MH370. The latest study showed that the southern end of the 120,000 square kilometre area under search was the last area where the aircraft could be found. In this area, 76,000 square kilometres of the sea bed had been scanned without finding anything resembling the wreckage of an aircraft; the remaining 44,000 square kilometres was expected to be covered before June 2016. He thanked China for its contribution of $20 million to the search.

On December 9th, the Australian media stated that a survey report on MH370 announced by Australia released an important message that the lost aircraft had suffered a serious technical failure caused by a power outage. The flight timeline showed that the power failure had occurred before MH370' s disappearance. At least one system, after restoring power 60 seconds later, continued to run and, in the subsequent flight, it sent a series of satellite pulses, with the last one transmitted 10 minutes before the plane crashed into the ocean. It was pointed out in the report that in an avionics system failure, the crew could do nothing but let the aircraft continue automatic 'zombie flight' until the fuel was exhausted. The right engine of the aircraft turned off first and 15 minutes later the left, after which the aircraft would have spiralled down into the Southern Indian Ocean.

January 2016

On January 24th, China's Daily Chinese network reported that a fragment 3 metres long and 2 metres wide had been discovered on the beach of Nakhon, southern Thailand, and was suspected to be from MH370. On the 26th, the Malaysian Ministry of Communications issued a statement that after a joint assessment by experts from the Ministry of Communications, the Civil Aviation Authority and Malaysia Airlines experts, the suspected wreckage did not belong to the missing aircraft. On inspection, the investigators found that the equipment number, wire number and bolt number on the wreckage does not match those of a Boeing 777.

On the 31st, the British Broadcasting Corporation website reported that China's search ship *East China Rescue* had set out on January 31 from Singapore for Australia to search a vast area of the Southern Indian Ocean with sonar and help the other three vessels, which still had not found anything. Australian Deputy Prime Minister Warren Trice said that China had offered the previous year to send a ship to join the search. The Chinese search and rescue ship would pull a 6 km deep sonar system. The search and rescue operation would continue until June.

February 2016

On February 17th, the British *Daily Mail* reported that if the aircraft could not be found in the targeted area, investigators would officially attribute the disappearance of MH370 to the pilots' abnormal behaviour, and define the event as a deliberate crash.

March 2016

On March 7th, fifteen families of the lost passengers submitted a complaint and the relevant evidence to the Beijing Railway Bureau Transport Court. On the 22nd, the Malaysian Minister of Transport stated that a metal plate printed with the words '676EB' and 'NO STEP' found by South African teenagers on a beach in Mozambique may be part of MH370's engine fairing.

May 2016

On May 4th, according to the Daily Express, the Australian Transportation Security Agency confirmed that if MH370's wreckage had not been found, the search would end at the end of June, leaving the search team only eight weeks. On the 14th,

Shenzhen Special Zone Daily reported that some wreckage found in Mauritius was confirmed as interior trim from the main cabin; the wreckage matched the decorative laminate of a work table at the front right cabin door of a Boeing 777. Aviation experts thought Flight MH370's fuselage had been torn open when it crashed into the sea.

June 2016

On June 11th, the *New York Times* website reported that Australia had decided to re-examine the flight distance of aircraft MH370. The search of the Southern Indian Ocean was drawing to a close, but no trace of the plane had been found. This forced people to make a final assessment on the assumptions used to determine the fate of the aircraft and the delineation of the search area.

On June 15th, the Australian Joint Coordination Centre released a report that the search may be delayed until the end of August due to poor weather conditions in the southern hemisphere after the arrival of winter, and the fact that the search had exceeded the priority area of over 105,000 square kilometres.

On the 20th, *The Guardian* reported that Australian, Chinese and Malaysian officials had previously reached an agreement, if there was no new reliable information, the search work for Flight MH370 would end after the current search. Families of the lost passengers insisted that the search must continue and urged Boeing to bear the cost.

On the 22nd the Xinhua News Agency, Canberra, reported that the Joint Coordination Centre in Australia had said some wreckage found in South Australia's Kangaroo Island on the 9th of the month did not match a Boeing 777.

July 2016

On July 21st, according to Reuters Sydney, the Dutch company's search and rescue personnel said they believed that the aircraft may have glided down rather than diving vertically. If so, for two years they had been searching the wrong waters.

On the 22nd, Reuters Kuala Lumpur reported that China, Malaysia and Australia had decided to suspend the search, but the three ministers reiterated that they had not given up hope.

In mid-July a third edition of this book *MH370 Should Be Here* was published, with much new material. Here the following views were further clarified:

First, Flight MH370 went missing at 1:25 and disappeared at 1:37, Malaysian local time..

Second, the aircraft encountered an accident during its normal cruising and an improper right turn resulted in its crashing vertically into the sea.

Third, it is now lying on the sea bed or in the trenches of the South China sea in an area of about 50 km radius around the point N7 degrees 25 points, E103 degrees 55 points, 80-120 metres from the sea surface.

Fourth, the South China Sea swallowed the plane as well as the 239 lives on board and shielded the plane's communication with the outside world.

Fifth, the seven satellite's 'handshakes' did not relate to MH370. Therefore, it was not surprising that no clues had been found to MH370 in the Southern Indian Ocean.

On the 31st, *The Guardian* reported that air crash experts said the flaperon found on Réunion Island showed that it was in the landing state, indicating that it was the 'rogue pilots' who had flown the aircraft into the water.

August 2016

On August 7th in the United States, *New York Magazine* stated the FBI data analysis showed that Zahari had flown this route less than a month before the plane crashed (evidence came from the hard disk data of the aviation simulator at his home); this is speaking evidence that the crash of Flight MH370 was the premeditated suicide of the pilot.

On the 9th, The Australian newspaper reported that Australian scientists had said that when the aircraft was flying south, it sent automatic signals and 'shook the hand' of the Perth ground satellite station. These signals may indicate that the aircraft could possibly have run out of fuel in Western Australia at 8:19 on March 8 and two engines were powered off. After the aircraft lost power, it dropped fast from a height of 35,000 feet at a speed up to 12,000-20,000 feet per minute, and finally crashed into the water and quickly sank into the sea. The Australian Transport Safety Bureau Chief Hu De said: 'a conclusion drawn from our analysis of these signals is that the plane was unmanned at the last moment.' He also suggested that the aircraft may have crashed in the 120,000 square kilometre priority search area.

September 2016

On September 15th, the *New York Times* reported that the Australian government had confirmed that a flap rushed from the coast of Pemba island, Tanzania (found in June 2016) was wreckage from the missing Flight MH370.

On the 16th, Malaysia's transport minister said that so far 22 suspected pieces from MH370 had been found in related waters in South Africa, Mozambique, Mauritius and Tanzania. Among them, the flaperon found in July 2015 on Réunion and the lateral flap debris found in June 2016 in Tanzania had been confirmed as from MH370; another four pieces 'almost certainly' belonged to it. Australian experts said that the drift model showed that the search area was correct, which also explained why wreckage would be found in the related areas.

Australian Transport Safety Authority (ATSB) experts confirmed that the information on the debris of the Boeing 777 aircraft was consistent with the manufacturing date of MH370, and therefore it was from the aircraft.

On the 18th, according to the Australian Associated Press, investigators disclosed that according to the analysis of a piece of MH370 wreckage, the aircraft, before crashing into the sea, had experienced a horrible death 'jump', from 35,000 feet straight down into the sea at up to 20,000 feet per minute without making an emergency forced landing or sliding. It was confirmed that no flap had been put down.

On the 21st, Malaysian transport minister Liow Tiong Lai released the news that the cabinet had decided to provide 15 million Australian dollars for searching the remaining areas for Flight MH370. So far more than 110,000 square kilometres had been searched, and the whole search programme was expected to be complete in December. So far Malaysia had allocated $100 million for search; Australia and China contributed an equal amount.

October 2016

On October 1st, The Australian exclusively published the United States flight safety writer Christine Negroni's article 'Good Night, Malaysia'. The author believed that the crash was not a conspiracy but a failure. After interviewing many pilots and analysing a number of flight safety cases, the author did a 'panoramic reduction' of MH370's flight the night it crashed and concluded that the cause was a sudden failure in flight. According to the author's analysis, after the plane cruised over Vietnam, it suddenly encountered an unknown fault. Through lack of experience, the 27-year old co-pilot, Fariq Abdul Hamid, did not know how to deal with the rapid decompression state of the cockpit, while Captain Zahari, then in the business class restroom, was eager to return to the cockpit but could not open the cockpit door as a result of hypoxia. By Now Hamid, who had only 39 hours' experience in the Boeing 777, was drifting in and out of unconsciousness. He planned to fly the plane back to Su State, Malaysia, and land at Langkawi International Airport, which he was more familiar with, but eventually because of his incapacity due to lack of oxygen, he flew the plane south across the ocean until the fuel was exhausted. As for the contact break between the flight and the satellite, the author thought it was because of a fatal design flaw in large aircraft: the electronic navigation cabin, located below the first-class cabin, often suffered a water seepage problem. The Australian Traffic Safety Administration Bureau had found several cases of water seepage in the electronic navigation cabin of Boeing 777 and Airbus aircraft.

On the 7th, the Kuala Lumpur Central News Agency reported that Malaysian and Australian officials had said today that the flap found on the island of Mauritius had been confirmed to be from MH370, through the serial number.

November 2016

On November 2nd, the Australian investigators released the latest report on Flight MH370 stating that when the plane crashed into the sea, it was in an unmanned state. The unopened flaps almost excluded the possibility that the aircraft was being flown manually when it crashed, and also proves the correctness of the current search area.

On the 2nd, the *Sydney Morning Herald* reported that the search area was likely to be further expanded to 34 degrees north latitude. The Australia Broadcasting Corporation reported that the Australian Transport Safety Bureau hoped to provide

30 million Australian dollars, equivalent to 155 million yuan, to continue the search work.

December 2016

On December 3rd, seven relatives of MH370 passengers from Malaysia and China went to Madagascar to encourage the local government to look for the remains of the plane. They planned to meet a tribal leader and the local residents in a coastal village to arouse their concern about the missing flight. A Malaysia lawyer said: 'Most of the families of the victims are unwilling to accept the worst unless we find more clues, although reason tells us that the plane has fallen into the sea and there is no possibility that the people survived, we cannot accept this fact emotionally.'

On the 13th, the BBC Chinese network reported that the Holland ship Fugro Equator had departed on December 12 from Australia's Freeman port and was expected to complete the final search mission in early 2017. Officials said the search mission would be suspended if the plane had not been found by then.

On the 19th, Associated Press reported that the international search teams had concluded that the crash site was likely not in the current search area, but rather further to the north. According to satellite communication data, experts estimated that the site was located along 'the Seventh Arc',

Based on the ocean drift analyses of more than 20 suspected pieces of MH370 wreckage washed ashore, the satellite data experts inferred that the original site of the wreckage was in an area of 25 square kilometres to the north of the current search area. Investigators were 'very sure' that the aircraft was not in the current search area, and were in favour of searching the new one.

On the 20th, the Australian Transport Safety Authority issued a report stating that the previously designated underwater search area was unlikely to contain the wreckage, and the possibility of finding it in the northern part of the search area was extremely high. This conclusion was drawn by evaluating and validating satellite data, drift models, and sonar data.

January 2017

On January 6th, Malaysian Transport Minister Liow Tiong Lai stated that the search would end in two weeks unless other significant clues were found.

On the 17th, the Australian, Malaysian and Chinese governments issued a joint statement saying that as no new information had been found, the current deep-sea search had been suspended. The final report on the disappearance of MH370 will be made public in a few months.

On the 19th, according to U.S. media reports, the sonar map obtained from searching for MH370 would help explore the floor of the Indian Ocean. Neville Exxon, a marine geologist at Australian National University, said: 'It is marvellous that an absolute disaster is bringing so much scientific research, and a lot of money has been put into them.' He pointed out that there were two oil and natural gas deposits in the search area, namely Broken Ridge and the Kerguelen Plateau. Understanding how the seabed is formed in the search area would provide clues for oil and gas exploration, and enable people to know where to look for oil and gas fields closer to the Australian coast.

March 2017

On March 4th, Malaysia held a press conference in Kuala Lumpur to commemorate the third anniversary of the crash. Jiang Hui, on behalf of the families of the lost Chinese passengers, handed a copy of the book 'MH370 Should Be Here' to Malaysia's transport minister, Liow Tiong Lai, and the media reporters on the scene as well as representatives of families of missing passengers from other countries. At the same time he distributed to them an open letter written by the author of the book, Mr. Long Wen, which introduces the main points of the book.

On the 8th, Malaysia's Annex 13 Security Investigation Team published its second interim statement which said that due to the fact that the main wreckage of the aircraft and its flight recorders had not yet been found, there was a serious lack of critical evidence to determine the reasons for the aircraft's shift from its intended flight plan.

On the 23rd, some QQ groups sent out a copy of a 'micro-blog text' which claimed that a Cantonese possessed confidential data on the MH370 analysis and investigation, stating that the plane had crashed into the Southern Indian Ocean at a position hundreds of kilometres beyond 'the Seventh Arc'. He claimed to have used a number of advanced theoretical calculations and derived the crash site within an accuracy of 20.2-100 square kilometres; this was an extreme position which aviation experts could not find credible. He demanded 500,000 Australian dollars for the data.

April 2017

On the 21st on Chinanews.com, it was reported that sea drift analyses of a Boeing 777 flap by the Australian authorities showed that the crash site was likely to be north of the previous search area. The analysis was consistent with a search report published in 2016 by Malaysia Airlines passenger aircraft. The report pointed out that compared with last year's report, Australian scientists, in this analysis, had used a more accurate drift model, but still reached the same conclusion, which once again verified the previous analytical results.

According to Britain's *The Independent* on April 22nd,

investigators said the most likely location of the missing aircraft had been found. The Commonwealth Australian scientific and Industrial Research Organisation claimed that the wreckage should be located in the northern part of the original 120,000 square kilometre search area, in a new search area of 25 thousand square kilometres.

August 2017

On the 17th, Chinanews.com reported that according to foreign media, MH370 had been missing for three and a half years, and the searching team had still not found the wreckage of the plane. On the basis of two newly- released research reports from the Australian Transport Safety Bureau (ATSB), the Australian authorities identified an area of 5,000 square kilometres which was very likely to be the final location of MH370.

October 2017

On October 3rd, the Australian Transport Safety Bureau (ATSB), on behalf of the MH370 search & rescue committee, issued a search-related final summative report. The report added up to more than 400 pages, recording in detail all the efforts from all sides to search for MH370. The report pointed out that the search had lasted for 1,046 days, covering a seabed area of 120,000 square kilometres, at a total cost of 160 million US dollars; by the time it had ended nothing had been found except three pieces of debris from a plane on the shores of the Indian Ocean, and the search team felt 'very sorry' for that. Although the report didn't explain the causes of the disappearance of MH370, it mentioned that the range where it could be found had been narrowed down to 25,000 square kilometres.

November 2017

On November 1st, according to *The Australian*, the Malaysian Cabinet agreed to set a special fund of 20-70 million US dollars for an American corporation, Ocean Infinity, with the premise that the corporation could find the wreckage of MH370 within 90 days. Last month, the Malaysian government accepted its prospectus with the principle 'No discovery, no money'. If the government signed the contract in the near future, the new search would start at the beginning of next year.

On the 16th, someone named Dennis Liu, also called A Last Hitting American, who wrote Devils' Trickeries — Investigation Report of the Truth of 911 Event, posted online an article called Investigation of MH370 (Closure) with more than 45,000 words. The article claimed that MH370 had been hijacked via electronic remote control. People on board 'were sorted according to a name list prepared in advance, and put into different cells which had been used to interrogate terrorists from Afghanistan, Iraq and so on'. Then they had invented a fake 'crash site' in the ocean, west of Perth,

On the 18th, three days after Investigation of MH370 (Closure) was posted online, an experienced pilot in Xiamen Airlines, after reading it, wrote: 'Investigation of MH370 (Closure) is nonsense!' After that the claim of 'hijacking via electronic remote control' was dropped.

January 2018

On January 3rd, many media reported that the Malaysian government would restart the search for MH370. The government had recruited Ocean Infinity, a US undersea mapping corporation, to restart the search. Ocean Infinity said they would focus on an area of 25,000 square kilometres north of the former searched spot. If the debris was found within the first 90 days of the search, Ocean Infinity would get 70 million US dollars; otherwise, they wouldn't get anything. The corporation planned to use pilotless submarines; their sonar scanning equipment could go down to 6,000 metres. The corporation was expected to search 1,200 square kilometres a day. The research ships of the corporation set off from port of Durban on January 2, and was expected to reach Perth on February 7.

On the 10th, the Malaysian government signed the contract with Ocean Infinity. If it found the plane, it would be rewarded with up to 70 million US dollars. Otherwise, it would get nothing.

On January 17, the Joint Coordination Centre in Australia declared that the underwater search had been suspended. After this, three bodies put in bids to start unofficial searches. After negotiation, Malaysia agreed to authorize Ocean Infinity to restart the search, according to the principle of 'No progress, no reward'. The amount of reward was decided by the location of the found MH370. If it was within the first 5,000 square kilometres, Ocean Infinity would get 20 million US dollar. The amount went up as the range went up. If it was found outside the 25,000 square kilometre area, Ocean Infinity would get up to 70 million US dollars.

A Norwegian research ship which took on the new search challenge set off from South Africa at the beginning of January. The ship had eight automatic diving devices which were equipped with hi-tech cameras and sonar and sensors. It would search at a higher speed, starting on January 17. Being able to search 1,200 square kilometres per day, the automatic diving devices could cover 25,000 square kilometres within one month.

On the 22nd, Ocean Infinity's search ship Seabed Constructor, equipped with eight automatic vehicles, reached the area to search. It aimed to finish searching 25,000 square kilometres within 90 days.

March 2018

On March 18th, Phoenix Satellite Television reported that a mechanical engineer named Peter McMahon had told the *Daily Star* that the position where MH370 crashed was 16 kilometre south of Round Island, north of Mauritius. On the 25th, in 'A QQ Group Concerned About MH370', someone with the internet name of 'Miracle' claimed that it had crashed into Gulf of Boni, south of Sulawesi, Indonesia. On the 26th, in the same QQ group, someone with a net name 'Flowers in the southern city blossomed.' claimed that MH370 had been captured by aliens, and it would come back on January 1 2262.

May 2018

On May 2nd, 'A QQ Group Concerned About MH370' reprinted a statement from Ocean Infinity: 'We have searched 80 thousand square kilometres, with no findings so far; we are still searching with an average search area of 1,300 square kilometres per day. On the 9th, the Malaysian Prime Minister Najib was relieved of office and 92-year-old Mahathir was elected as Prime Minister once again. The transport minister Liow Tiong Lai was replaced by Anthony Loke Siew Fook.

On the 14th, according to *The Independent*, a renowned air safety expert drew a conclusion and affirmed that the pilot of MH370 had intentionally made the flight crash. One of the search and rescue experts said that he had elaborately planned a murder and a suicide flight. On the 17th, CRI Online reported that the British engineer and mathematician Robin Stevens had put the aircraft's last position at near S39° 2, E88° 36'.

On the 29th, the *Deutsche Welle* web page reported that the US undersea mapping corporation had decided to end the search in the Southern Indian Ocean after more than three months. Ocean Infinity's CEO, Oliver Plunkett, said they had searched more than 112,000 square kilometres without finding the plane. They now had to stop the search with a heavy heart.

June 2018

On June 8th, it was reported from Kuala Lumpur that Seabed Constructor, which was in charge of the search for MH370, had ended its search set off back to Australia without no result. On the 22nd, Oliver Plunkett declared that the seabed data collected during the search would be donated to Japan's GEBCO Fund to support the 2030 plan.

July 2018

On July 30th, 1603 days after MH370's disappearance, the Malaysian Government released to the world as well as to the related families a long-awaited report. With 822 pages in the main body of the report and another 200 pages in the appendix, the report was over 1000 pages in total.

The report recorded the investigation and analyses of various information, including the crew, the safety of the flying system, satellite communication, the cargoes as well as three pieces of "confirmed" debris.

Kok Soo Chon, leader of the investigation team, said in the press conference that a number of concerns still remained unknown due to the lack of evidence, especially from the flight recorder and major debris from the plane. As for the plane itself, the captain, the first officer and other aspects, there was nothing abnormal found. However, 'unlawful interference by a third party' could not be ruled out. The plane was presumed to have crashed into the Southern Indian Ocean, but the second period of searching before the release of the report failed to find it.

The truth will not come out until the wreckage is found. The investigation team may be dismissed if there is no new evidence.

The report announced that the causes of the crash could not yet be determined.

August 2018

On August 7th, according to the *Daily Express*, French Aviation and Transportation regulators blamed MAS's report about MH370 released on July 30th, saying that the report had swept away the prevailing view that the plane might be damaged and the pilots should be partially responsible for the event. The French side thought there was no further interpretation of the view that 'unlawful interference by a third party' could not be ruled out. Also, the French side decided to conduct relevant investigations regarding the technical data in the report. The 'interference' of France was based on the fact that there had been four French passengers on board. France was allowed to conduct the investigation into the event.

September, 2018

On the 3rd, the Daily Mirror reported that British technologist Ian Wilson said that he had spotted the main body of MH370's wreckage on Google Maps. It was on the border between Khêt Pursat and Kampong Speu Province, Vietnam: N12.089139', E104.151806. The aircraft so many people were concerned about was claimed to be found.

On the 6th, the authorities of Cambodia denied the statement. It was mistaken. Later it was called by netizens a rumour drawing the most attention in September, 2018.

APPENDIX 4

A common-sense approach to radio communication

In radio technology, the word 'waveband' has two definitions. One refers to electromagnetic waves, such as long wave, short wave, ultrashort wave and so on. The other is the operation frequency range division of devices like transmitters and receivers. If the operation frequency range is divided into several parts, these are also called wavebands, for example, three-band radio.

Wavebands are also called spectral bands or spectral zones. In an electromagnetic waveband, a continuous electromagnetic wave with a definite wavelength range is the basic unit of the wavelength range of the sensor spectrum channel. In remote sensing technology, the electromagnetic spectrum is usually divided into large and small sections: large ones called spectral regions, such as the visible region, infrared region and so on, medium-sized ones like the near-infrared and far-infrared regions and small ones called wavebands, while the narrowest is the spectral line. Bands are usually represented at a specific wavelength range value, for instance, the fourth band of a landsat multi-band scanner is 0.5 to 0.6 microns. They can also be represented by numbers or letters – for example in the microwave region, L, S and K respectively represent wavelength ranges of 17.63~26.76cm, 7.39~11.52cm and 1.13~1.67cm. When electromagnetic waves are divided by frequencies, they are called frequency zones or frequency bands.

Radio waves generally refer to electromagnetic waves ranging from 100,000 metres to 0.75 millimetres. According to the characteristics of electromagnetic wave transmission, it can be divided into ultra-long wave, long wave, medium wave, short wave and ultra-short wave.

Radio frequency bands are used in radio and television: in China, the waveband of medium-wave broadcast is approximately 550-1605kHz; that of short-wave broadcasting is 2-24MHz; that of FM radio is 87-108MHz. Broadcast includes two frequency bands, 'very-high frequency band' (VHF) and ' ultra-high frequency band' (UHF). The very-high frequency band has 12 channels, whose frequency ranges are 48.5-92MHz for channels 1-5 and 167-223MHz for channels 6-12.

The UHF band has 56 channels from channel 13 to channel 68, and its corresponding frequency range is 470-958MHz. Customarily, 'VHF' is used to mean very-high frequency, 'VL' channels 1-5, 'VH' for channels 6-12; 'UHF' for ultra-high frequency.

There are 6 frequency bands used in internationally-defined satellite radio and television. The main band is 12000MHz. In this band, satellite radio and television services are protected. Wavebands are divided as the following table suggests:

HOW WAVEBANDS ARE DIVIDED

No.	wave band (frequency band)	English Abbr.	wave length range	frequency range	application range
01	extremely long wave (extremely low frequency)	ELF	100—10 megametres	3—30HZ	underground remote sensing, underground communication, communication from upside to submarine
02	super long wave (super low frequency)	SLF	10—1 megametre	30—300HZ	1.coast-submarine communication; 2.maritime navigation
03	ultra long wave (ultra low frequency)	ULF	1000—100 thousand meters	30—3000HZ	geological exploration, earthquakes
04	very long wave (very low frequency)	VLF	100—10 thousand meters	3—30KHZ	navigation, time mark, audio telephone and so on
05	long wave (low frequency)	LF	10—1 thousand meters	30—300KHZ	1. medium distance communication in aerosphere; 2.underground stratum communication; 3.maritime navigation。
06	medium wave (medium frequency)	MF	10—1 hundred meters	300—3000KHZ	1.broadcast; 2.maritime navigation
07	short wave (high frequency)	HF	100—10 meters	3—30MHZ	1. long distance short wave communication; 2.short wave broadcast
08	very short wave (very high frequency)	VHF	10—1 meter	30—300MHZ	1. ionospheric scatter communication. (30-60MHz) ;2.meteor trail communication (30-100MHz) ;3. man-made ionospheric scatter communication (30-144MHz) ;4. communication with outside aerosphere, outerspace flying objects(planes, missiles, satellites); television, radar, navigation, mobile communication.

No.	wave band (frequency band)	English Abbr.	wave length range	frequency range	application range
09	decimeter wave (very high frequency)	UHF	10—1 decimeter	300—3000MHZ	1.troposphere scatter communication (700-1000MHz); 2. small volume (lines 8-12) Microwave relay communication (352-420MHz); 3.medium volume (line 120) Microwave relay communication (1700-2400MHz)
10	centimeter wave (super high frequency)	SHF	10-1 centimeter	3-30GHz	1.large volume (line 2500、line 6000) Microwave relay communication (3600-4200MHz, 5850-8500MHz); 2.digital communication; 3.卫星通信; 4.waveguide communication
11	millimeter wave (extremely high frequency)	EHF	10-1 millimeter	30-300GHz	communication through aerosphere
12	decimillimeter (top frequency)		10—1 decimillimeter	300—3000GHZ	short path communication
13	ultraviolet rays, infrared rays and visible light			10^7–10^5 GHZ	cable and laser communication
14	X-ray与r- ray				medical science

Note that decimetre waves, centimetre waves, millimetre waves and decimillimetre waves are all called microwaves. Some people classify the decimetre wave as 'superwaves'; others put all of them together and call them 'mixed waveband'.

APPENDIX 5

A selection of readers' comments

What I learned from Mr. Longwen's 'MH370 Should Be Here.' On finishing the first chapter, I was fascinated by this book. In my radio engineer's eyes, with over half a century of social experience, I couldn't help feeling, when I examined this book with both a rich science and technology content and mysteries, that everyone would find it worth reading. What we are most concerned about is where the ultimate crash site of the aircraft is. But there are many other aspects worth reading.

You can easily appreciate the whole picture of the event. The book collects almost all of the information about the Malaysia Airlines MH370 event: the situation of the flight, the list of missing persons, the events after the crash, the search situation, the equipment of all communication systems; also the analyses of the event as well as forecasts on the future results of the event.

You can learn radio positioning technology. This is quite valuable for readers who do not understand it. Previously, radio positioning technology was not only widely used in military, but also applied to disaster relief, shipping, both which are not quite relevant to ordinary people. With the development and application of satellite positioning technology, especially the wide use of mobile phone mobile communication, the car's automatic navigation, radio positioning technology is associated with everyone and is related to our daily life since almost everyone has a mobile phone and every family owns a car and mobile phones and cars use radio positioning technology.

You can understand the intricacies of international relations. The MH 370 event affects the world, with scores of countries directly involved. The event involves the interests of all parties, which share common responsibilities and obligations, but also consider their own gains and losses. These two considerations will be reflected in the handling of the event. For example, Malaysia, as the main country involved in the event, has to both find the plane and consider compensation, take into account its national reputation and still manage a balance between countries, a real dilemma. For the US, the plane was made in the United States, a responsibility the United States cannot get away from; if the crash was due to the aircraft's hardware problems, its responsibility is greater; if it is aviation management, it is smaller. And Vietnam is not willing to allow a large number of warships and aircraft from other countries to search in their own territorial waters, because of national geographical secrets. China had a large number of passengers on the plane; naturally it has many more responsibilities and obligations. These different interests and demands cannot be all laid on the table. Therefore, in the handling of the event there will be game-playing between countries. This book clearly shows to us readers these under-the-table things. Readers can learn some political wisdom.

You may know the gains and losses of our country in handling this matter. China has been actively involved all along, investing a lot of manpower and material resources, but has not found the plane. It's inevitable that many people will have complaints. The author analysed the question very cleverly, talking about losses and gains in a simple and clear manner. The reader may not only understand our country's behaviour, but also learn a scientific and comprehensive way of analysing problems. It broadens our horizons.

The author also talks about what the international community should do to improve aviation safety after this event. For example, aircraft manufacturers should be forced to install automatic reporting and tracking systems within the cost of the aircraft rather than not install them to lower the sale price.

A global surveillance and tracking system for civil aircraft, with search and rescue systems, should be established. We should strengthen the management of civil aviation pilots and air attendants, to prevent them from boarding while sick.

Of course, the most important thing is how to find the vanished aircraft. See how the author analyses and infers what his conclusion is. The author concluded that the first site is the area below the established route in a radius of 100km around the area where MH370 was at one o'clock, about 600 km from Kuala Lumpur. The key position is in the southern waters or in the deep mountains and forests of Nam Can, southwest of Ho Chi Minh city. Second place is the position where Malaysian radar last detected the plane, including Lara Island, Danasina Island, the Spratly Islands area, East Malaysia and Kota Kinabalu and the nearby mountains. These two are based on radar measurements. The third place is 600 kilometres south of Albany, Australia. This is based on the plane's computer problems; the aircraft's course went back, in the opposite direction to Beijing.

The author is not optimistic about finding the aircraft in the west of Perth, the Indian Ocean. That is, he does not believe the judgment made by Inmarsat experts on radio positioning by satellite Doppler technology.

There are roughly two kinds of radio positioning technology:

One is the traditional cross-positioning described in the book. That is, the direction measured by more than two radio direction finders at different locations. Because of the different location of the direction finding, the intersection the intersection is the location of the object to be measured. In theory, two directions can be crossed, and of course, the more directions, the higher the reliability. The angle of intersection between the point of direction finding is best at ninety degrees for the object to be measured. If two direction finding points are on the same line as those being measured, they cannot be crossed. Therefore, the angles between the three are also very important. The author concluded that the plane landed in the Vietnamese sea, according to the almost simultaneous detection of Malaysia Airlines 370 by the radars of the Malaysia, Vietnam and Thailand. Radar not only has a detection function, it can measure direction. It should be said that the three radar alignment areas are quite reliable. That's the main reason why the author thinks MH 370 is there.

The other is Doppler technology positioning, a new technology emerging recently. By measuring the Doppler effect, we can determine the relative speed of the transmitted signal and the satellite that receives the signal. Although it has no alignment, no crossover, when there is a shift between the sender and receiver of the signal, the frequency of the signal changes. The frequency change of the signal is proportional to the relative velocity, so the velocity can be inferred from frequency variations. In fact, the Doppler effect has long been used to monitor all moving objects such as hurricanes, aircraft, currents, etc. Similarly, the signal from a lost plane is 'sharp' or 'deep' (although the difference is minimal), and it can be judged at that moment whether the aircraft is near or away from the satellite.

It is not that the author does not value Doppler's technical radio location. It is the authenticity of the 'handshake' signals of aircrafts and satellites and the reasoning of the researchers that the author doubts. However, Inmarsat experts are quite confident of their conclusions, saying that they are using several aircraft for comparison tests. They use the Doppler principle to calculate the approximate distance between the aircraft and satellite signals; they compute the position when the aircraft sent out signals according to the exact location of the satellite and the aircraft's known location, and finally work out the plane's trajectory with a series of point positions. If the trajectory is continuous and consistent with the flight path of the aircraft, this conclusion is more reasonable and more believable. I think. Experts in maritime satellites must put forward the authentic evidence on which the 'handshake' signal is based to rule out the possibility of some signals not having been issued by MH370 and how sure they are about the accuracy of the distance data they calculated.

I think the data measured by the three radars must be reliable. The point is, did the plane continue to fly after it disappeared from radar. Analysis of the data provided by maritime satellite is based on that the aircraft continued to fly; however, there is no other evidence except what the maritime satellite experts themselves have said.

The book, whether in information, science and technology, logical thinking, or the overall view and the practicality of looking for the missing aircraft, is worth reading. Since Long's view is justified, and passed to the relevant departments of our country, why is it still ignored? Maybe there is interference from national interests: Vietnam does not want other countries to search in its backyard; Malaysia bears a responsibility, the full management responsibility; the United States shoulders the responsibility of manufacturing. If the cause of the event is unknown, the responsibility is uncertain, the relevant parties have more space to handle the event: they may pass the buck or muddle with their duties. This should be the reason that some interested countries failed to perform their duties. In this way, only the passengers of the missing aircraft suffer. Longwen's proposal should have been acknowledged by China's relevant departments, so why didn't they adopt it? I think voice power is not in our hands. Coupled with the complexity of international relations, Malaysia must take care of the interests of all parties. Although the air crash was a big event, international relations is bigger.

This is a book full of mysteries and scientific and technological content. It is also a book of informative documentation for the whole event, and a proposal to strengthen aviation safety management around the world. The technical, practical, social and considerable historical significance of this book is surely a guarantee that many people will carefully read it if they are interested in continuing to search for MH370, or in strengthening the research on aviation safety work, or studying Doppler satellite radio positioning technology, or writing or filming the event based on the books, dramas, films and television programmes.

Time will prove this is a book that history will mention from time to time. While reading the book, I wrote a poem dedicated to those reading it.

Air accidents are essentially rare, each with peculiar causes. This book explodes the myth.

2015/05/29

Lei Haiji, pen name: Zhuang Xishui, Dongshan Red Leaves, male; born in Jinxian County of Jiangxi Province in October,

1943; enrolled in the PLA technical engineering academy in 1961. Served as the general staff of PLA Political Committee, reaching the rank of colonel. Published hundreds of poems and essays and articles in more than forty domestic and overseas newspapers and periodicals such as Chinese Poetry, Writer, Poetry and so on. His poems repeatedly won national and provincial awards, and were repeatedly selected by the Chinese Poetry National Seminar, Chinese Military Poetry Seminar. He also authored the two books 'Poetry, A Quick-start Guide' and 'On Poems, Quotations of Ancient and Modern Famous Poets'.

(telephone 18611316231, address: Room 802, 2 floor, No.6 Building, South Shili Community, Chaoyang District Beijing zip code 100016)

This article was published on Sina blog on August 23, 2015 slightly modified.

SPEAKING FOR THE CHINESE PEOPLE

MH370 event, Chinese monograph by Netizen, A Leading Horse

On March 8 last year, Malaysia Airlines Flight MH370 from Kuala Lumpur to Beijing, carrying 239 passengers and crew, of whom 154 were Chinese citizens, disappeared in the early morning, within range of Malaysia, Thailand and Vietnam's radar. It is a year since the event, but so far, the plane is still missing. The whole event is complicated and confusing, and everything remains a mystery. On January 29 this year, the Malaysian Civil Aviation Authority Director Azerbaru Ding, on behalf of the Malaysian government, officially announced that after long analysis and speculation, according to the Chicago Convention provisions, it is believed that MH370 crashed, and all 239 passengers and the crew are presumed dead. According to the data, the plane was considered to have run out of fuel in a region over the southern Indian Ocean. It is now at the bottom of the sea. The official conclusion immediately exploded the calm of world opinion.

Over the past year, countless media and individuals in the world, have spread and published news, comments, analyses and speculation. Some have even authored books about this event. Soon after the event, two troublemakers from Australia and New Zealand's published monographs elaborating the matter. In China, the country with the largest number of victims, no one bothered to voice his opinion, a sharp contrast with the international hot spots. This is a situation of helpless indifference rather than rational silence. Fortunately, on New Year's Day this year, Hong Kong Kunpeng Publishing Co. Ltd. published the monograph 'MH370 Should Be Here —Analyses of Its Disappearance and Whereabouts', written by the mainland author Long Wen as a memorial to the compatriots on the crashed plane, and also as the civil voice of the MH370 event. The author insisted on collecting the data carefully, drawing and analysing research patiently and making judgments based on science and the facts. To avoid the interference of different opinions, and create a logical and unbiased point of view, the author adopted the perspective of radio frequency measurement technology, followed the scientific laws of radio wave transmission, and finally argued that the key search area should be the surrounding sea waters and land south of Nam Cam, Vietnam, below the scheduled route of the aircraft. This book gave detailed analyses of the seven focuses of foreign public opinion and reasoned with them one by one; it also refuted 20 other kinds of arguments based on sound facts.

After the event, within three months from March to July, the author, out of moral responsibility, delivered 17 comments on the network and repeatedly presented his suggestion to the relevant state departments and even directly to the highest leaders, in addition to writing three monographs. After all, the author is a civilian, so it is natural that his three monographs should find nowhere to get published, even if the views in the books are 100% correct. It is difficult to reach the decision makers, not least because their solutions are just on paper. It is not pessimistic, but most probably his opinions will end here. Anyway, the author's firmness and self-confidence are still respectable. 'I predict that MH370 will be found in an appropriate time by fishermen, the crew of a boat, explorers, hunters or animals, intentionally or 'accidentally' and may be announced in a 'clever way', he says.

Teacher

'I am instantly fascinated by the title of the book, it's really admirable to write such an unpopular but interesting book that attracts people's attention. As an instructor, I am very proud'.

Yunnan Dadi, General Aviation Corporation,
Chairman Li Mingfa

The book 'MH370 Should Be Here' I have read carefully. Its writing, structure, aviation expertise and the final conclusion are impeccable. I think it is a good work. The rest is left for later generations to figure out; after all, different people have different opinions.

MH370 WeChat group, Xiaodong

I have read your book, which is beneficial. In the past, I had only a smattering of knowledge of the Malaysia Airlines event, but after reading it, I fully understand the event. The words of the book condensed your efforts; in just a few months, you collected a lot of materials, data and pictures and completed profound and simple analyses and speculations as well as this book. I deeply admire it. It offers vivid description, a profound knowledge, smooth ideas and a logical structure, as well as simple to in-depth analyses and convincing reasoning. Compelling, in a word. It is a good book worth reading.

Reviews by *Shenzhen Evening News* and *Chinese Culture News* on July 17, 2015

Some important members of the Futian Writers Association believe that living in the current busy life, Longwen, a lover of writing, is worthy of admiration for his adherence to the creative spirit, especially a scientific proposition in the spirit of literature.

A QQ Group Concerned About MH370
A'an, at 11:55, September 18, 2016

All the times in your book come from the authorities, and none of them is correct! As to your assumption that the signal failure was caused by the plane's vertical crash into the sea, this view is not established, for the sinking could not be instantaneous but would last at least half a minute even if the vertical speed was at the extreme limit! And the answering machine and other equipment might send out response signals and broadcast signals dozens of times in half a minute.

The satellite signal records absolutely have correspondence with MH370, and are unique to MH370 instead of not being irrelevant. This is absolutely the same relation as our cell phone's SIM card to its unique PIN code.

Thanks to China at 10:31, December 4, 2016

Now almost everyone believes that the plane crashed in the Southern Indian Ocean, and nobody believes the plane was in the Gulf of Thailand. Your edition of July 2016, I believe many people have read, but they are not convinced. No one like you should dare to deny authoritative conclusions!

Acknowledgements

Yu Haibo (drawing), Lei Haiji, Yang Damo , Liu Panpan (drawing), Li Surui, Peng Lingyang, Yang Bo, Feng Guohua, Ban Guochun, Zhong Weiting, Gong Ping, Dai Xiuli, Ao Qiang, Fang Yanwen, He Yunfan, Jiang Hongyan, Liang Guanglin, Xie Meiju, Hu Yanjiang, Liu Chuanchun, Xue Tingfang, Wang Dongling, Li Tao, Lin Jinwei, Rao Chunping, Du Hong, Wu Xianjun, etc.

Contact number: 0755-82933840 (Mr Gong).
Contact Email: gxxgdsz100@126.com
13926598998 (Mr Zhou)

Postscript

After I finished this book and sat in meditation, I felt more and more strongly that the decision to give up the South China Sea to search the Southern Indian Ocean for the whereabouts of Flight MH370 was wrong from the very beginning. It is just like the United States' excuse to invade Iraq, that Iraq possessed weapons of mass destruction. They sent troops to Iraq, only to overthrow the Saddam regime and convert a stable society into a mess. Have they found mass destruction weapons? No. Why? Because Iraq had no facilities for the manufacturing of such weapons. The United States has the ability to manufacture and store weapons of mass destruction. If you go to the United States, you will easily find them.

The same is true for MH370. Because the Southern Indian Ocean does not have the condition for MH370 to crash, we cannot expect to find it there.

I know where MH370 is. It didn't drift out of the South China Sea, nor did it fly into the ocean. MH370 is in the southern waters or on a sparsely populated island reef, or in the deep mountains or forests of Nam Can, southwest of Vietnam. As for the exact longitude and latitude, there are detailed descriptions in the book. This location is determined by scientific and technological means and concrete data, and has sufficient scientific basis. As for the cause of the disappearance, it is described by reasoning and deduction, only for reference.

I wrote this book about MH370 not because I am whimsical, or delirious, or fishing for fame. It is based on my 26-year military career, 20 years of police practice, six years of the accumulation of assessment work and the unswerving pursuit of Mao Zedong's correct thinking, as well as my wish to find the missing aircraft and those on board as soon as possible.

To be honest, even I can't understand why I am so concerned about the disappearance of MH370, so obsessed with it. Why did I yearn day and night to compile this book? Some people say that I am connected by destiny to MH370; some people do not know my real name, and simply call me '370'. If one day, the main fuselage of Flight MH370 is found and its whereabouts are as I described, I really want to express my gratitude to the Communist Party of China for its many years of cultivation, and to my comrades, colleagues, friends and family folks for their care, love and support. If the result is not as analysed by the author, I will find the gap, continue to learn, keep pace with the times, live and learn.